D1543264

COCKTAILS AND CONVERSATIONS
DIALOGUES ON ARCHITECTURAL DESIGN

CURATED BY **ABBY SUCKLE & WILLIAM SINGER**

Mahomet
Public Library

© 2018 by American Institute of Architects New York Chapter

All Rights Reserved. No portion of the work may be reproduced or transmited in any form or by any means, electronic or mechanical, including photocopying and recording, or by any information storage or retrieval system, without permission in writing from AIANY.

ISBN 978-1-64316-280-5

Orders, inquiries and correspondence should be addressed to:

American Institute of Architects New York Chapter
Center For Architecture
536 LaGuardia Place
New York, NY 10012
(212) 683 0023, info@aiany.org

Printed in the United States

MAHOMET PUBLIC LIBRARY DISTRICT

3 3031 00170 8052

DEC 1 7 2018

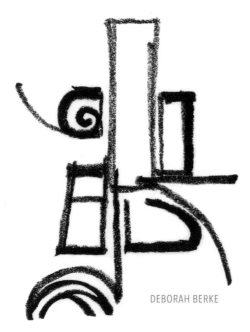

DEBORAH BERKE

BRAD CLOEPFIL

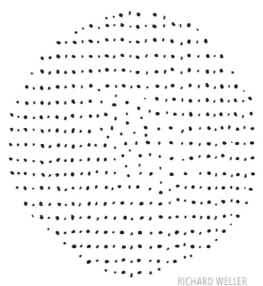

RICHARD WELLER

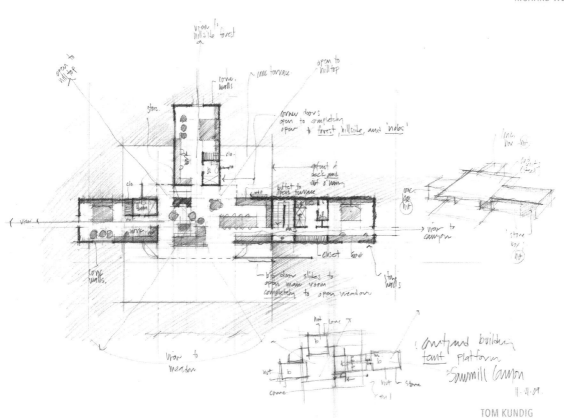

TOM KUNDIG

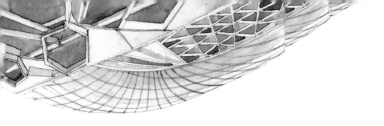

CONTENTS

The world may view architects' idealism and aspiration as idiosyncratic, hopelessly romantic, if not naïve. Architects are constantly browbeaten for daring to dream oversized dreams. Why this slavish devotion to design and aspiration, the skeptic asks, when mean, cost-driven functionalism is all that's being asked for? Architects don't have many venues to discuss what makes architecture meaningful, how to "practice" in a world determined to bury aspiration under mandates and me-tooism. That's the genius of Cocktails and Conversations and the Center for Architecture in New York.

Audiences are happily liberated from over-serious formats such as academic lectures. Instead, they are treated to a rich back-and-forth between an architect and an insightful interlocutor that has proven to be both amusing and substantial. Architects too rarely let their hair down in such an informal format. A delicious drink aids the flow and takes participants and audience alike away from the day-to-day exigencies that designers confront: shrinking budgets, building codes, change orders, onerous schedules. Participants in Cocktails and Conversations take a few minutes to ask, Why do we do this? How do we confer meaning? What's truly significant? How do you create meaningful places in the cacophony of competing interests and tastes?

This book shows, in many rich and diverse ways, how architects truly serve our societies and our cities. Pour me another, please.

—James S. Russell, *FAIA*, NYC Department of Design & Construction, formerly *Bloomberg News*

As an architect, **Hugh Hardy** was unfettered by the conventional and expected; he was a master at creating (and restoring and adapting) spaces that are vivid, dramatic, alive. As a New Yorker, he defined the idea of civic. The long list of organizations and institutions he was associated with, and even more importantly, how much of his enthusiasm and time and critical intelligence he gave to them, is profound evidence of his generous character and unwavering commitment to the future.
—**Rosalie Genevro**, Executive Director, Architectural League of New York, July 2018

I was fortunate to know **Walter Hunt** as a professional who I worked with as well as competed against for projects. We were co-chairs of the Advisory Council to create the Center for Architecture and co-chairs for the Capital Campaign. Through all these experiences, I was honored to have the opportunity to appreciate his special qualities as a leader and as a fine human being. Walter will be missed by all who knew him personally and professionally, and will be remembered for all the wonderful things he contributed and accomplished in his lifetime. My deepest and sincere condolences to his family.
—**A. Eugene Kohn**, *FAIA*, Founder & Chairman, Kohn Pedersen Fox Associates, 2016

I want to say a few words about **Jason Sheftell**. He was the real estate reporter for the *New York Daily News* and I only met him through industry events. I sat at a table with him at the 2011 AIANY New York Design Awards luncheon. And then I would meet him on occasion at different events around the city. So I didn't know him that well, but he had a great spirit. I know he was loved by a lot of people and he was important to the profession. He participated in Cocktails and Conversations in April 2013 with Audrey Matlock. We all went out to dinner afterwards at the Odeon and had a lovely evening. He died unexpectedly a couple of weeks later. They don't know why he died. He was 46. Maybe we'll just spend a moment thinking about Jason.
—**Diana Darling**, Publisher, *The Architect's Newspaper* - At the Cocktails and Conversations program, May 2013

Bing Thom and I bonded over Louis Kahn. I first met Bing when I was working on the FDR Memorial and was hoping to renovate the old Smallpox Hospital into a visitor's center. A mutual friend introduced us, and we hit it off immediately. Though that project never materialized, we vowed to find a way to work together. I nearly had the chance a few years later, and I feel cheated that now I will never have the opportunity.

Bing was a true architect in all the ways that matter. He was a humanist and a master builder. He believed in the power of architecture to make positive change in the world, and he moved through the world with a deep curiosity and an openness. It was a privilege to have had even the short amount of time with him that I did. I think of him so often, and find myself missing both Bing and what he had yet to create.
—**Gina Pollara**, Principal, GPollara Consulting, June 2018

I had the privilege of collaborating with **Bing Thom** for close to 29 years. It was an extraordinary experience. While he was very much in the West Coast Modern tradition of his longtime teacher and mentor Arthur Erickson, he broadened the definition of architectural practice, taking an interest in all aspects of the built environment and the process of building. His endless curiosity and generous nature made him very popular with everyone, from the highest political officials to the laborers on his building sites. He was always able to inspire us to push boundaries in new and exciting ways—always using architecture to better the human condition, improve our communities, and nourish our spirits. His broad interests and approach were reflected in his cosmopolitan team, whom he would frequently brag about, noting that his 50 colleagues spoke more than a dozen languages and hailed from a similar number of counties. He said that this plurality of backgrounds always ensured that every project was considered from a unique perspective and generated unusual results. His favorite saying at any client meeting was: "This has never been done before," and somehow he convinced us all to make it happen.
—**Michael Heeney,** President and CEO, Surrey City, June 2018

DEDICATIONS

When we started Cocktails and Conversations, we filmed the programs for many reasons. We filmed them because we thought architectural thinking deserved a wider audience than the number of people who could (and would) find their way to Tafel Hall at the Center for Architecture on a Friday evening. We filmed them because we thought that sometime in the future a young architect would want to hear the voices of some of the most interesting, provocative, and thoughtful practitioners and critics of our time. We filmed because we thought there should be a record, without realizing that, in some cases, it might be all that we would have. Sadly, over the course of the six years of programs, our architectural community shrank. It is difficult to imagine that these moments turned out to be parting snapshots of three architects and a journalist who were soon to leave us. All four were terrifically inspirational to us.

HUGH HARDY *1932-2017*
There are probably very few architects in New York City who haven't intersected with Hugh during the course of his long career; they worked for him, collaborated with him, served on committees or panels with him. All of them will say that he was articulate, gracious, and, perhaps justifiably, New York's best "civic booster."

WALTER HUNT *1941-2016*
To Gensler, he was the consummate team player who joined the firm in its early days in San Francisco and became instrumental in transforming it from a small interiors practice into one of the leading and largest architectural firms in the world. To the AIA, he was a former Chapter President, Center for Architecture Foundation President, and board member of AIA New York State. Without Walter, there would probably be no Center for Architecture. When AIANY occupied a couple of donated desks in a borrowed office on the 6th floor the New York Design Center in the late 1990s, Walter helped conceive of a storefront to promote design and architecture in New York. Walter loved Cocktails and Conversations, and came to more programs than anyone else.

JASON SHEFTELL *1967-2013*
In architectural circles, journalists, especially with popular newspapers, are usually considered necessary evils. Architects complain bitterly about the media and how they are misunderstood. Not with Jason. He was one of the most enthusiastic reporters in the city who broadly defined real estate into anything about the built environment. He wrote about the usual subjects: the developments, high rises, mansions, and about the less usual, like houseboats and public art.

BING THOM *1940-2016*
Because we live and practice in New York and travel extensively, we consider ourselves highly cultured and knowledgeable. But we are actually quite parochial, a fact that sadly struck a chord when Bing Thom passed away. Even though he would serve on our juries and our boards, his firm received the 2010 Canadian Architect Firm Award, and he won the 2016 Royal Architectural Institute of Canada Gold Medal, he was not particularly well known in our architectural community. He was a lovely man in person, full of passion, thoughtfulness, intelligence, generosity of spirit, and a belief in the power of architecture to transform. We are glad we had the opportunity to meet him and filmed the evening, and sad that it is all we have.

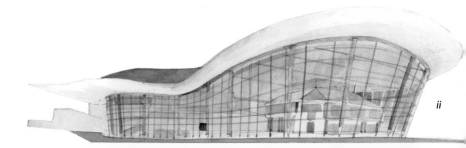

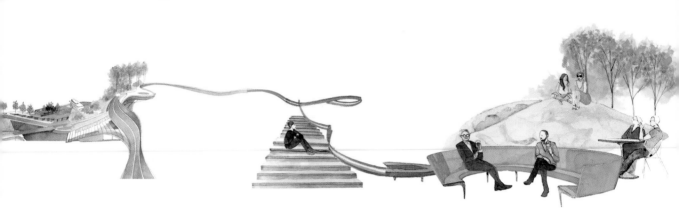

WITH SPECIAL THANKS TO:

All the participants in the series. Not only did they return our emails, but they provided us with fun and provocative evenings.

Design:
Kritika Dhanda, *Assoc. AIA*

Original Illustrations:
Bishakh Som

Design Direction:
Anne Lewison, *AIA*

Consulting Editor:
Kristen Richards, *Hon. AIA, Hon. ASLA*

Cocktail Photographs:
Marc Falzon

Bartenders:
Toby Cecchini, **Eben Klemm**, and **David Moo**

We want to thank our partner **cultureNOW**,
Our supporters **John Herzog**, **Catherine Sweeney Singer**, **Alex Bachrach**.
Our audience and everyone who helped out with all 40 programs.

We also want to thank the individual program sponsors:
AXOR; **IBC Group**; **Kramer Levin**; **Lasvit**; **Mechosystems**; **One Fine Stay**; **Porcelanosa**; **Reed Construction Data**;
The Architect's Newspaper; **Weidlinger + Thorton Thomasetti**

Current AIANY Staff: **Benjamin Prosky**, *Assoc. AIA*, Executive Director; **Suzanne Mecs**, *Hon. AIA NYS*, Managing Director; **Kamaria Greenfield**;
Yvette Sanchez Perez; **Philip Stevens**
Former AIANY Staff: **Rick Bell**, *FAIA*, former Executive Director; **Cynthia Phifer Kracauer**, *AIA*, former Managing Director; **Eve Dilworth Rosen**;
Kelly Felsberg

WITH THANKS TO:

Presidents of the AIA New York Chapter

2018	**Guy Geier, II**, *FAIA*
2017	**David Piscuskas**, *FAIA*
2016	**Carol Loewenson**, *FAIA*
2015	**Tomas Rossant**, *AIA*
2014	**Lance Jay Brown**, *FAIA*
2013	**Jill N. Lerner**, *FAIA*
2012	**Joseph J. Aliotta**, *FAIA*

ABOUT COCKTAILS AND CONVERSATIONS

One Friday night about six years ago, we found ourselves standing in the Center for Architecture's Tafel Hall sipping white wine from plastic tumblers. We had just arrived after a late afternoon meeting at the Rubin Museum of Art where we stood in the atrium while the museum transformed itself into a party venue. Tables were moved, bartenders began setting out glasses, and the space began to fill up. We remarked that it was amazing that every cultural institution of significance in New York City seemed to have a fun Friday evening event involving drinks while, sadly, the lights at the Center for Architecture were turned off. Everyone standing around commiserated with us. We suggested that architects are fun and like to talk about design—and they like to drink. Would it be possible to pair an architect with a journalist and have a bartender create a drink in the spirit of the architect's work?

Charles Renfro of Diller Scofidio + Renfro was standing next to us was, and immediately volunteered to be the inaugural guinea pig. He suggested a pairing with Justin Davidson from *New York Magazine*. Next to him was Andrew Pennington from Porcelanosa, who agreed to underwrite the first program—and in an instant *Cocktails and Conversations* was born. We proceeded to invite architects and landscape architects to share their ideas about design with an audience. We paired them with people who "read" the built environment: journalists and critics who distill and explain it to us; historians who frame it in time; and clients who commission it. The programs have been provocative, inspiring, and lively—and definitely fun.

Abby Suckle, *FAIA* **and William Singer,** *AIA*
Co-chairs, AIANY Architecture Dialogue Committee

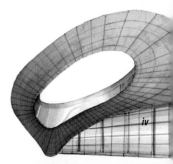

iv

INTRODUCTION

Since we happily sampled everything our guest bartenders concocted, it is very likely that we heard some of the conversations in a haze. Which meant that when it came time to curate this book, we turned to the videos. Sober, the scope and scale of what we had actually assembled was a revelation.

The Big Picture is extraordinary. It never occurred to us that what we had really done was to make a book about how to design. Architecture is about solving complicated problems with a lot of moving targets. While architects can be remarkably articulate in person, their written words may not always be as eloquent. Little has been written about how to design, especially from those who are practicing at the highest level. The mosaic of conversations presented here raises many of the issues that impact design in thoughtful, intelligent, engaging, and provocative ways. All of the ducks have to be in a row or the design won't work. Good design doesn't happen in a vacuum. The client has to be on board, and the contractor has to want to build it.

How do you become an architect? Many paths are laid out, some surprising and some straightforward. Bart Voorsanger was an orphan, Steven Holl, a hotheaded teenager, and Rob Rogers had architect-parents. But growing up is only part of it. Every architect had someone who saw their potential, recognized their talent and passion, and took them under their wing to help shape their thinking—someone who taught, nurtured, and mentored them. Sometimes it happened in school and sometimes at work. It is no surprise that a number of big names pop up; occasionally it was two degrees of separation. Charles Moore spent his life crisscrossing the country establishing firms everywhere. Who knew that his mentor was Louis Kahn, and one of his students at Princeton was Hugh Hardy. Morris Adjmi learned from Aldo Rossi and ran his U.S. office. Frank Harmon and Steven Holl worked for Richard Meier, Bill Pedersen for I.M. Pei, and Richard Weller collaborated with Daniel Libeskind in Berlin.

If you do the math, winning a competition is an architectural lottery jackpot. Competitions launched multiple careers: David Adjaye (Idea Store Chrisp Street, London); Steven Holl (Kiasma Museum, Helsinki); Marion Weiss and Michael Manfredi (Seattle Art Museum Sculpture Park); and Louisa Hutton (GSW Tower, Berlin).

Where do clients come from? Andrea Leers and Jane Weinzapfl say they were advised to go after public buildings early in their careers, when they were one of the few women-owned architecture firms in Boston. Belmont Freeman, Scott Marble, and Claire Weisz are some of the architects who give credit for commissions to New York City's Design and Construction Excellence Program. David Piscuskas and David Adjaye started out by designing houses for artists. Tod Williams and Billie Tsien speak about how they won the Obama Presidential Center project, crediting chemistry and being a couple. And some jobs are self-generated, when an architect sees a need or wants to study an issue.

Where does inspiration come from? The big takeaway is that it can come from anywhere—the important thing is to have an open mind, to be receptive. It begins with the voices of the stakeholders: the client, community, user groups, donors, etc. Frances Halsband points to her research in understanding the program and the setting, particularly when she's adding to a historic building. Deborah Berke says that she looks at the setting. Masimiliano Fuksas tells a story about how a package wrapped in folded paper inspired a roof design. For Todd Schliemann, it can come from the projects that didn't get built—or the failures. Audrey Matlock says something similar when she talks about her losers.

What role does drawing play? Frank Harmon uses it to understand a problem. For Daniel Libeskind, a drawing is the beginning of a design. Steven Holl talks about his conceptual sketches. At the other end of the spectrum, Jeanne Gang thinks about portraying future buildings in virtual reality, and whether VR tells the truth about what a project will really be like.

What is the role of research? Traditionally, architectural research is focused on program and fabrication. Many architects like the opportunity to explore a new program type, such as learning everything one can about airports or museums. Brad Cloepfil describes developing the program for Canada's National Music Centre. Scott Marble talks about experimenting with Building Information Modeling (BIM) and digital fabrication. David Benjamin is interested in zero waste, and using agricultural by-products to grow a building material, in this case a brick for a temporary pavilion at MoMA PS1. Tom Kundig uses small projects to explore large design issues.

Peter Gluck acts as his own general contractor, which streamlines the building process, making it more cost-effective for his clients. There are also conversations about craft. Tom Kundig talks about getting expertise in metal fabrication from a Texas hot rod culture. Gregg Pasquarelli discusses how his firm designs computer programs to fabricate complicated forms, and how to realize projects that are more innovative than existing building codes permit.

Many of the architects address preservation issues. For Hugh Hardy, it was navigating the multiple challenges of preserving a portion of the Greenwich Village townhouse that the Weathermen accidently blew up. Morris Adjmi addresses the NYC Landmarks Preservation Commission itself. Belmont Freeman talks about preserving modern architecture. At UC Santa Barbara, John Ruble updated Charles Moore's Faculty Club, which Ruble admits should have been a temporary building. Frances Halsband speaks of small insertions in historic buildings.

Several architects focus on the challenges and rewards of practicing globally. How do you maintain your voice and authenticity when designing a project in an unfamiliar city? Rob Rogers fondly recalls a road trip across America after architecture school. Enrique Norten has offices in New York and Mexico City, and shares the differences he's encountered working in each place. David Adjaye moves between Africa, London, and New York.

Everyone mentions the value of having a good team with a dedicated staff and a strong office culture. They always tend to hire consultants who help them push the envelope. The same engineers' names kept popping up, for instance. We included landscape architects because boundaries are blurred and the conversations are broader—and because everyone is concerned about resiliency and sustainability.

What is the role of the Academy? Uniformly, the architects enjoy teaching because it was a reliable source of income when they were starting their careers and broke, and became a way to explore multiple design ideas as they matured. They like the vibrancy and seeing students' different design approaches to a project. Richard Weller says it gives him the luxury of exploring an idea without a client, and he can head in any direction he likes.

The political process plays a role. There are community groups and design review boards that must be navigated for public projects. Two weeks after the 2016 election, Michael Murphy and Michael Sorkin devoted their evening to a hard look at architecture and politics, and the impact beyond getting whatever commissions would be doled out by the Trump Administration.

This book doesn't give enough real estate to those who were the other half of the conversations: the journalists, professors, historians, curators, clients, and people whose job it is to frame design issues for the public. They, too, were extremely articulate. Their voices are more muted only because of space constraints.

Architects tend to photograph their projects at dawn the day before they open, when the buildings are unoccupied and extremely clean. The photos are always visually stunning, but they tend to look alike. The buildings will never look this good again. We were searching for a way to frame the discussions and unify the presentations to bring more personality and informality to the book, and to reflect the spirit of the Cocktails and Conversations programs. For cohesion, the watercolor illustrations by Bishakh Som that place the architects in their buildings are our interpretations of the architects' work.

Architects are famous for talking about how they sketch the essence of an idea for a building on a napkin. So, we asked every architect to send us a napkin sketch. These are presented in the book—and will find their way to being a set of cocktail napkins soon.

Even though we represent the American Institute of Architects, we are colleagues and fellow architects—in other words, friends and family. This book is not a PR machine for the architects. These are the architects' voices, lightly edited from the conversations themselves.

Abby Suckle, *FAIA* **and William Singer,** *AIA*
Co-chairs, AIANY Architecture Dialogue Committee

CHARLES **RENFRO**

Charles Renfro is a Partner at **Diller Scofidio + Renfro** whose work includes the High Line and Lincoln Center, both in NY, The Broad in L.A., and Zaryadye Park in Moscow. He is the recipient of WSJ Magazine's 2017 Architecture Innovator Award, the Texas Medal of the Arts Award, and is a National Academician. He is President of the Board at Storefront for Art & Architecture in NY.

JUSTIN **DAVIDSON**

Justin Davidson, author of *Magnetic City: A Walking Companion to New York*, has been the classical music and architecture critic for **New York magazine** since 2007. Before that, he worked at *Newsday*, where he won a Pulitzer Prize in criticism and an American Society of News Editors award. He earned a doctorate in music composition at Columbia University.

MERGER: BRICKS + MORTAR + PIXELS

CR: Architecture should always be thoughtful and risk-taking. New York has been at the forefront of making policy in the realm of public-private partnerships, which makes different kinds of public spaces possible and gives them a creative edge.

CARRÉ SQUARED
By Toby Cecchini

1 part **H by Hine Cognac**
1 barspoon **Cynar artichoke liqueur**
1 part **Rittenhouse Bonded Rye**
1 barspoon **Marriage Freres Marco Polo black tea tincture**
1 part **Laird's Straight Apple Brandy**
2 dashes **Angostura orange bitters**
1 part **Dolan Blanc white sweet vermouth**
2 drops **Rosewater distillate**
Garnish with a **thin lemon twist**
Combine all ingredients in a large mixing glass over ice and stir together for 30-45 seconds. Strain into a double rocks glass over one large ice cube and garnish with a lemon twist.

For Charles, our inaugural architect, I had to concentrate on one of Diller Scofidio + Renfro's myriad projects. And so I chose the High Line, a turn-of-the-century structure lightened and repurposed for a modern stroll. In so doing, I took a parallel approach to an old turn-of-the-century cocktail, the Vieux Carré, and reinterpreted it accordingly.

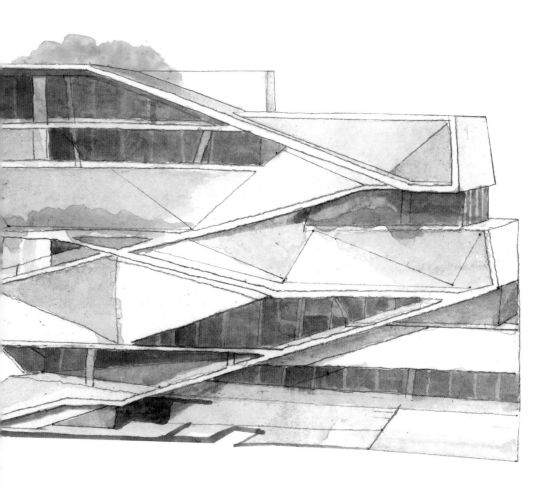

We are conditioned to think that a view costs a lot.

I think of the High Line as an apparatus for viewing, a kind of media device that reframes the city. It extracts elements of, or people from, the city. It also presents you to the city. In a lot of places you don't even realize that you're on stage and being watched. They're frames that work symbiotically in both directions and, in a way, turn this everyday life into a mediated event. We're trying to capture the effects, the impact, that an early age of media might have been able to deliver.

At the **High Line,** we came up with the concept called **Agritecture,** whereby we wanted to both harken back to the Industrial Age of the High Line, and also project forward into an era of digits and fuzziness.

THE HIGH LINE, NEW YORK, NY

We won the Lincoln Center commission because we were the only people who said, **we love Lincoln Center.** We love its diurnal rhythms, the pulse of life, how it changes from day to night, and that people spill out of these buildings at regular intervals. What we wanted to do is bring life back to Lincoln Center. Our objective was to make it more transparent.

A new media element embedded in the stairs becomes the front door of Lincoln Center.

LINCOLN CENTER FOR THE PERFORMING ARTS, NEW YORK, NY

JD: In New York, it's pretty much a given that every time you see them start to demolish a masonry building, you're going to get a glass building there instead.

One of the cheapest things you can do is to make a building out of glass. **We're trying to challenge some of the accepted qualities and performance characteristics of glass to elevate the experience.** We've always tried to make glass appear to do things proactively and challenge expectations. There is so much research being done in glass. It's electronic. You can dim it. You can make it opaque. You can break it, and you can drink from it. In a way, nobody questions what it does.

THE BROAD, LOS ANGELES, CA

INSTITUTE OF CONTEMPORARY ART, BOSTON, MA

To me, **making space by extraction, or building up space that is not filled to capacity, makes places great.** If you look around most commercial spaces, they're mostly just skin jobs. It's very hard to make fantastic, innovative architecture in the commercial sense in New York because everything is so tightly knitted together—the density, the fact that every cubic foot is counted in the value of the land purchased for a project and its zoning. Therefore, it's impossible to extract volume out of your building or else the owner won't make money. So typically, **great architecture is made with great space, I would say. Sometimes, it's made with great materials and joinery.**

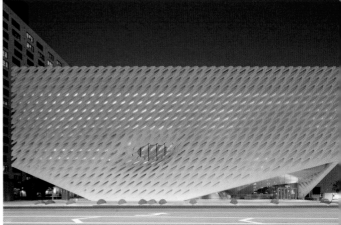

Back in 2000, when we did the Brasserie Restaurant, people were afraid of security and having their pictures taken and broadcast. It's interesting how times have changed. **Now people are upset if their image isn't in public.** They post 50 times a day. Lack of attention is the thing that we're now all afraid of.

Social media is free, it's cheap, it's entertaining, and it drains our critical life of actual, educated information and good writing.

I still think that there's room for media to act powerfully, but it's a little bit like glass. It's everywhere and everybody just accepts that transparency is the order of the day. Media means information and knowledge, and information could fall into the wrong hands. If you treat it carefully, you can still be very powerful.

JD: You can't have juxtaposition without contextualism. **If New York turned into an architecture park, it wouldn't be New York anymore.** *This is a large and complex city, and much as I love certain works that assert themselves, they wouldn't be able to assert themselves if that fabric weren't there.*

ROY & DIANA VAGELOS EDUCATION CENTER, NEW YORK, NY

JD: You said that you know there was a fear of surveillance and now we seem to love it. How has that changed your practice? And now that the technology you were thinking of has become reality, are you doing things differently, because of not just the technology, but how we think of it?

We have been transitioning the work that we do in three dimensions into media devices. **We've always been interested in the merger of bricks and mortar and pixels and never the stand-alone pixels.** Since we conceived of the LED screens at Lincoln Center, they've become ubiquitous in our cities.

ZARYADYE PARK, MOSCOW, RUSSIA

BLUR BUILDING, SWISS EXPO 2002, YVERDON-LES-BAINS, SWITZERLAND

Paris has a lot of standout pieces of architecture, and yet it also has one of the most consistent urban fabrics, which took top-down legislation. They made the city a pretty nice place.

CLAIRE
WEISZ

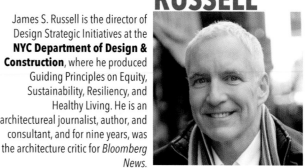

Claire Weisz is an architect, urbanist, and founding principal, along with her partner Mark Yoes, of NYC-based **WXY architecture + urban design**, which focuses on innovative approaches to public space, structures and cities. They were among the Architectural League of New York's 2011 Emerging Voices, and recipients of the League Prize.

JAMES S.
RUSSELL

James S. Russell is the director of Design Strategic Initiatives at the **NYC Department of Design & Construction**, where he produced Guiding Principles on Equity, Sustainability, Resiliency, and Healthy Living. He is an architectureal journalist, author, and consultant, and for nine years, was the architecture critic for *Bloomberg News*.

DESIGN DOES DRIVE CITIES

CW: You are marked by time, place, and news events, what was on television when you grew up, what you drive by, and walk by. What was in the American landscape was not what we were looking at in architecture school. The world of architecture was completely hermetically isolated. We looked at spaces that, for those of us who grew up in the middle of the prairies, had absolutely nothing to do with our prior experiences and natural environments. We figured out that our industry and nature were industrial, which really ran in the face of much of what we loved in architecture school. We learned that a building has to be more than a building. A landscape has to be more than a landscape. A railing has to be more than a railing. A sign has to be more than a sign. That's what architecture is about.

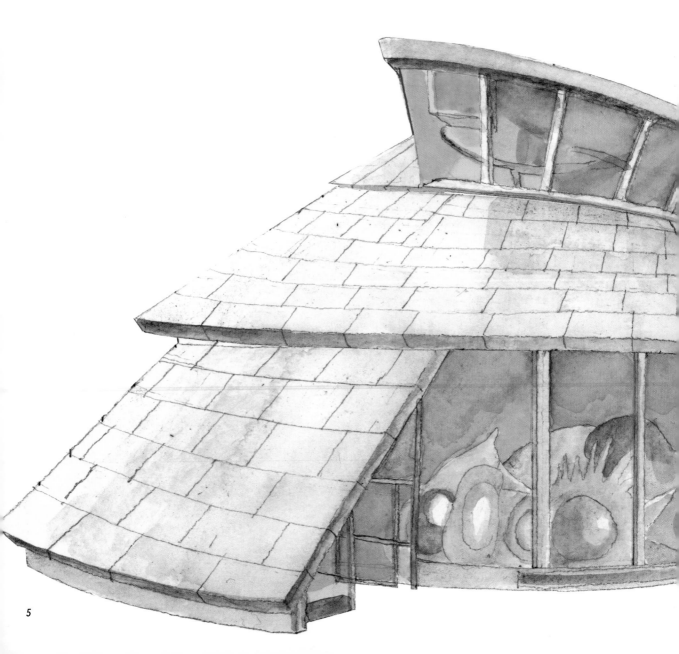

THE CLAIR POOL
By Toby Cecchini

2 oz. **Anchor Distilling Hophead Vodka**
1 oz. **Cocchi Americano**
2 **Fresh shiso leaves**
2 Dashes **Pomelo/Seville orange tincture** (orange bitters, for home use)
Tear shiso leaves into pieces and lightly muddle in the bottom of a mixing glass. Add ice, then liquid ingredients and stir for at least one minute. Strain into a chilled martini coupe. Garnish with a twist of lemon peel.

Something watery and limpid, with green elements, was called for to invoke Claire's reimagining of the Rockaway Boardwalk following Hurricane Sandy's destruction. She is an avowed fan of the vodka martini, so I riffed on it liberally.

BRONX CHARTER SCHOOL FOR THE ARTS, BRONX, NY

Look at how far New York City has been able to come in terms of the dialogue about public work. The kind of work many of us always thought was incredibly sexy and interesting. No one else believed us, especially people like Mayor Giuliani who were telling the Department of Design and Construction that they had to spend as little as possible on something, and if it looked good, that must mean it's expensive. What's really changed is that **the role of design is now understood and maybe the larger economic and cultural context.** We do have to thank Frank Gehry and Zaha Hadid and a number of architects for demonstrating that **design does drive cities**.

We do very tiny projects. We tend to get projects that other people think of as re-roofing projects or parking lot projects, and it turns out they're actually **public space projects**. We try to figure out what they should be. **Who am I? It's a question for institutions, just as it is for architects.**

JR: Constraint is character building. I just love the notion that designing a restroom facility, a comfort station suddenly becomes a whole other thing.

SEAGLASS CAROUSEL, NEW YORK, NY

FAR ROCKAWAY PARK, FAR ROCKAWAY, NY

Some of the smartest people in the city work in city government. So even if you are tearing your hair out about the project, it's usually pretty interesting to be in a meeting.

Every project is an excuse to get to know about something that you didn't before, and I think that's a great thing. It's hard to convince people of the idea that architecture teaches everyone something during the process; it's something we still have to get over.

A lot of the work we're doing now is actually non-physical projects. **In our digital society Big Data rules.** No one understands it physically. It's really important to dabble in what is the physical overlap with all of this information out there. What will architecture mean in the next five or six years? Architects are in an interesting position because they actually know something about the space between here and there.

WXY URBAN FURNITURE SYSTEMS, NEW YORK, NY

"The only way to get to know a site is to sleep on it, and to sleep on it in every season of the year, before you start working on it."
—Dan Kiley

Right now, unfortunately, people assume that after five minutes, you're supposed to understand a place. I think one of the reasons we've done so much work in New York City is because we're starting to understand it. And it's been 19 years working in New York.

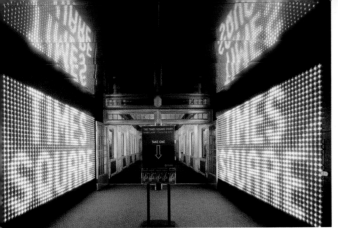

TIMES SQUARE VISITORS CENTER, NEW YORK, NY

We don't understand how important what we throw out is, as a resource. We spend so much money trucking all of our garbage to Pennsylvania that we're unable to pay for other things, and we don't charge people for the amount of garbage they throw out.

Trash is becoming so valuable that we're going to end up figuring out how to deal with it. Because we're going to have to.

It isn't about just looking at the end of Sanitation as facilities, but really supporting the city by **spending money on infrastructure.** There's a huge budget constraint in the city on making these big investments.

I meet people who fundamentally think that apps are going to solve everything. But, in a sense, all they want is to track people's whereabouts, believing that they can then design cities around people's movements. They now also have **new ways of tracking desire.**

An app might get me to buy something, but it won't get me to go somewhere. People haven't figured out that sometimes we move around to avoid things. Replicating movement affected by negative aspects in the city is not a good idea.

BRONX EMS AMBULANCE STATION, BRONX, NY

SPRING STREET MANHATTAN DISTRICTS 1/2/5 GARAGE AND SALT SHED, NEW YORK, NY

Architecture is a dialogue. If you don't get emotional because you don't care about it, and if someone on the other side doesn't care either, you are toast. Whenever you see an architect building in the public realm, there are a lot of people who championed it to make it happen.

JR: I would second that. Especially with controversial projects. Brilliant clients can help the architect come up with a design that is more acceptable. **Brilliant clients will also dive in and help you make it happen.**

XINJIN BRIDGE, CHINA

I love the idea of designing a Sanitation Transfer Center.

In the case of Spring Street, it's a **Sanitation Maintenance Garage.** You really have to give credit to the Bloomberg Administration and its smart public servants. We can't simply put all of the trucks and garbage in the Bronx. It's not fair. On the other hand, a garage is not a place where garbage is dumped. It's where trucks are cleaned and stored. People don't want to parse that.

AUDREY MATLOCK

Audrey Matlock leads **Audrey Matlock Architect**, a New York City-based studio committed to fusing architecture, technology, and contemporary culture. Her project base is international with a range of building types. Her firm has won more than 30 design awards, including 10 from the AIA.

JASON SHEFTELL

The late Jason Sheftell was the real estate editor and chief design, architecture, and neighborhood writer for the **New York Daily News**, where he created and launched the paper's *"Your Home"* section more than five years ago. Since then, the section has changed the way real estate, neighborhoods, and design have been covered in New York.

THE ONES THAT GOT AWAY

AM: I think architecture does have its rewards, which is why we all stick with it. Architecture is endlessly fascinating. You never run out of things to think about, new experiences, new challenges, new things to dig into. We brush shoulders lightly with politics, with economic issues, social issues, artistic issues, construction issues. That's why it's interesting. That's why we do it—it has greater rewards than just money. There are so many other things we could have chosen to do to make all that money we should be making.

CROSS-ISLE EXPRESSWAY
By Toby Cecchini

1 oz. **Plantation 5-year Barbados Rum**
1 oz. **Smith & Cross Navy Strength Pot Still Jamaican Rum**
1 1/2 oz. **Lime-ginger cordial**
1/2 oz. **Fresh lime juice**
1/2 oz. 1:1 ratio **simple syrup**

Shake all ingredients together over ice and strain into a double old fashioned glass with one large ice cube. Garnish with half a spent lime hull and three spritzes of Laphroaig 10-year Cask Strength scotch.

Warning that she only occasionally drinks Dark 'n' Stormys—and that she was fine with anything but scotch—I had to take a playful jab at Audrey by concocting a type of Dark 'n' Stormy with a wisp of an Islay malt overlay: island to island, as it were.

The word **practice** is a very curious word to describe what we do. The dictionary defines practice as rehearsal, exercise, preparation, training, run-through, drill, repetition, and, in a sentence, uses it as "practice makes perfect." Sadly, it's a very good description for much of what we do—lengthy proposals, unpaid design studies, poorly-paid competitions, projects lost to someone who undercuts our fair fees, who uses unpaid interns. And **sometimes it seems only a fraction of our very hard work results in real projects.** So, we certainly do get a lot of practice. And tonight I thought we would show some of our practice here. **The ones that got away. The war stories.** The ones lamented over cocktails with our friends and colleagues.

BAR HOUSE, EAST HAMPTON, NY

CATSKILL MOUNTAIN HOUSE, CATSKILL, NY

I made my treehouse from scraps from the farmhouse my parents were renovating. I've always been fascinated with relationships between indoor and outdoor spaces, and how specific landscape conditions inform architecture. There's a 12-foot-long terrace on the 7-by-7-foot house, so my interest in long-span structures goes way back. There was a roof deck reachable by a hatch with a latch to keep people out. I've always been interested in construction strategies and materials, testing new ways of thinking about them, which you can see in the treehouse. I've taken clapboards and rotated them vertically, so they overlap, but aligned vertically. That was kind of a radical idea back then, as a matter of fact. Functional design has always been important to me; there are even screens and shutters on the windows in my treehouse.

Alcohol loosens the tongue, so they say. Since we are all here drinking together this evening, I thought I would share some of my past with you and start by giving a public presentation of **my very first building, a treehouse that I designed when I was ten.**

MEDEU SPORTS CENTER, ALMATY, KAZAKHSTAN

ARMSTRONG VISITOR CENTER, LANCASTER, PA

Though treehouses are usually higher, I've been partial to low-to-the-ground residences, especially ones that have protected space underneath. As we all know, any good building today is adaptable; several years later this became a favorite party place for my young teenage friends. So this was a practice run for some of those skyscrapers I began to work on 30 years later, and possibly the inspiration for a recent project in the Hamptons: a low-slung house in the trees with a long span, roof terraces, space underneath, and sunscreens. This treehouse has continued to inspire my work going forward.

A few years after the treehouse, we designed our first invited and paid competition. This project was driven by an idea about a physical model to describe women's history. It was organized in two spirals that wove historical events together in a non-linear way. We did not win. The museum was never built. It was cancelled. It was a political hot potato. One thing about this project that we particularly mourned was not getting to build the flowing glass façade that we worked so hard with Arup to develop. **Sometimes lost competitions spawn ideas that resurface in later projects.** Several years later we were able to revisit this concept in the Chelsea Modern, where we developed an undulating infill façade to horizontally weave together this kind of diverse neighborhood context.

Sometimes they come back in another form, so some good comes out of these losses. Sometimes we lose the battle, but we build the project. 57 Irving Place, a residential project, was a victim of the economy and only recently completed. We had a really interesting proposal where the living spaces could open to the exterior with large sliding glass walls on tracks. We were really excited about it. But our client did not share our enthusiasm. And the brokers concurred that no one would ever buy into this. Lo and behold about a year later, there were previews in the media for an apartment building designed by Shigeru Ban where vertical sliding panels open living spaces to the exterior. History tells us that they sold like hotcakes for a massive amount of money. So always listen to brokers [said sarcastically].

57 IRVING PLACE RESIDENTIAL TOWER, NEW YORK, NY

CHELSEA MODERN, NEW YORK, NY

JS: Where do your inspirations come from?

The site is primary. I don't think one building can work in two sites that are even remotely similar. For that reason we've taken a different approach to many projects. It might be the same building type, but the site would indicate a different way of beginning that project.

I'm very interested in program. I'm very interested in what happens in the building. I'm fascinated with skyscrapers as structures, as a type of technical spatial challenge. For other reasons I love projects that have really rich programming that can be a huge inspiration for how to start a project.

JS: The role of an architect defines the way we're going to live and how we look at programs and institutions. Isn't that part of the architect's role, or is it a part of the institution's role?

One of the reasons that people don't like architects is that we tell them how they're supposed to live. We tell them how they're supposed to do things. That's a criticism that I've often heard about architects, from non-architects. A good client hopes that what we will do is take their concepts about how they want to use the space and turn them into exciting spatial ideas.

BRAD CLOEPFIL

Architect, educator, and principal of **Allied Works Architecture**, Brad Cloepfil founded AWA in his native Portland, OR, in 1994, and opened the New York office in 2003. He has a Bachelor of Architecture from the University of Oregon, and a Master of Science in Advanced Architectural Design from Columbia University.

DAVID VAN DER LEER

David van der Leer is the executive director of the **Van Alen Institute** in NYC, which develops projects that explore the relationship between the built environment and the human being. He was previously associate curator, Architecture & Urban Studies at the Guggenheim and initiated the BMW Guggenheim Lab.

MAKING BUILDINGS

BC: For me, you either seek an architectural challenge or you're offered an architectural challenge. You ask the question about what a building can reveal, what understanding can it serve. How many times do we go into a building of any era that reveals something to us, whether it's a sense of place, a sense of ceremony, a sense of awe, or a sense of beauty? Or something that could contribute to a conversation about our culture or lives or the way we gather or the way we build? That it's cool is just not enough for me.

THE CLOEPFIL RHUBARB GIMLET
By Toby Cecchini

2 oz. **Plymouth Gin**
2 oz. **Rhubarb/vanilla syrup**
1 oz. **Fresh lemon cordial**

Mix ingredients in an ice-filled shaker and shake until well-chilled and diluted. Double-strain into a stemmed cocktail or martini glass, and garnish with a twist of lemon.

Combining Brad's Portland, Oregon, roots (rhubarb) with a fresh lemon cordial yielded this cross-up of a Plymouth Martini and a gimlet he insisted upon. I also couldn't resist the waggishness of giving Brad Cloepfil, this big, western, virile fellow, a pink drink that perfectly resembles a Cosmopolitan.

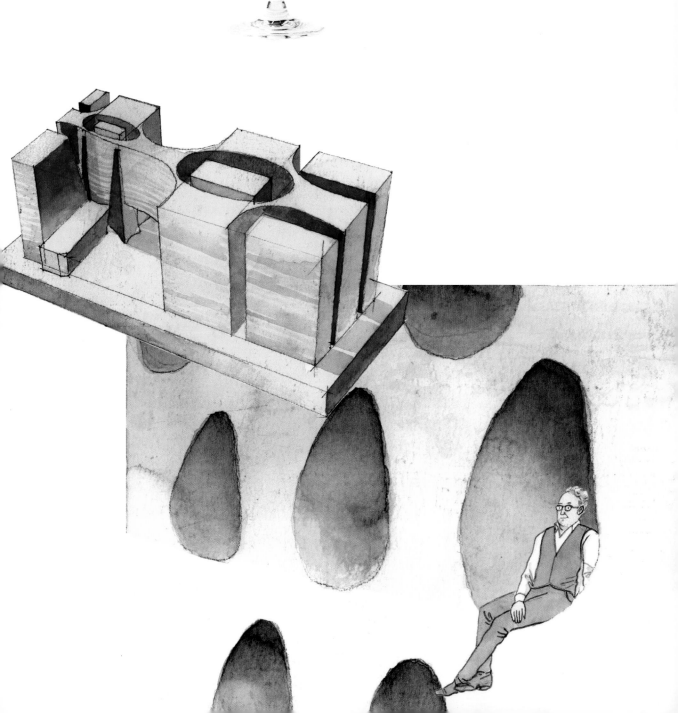

I was giving a talk at the opening of the Seattle Art Museum. I don't remember the context of what I was saying, but I mentioned that there was only one thing that would make it better. This would be **if I could have a martini while giving a talk.** Someone ran across the street to a strip joint called the Lucky Lady, and returned with a martini for me which they set on the podium. That was the only time this ever happened until tonight. **Really, it is a dream come true.**

NATIONAL VETERANS MEMORIAL AND MUSEUM, COLUMBUS, OH

DUTCHESS COUNTY RESIDENCE GUEST HOUSE, DUTCHESS COUNTY, NY

It's interesting because clients don't always know the answers to those questions. **In our culture, architecture is such a commodity.** I guess it always has been, but it certainly seems to be right now. They actually need something for the architecture to serve, other than whether it's a museum or library.

There are bigger questions that the architecture can engage with clients. It's not common, so it's important to bring them along.

DvdL: When I was listening to the story about the drink, which was so beautifully told, I was wondering what skills do you pull out of your bag when you come up for a difficult client interview? What do you show or tell them to convince them that you have a good idea?

I ask them questions. **What do they hope for the architecture? What are they striving for? What's their aspiration for the building? Why are they doing this project?** It's very interesting. Often when clients hire architects for museums, they don't talk about the fact that they want to make beautiful galleries. They say: "We want to hire an architect because we want to raise money." Or, "We want it to be an icon." There are a lot of architects who can make icons, whatever that is. Or because such-and-such a city needs a new museum. To turn it around, I ask them to begin an exercise of being introspective, because you have to be introspective to do a building. I need that information to design a building. I can't come in with, "We will take care of you, no problem. Call us in a couple of years and we'll have the design done and it'll be great. "

NATIONAL MUSIC CENTRE OF CANADA, ALBERTA, CANADA

SOKOL BLOSSER WINERY TASTING ROOM, DAYTON, OR

When we entered the competition for Canada's National Music Centre, we Googled it. It doesn't exist. There is no National Music Centre. What is it? Nobody even knew how big this building was. It was a big question mark, which most architects would run away from. It's a question that we were asking together with the client. We looked at museums and music institutes all over the world. It became a conversation about the programming, the architecture, and the aspirations of a nation and what it means to manifest their cultural ambitions.

15

We're also being educated. You research and invent a new building typology that doesn't exist. You do it together.

It's important to me to find places, spaces of great introspection. We don't have that many in our culture. I think the New York Public Library has some of those kinds of spaces. We seek those rooms. In Denver in particular, there are all of these buildings trying to make very broad, very public, very loud statements. The Clyfford Still Museum is a small building, but it showcases powerful, spiritual work—that we had a chance to spend time with that work and create that kind of intimacy was a treat.

U.S. EMBASSY MOZAMBIQUE, MAPUTO, MOZAMBIQUE

CLYFFORD STILL MUSEUM, DENVER, CO

The West is so important to me, and the **best elixir is the landscape,** where I regenerate. I prefer to be out in an unbuilt environment. It's the calmness, sense of awe and stillness and scale that creates introspection. Isn't it funny that **some of the most introspective times of our lives are in the biggest places**? Grand Canyon, Gothic cathedrals—losing the sense of your own scale is when you become the most introspective.

When I was growing up in the West, the cities were inconsequential as built places. In the West, there are some of the greatest acts of architecture you could imagine without any architects—huge infrastructure projects, the freeways and the dams, were just mind blowing. Their impact is greater than anything we can imagine. They are spectacular.

I do think that in the cacophony of our lives, you have the opportunity for architecture to filter out some of that noise, to be more of a **vessel of discernment**, to choose what to let in and let out, and not compete with all the other noise in our lives. It's nice to have architecture as acts of editing. That's one thing architecture does best.

I would love to think that it's always the architecture that creates a great room—that's what we all hope for as architects. I would love to think it was the beauty of that empty room. But it's not. It's the curation of the art collection, performance of the play, the music, or the dinner party that makes the space special. The fact that it gets superimposed over the architecture is very interesting. For me, it becomes the conversation and a study of where to stop the architecture. **Don't make the architecture the conversation**. The architecture is not the play, not the dinner party. It is only the vessel, the vehicle, the instigator, the facilitator.

CLYFFORD STILL MUSEUM, DENVER, CO

CLYFFORD STILL MUSEUM CONCEPT MODEL

DvdL: I do a lot of studio visits. I like meeting the people behind the work because the work seems to speak more. Office culture is interesting because people are incredibly dedicated and work very long hours.

We have an extensive bar at both offices, and one day a year we drink all day. Our staff works incredibly hard, and we don't pay them enough. But it's a very collegial culture—we're having a lot of fun, a tremendous amount of fun. Maybe it's similar in other offices—if you survive the pressure, there are such strong bonds formed that even when they get off work, they often spend time together.

RICHARD
WELLER

Richard Weller is the Martin and Margy Meyerson Chair of Urbanism and professor and chair of Landscape Architecture at the **University of Pennsylvania**. He is the former director of the Australian Urban Design Research Centre, and former co-director of the design firm Room 4.1.3, acknowledged with a Penn Press monograph in 2005.

WILLIAM
MENKING

Founder and editor-in-chief of *The Architect's Newspaper*, and professor at Pratt Institute, William Menking has organized, curated, and written catalogues for exhibitions on architecture and urbanism in the U.S., England, and Europe, including *Archigram: Experimental Architecture 1961-1974*, and the U.S. Pavilion at the 2008 Venice Architecture Biennale.

DREAMSCAPES AND WAKE-UP CALLS

"Philosopher, practitioner, visionary. Richard uses the tools of layers of process, of analysis, of integration to address areas where rapid urban growth and biodiversity are in direct conflict with each other. He calls this socio-ecological drama. His work engages fiercely with the multidimensional layered nature of cities and landscapes, and positions the landscape architect as the great conductor of an orchestra of the most varied physical and social instruments." —Laura Starr, *FASLA*, Starr Whitehouse Landscape Architects

THE ANTI SOUTHSIDE
By Toby Cecchini

2 oz. **Absolut Vodka**
3/4 oz. **Lime**
3/4 oz. **Ginger syrup** (1:1 ginger juice and sugar)
1/4 oz. **Cucumber juice** (this I extracted right before the event, so it would be fresh)
6 **Mint leaves**

Place all ingredients in a shaker filled with ice and shake ferociously for 10 to 20 seconds. Strain into a large rocks glass with fresh ice cubes, leaving room to top off with 4 oz. soda water. Garnish with a mint sprig top, a thin slice of cucumber, and a lime wedge.

As Richard was our first landscape architect, I went for a super-clean and super-green hybrid of a Moscow Mule and a Southside, using both freshly extracted cucumber and ginger juice and a spritz of soda atop.

There's a little box in the garden, which is a camera obscura. You go inside this little building and you see the world flipped upside down. As a rule, **there is nothing in this garden that is not already a representation of landscape.**

What is landscape architecture's larger calling? I've never done projects just because of commercial need. I admire people who do run commercial practices and maintain a level of creativity. **That's not easy.**

I've had the luxury of being able to always have one foot in the academy and one foot in practice, so I've been able to be selective. **I've had the luxury of time.** I've had the luxury of choice. And I have explicitly only done projects when I felt like there was a research question of some importance in the project.

My journey started from what you might call art work and a strong interest in representation right up to a very large-scale kind of operation. Now, I'm much more interested in the potential of what we refer to as planning, and how that can influence policy and be a very active agent in terms of social and economic change.

Most landscape architecture that you see seems to feel the need to represent nature. There will be varying degrees of abstraction in that representation, but, typically, almost every landscape project will try to represent nature. The Garden of Australian Dreams explicitly refuses to do that—**there is no representation of nature.**

**THE GARDEN OF AUSTRALIAN DREAMS,
NATIONAL MUSEUM OF AUSTRALIA,** CANBERRA, AUSTRALIA

We won the open competition, with the architects Ashton Raggatt McDougall, for the Garden of Australian Dreams at the National Museum of Australia, a museum that encapsulates the national narrative. What was at stake here, in terms of meaning, was quite high. The architects broke the program up into a series of chunks, and used different buildings to create a chaotic compilation of architectural forms. This is no-holds-barred stuff. The client expected a garden, right? Flowers and plants, just nature, for goodness sake. Please. It's not. Children love it. They treat it as a playground. They don't realize they're running around on a huge map of the nation that has massacre sites and all the rest of it emblazoned into the surface. The word "Australia," taken from our national currency, is written in reverse.

**THE GARDEN OF AUSTRALIAN DREAMS,
NATIONAL MUSEUM OF AUSTRALIA,** CANBERRA, AUSTRALIA

The garden opened and, of course, everyone panicked. The government said, "What the hell have you done?" Then, everything became more meaningful. And to this day, the museum will ring me up and say, "You know, we've just seen **a pigeon sitting in one part of the garden. What does it mean?"**

**THE GARDEN OF AUSTRALIAN DREAMS,
NATIONAL MUSEUM OF AUSTRALIA,** CANBERRA, AUSTRALIA

**THE GARDEN OF AUSTRALIAN DREAMS,
NATIONAL MUSEUM OF AUSTRALIA,** CANBERRA, AUSTRALIA

I like doing memorials because they raise the bar so high for your choice of metaphor and allegory and symbolism. **The translation of meaning into form is never more acute than when you are doing something like a memorial.**

Our Tsunami Memorial competition entry was based on the tension between **cosmos**, the Greek word for order, and **chaos**. We've become more familiar with chaos now, as a new form of order, through mathematics. But when the natural world acts up, like the Thai tsunami or Superstorm Sandy, we hate nature. We cannot comprehend that level of chaos. Of course, we better get used to it because it appears that the planet is starting to unleash all sorts of chaos on us.

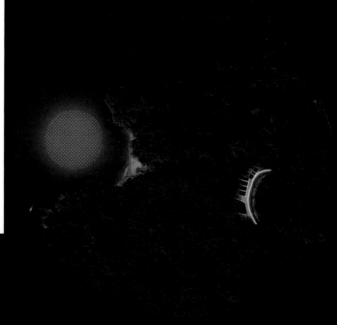

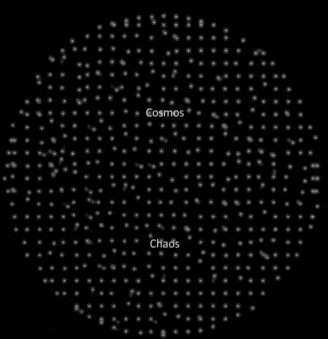

TSUNAMI MEMORIAL COMPETITION, THAILAND

There are now larger issues on global, national, and bioregional scales that we need landscape architects to speak to. To map.

There's a nice tension between the disorder of the diagram and the ideal of perfect order, which appeals to the human mind, as it has done throughout history.

When I lived in Berlin, I did quite a lot of competition work with Daniel Libeskind, including Potsdamer Platz. I think that Libeskind drew one of the bravest drawings I've ever seen for that site. Irrespective of what you think of his work now, back then, he was on fire. And doing such risky, intelligent work.

New urbanism is appealing to people on a range of levels because nostalgia is always particular. It's sugarcoated, but we're dealing with urban challenges on a much greater scale than I think new urbanism has even broached yet.

I'm talking about engagement. I'm talking about going into a certain situation and looking at its ecology, infrastructure, population growth, projections, and economies of scale. These are the things to talk about, then apply the creativity of design to those problems. I don't see why that's so hard.

TSUNAMI MEMORIAL COMPETITION, THAILAND

TSUNAMI MEMORIAL COMPETITION, THAILAND

ROB ROGERS

Rob Rogers, founding partner of **ROGERS PARTNERS** Architects+Urban Designers, explores the overlap of disciplines: the spaces where architecture, landscapes, and the public realm converge. Designing around the country, the firm creates work built on research, analysis, discovery, and shared experience.

SUSAN S. SZENASY

Susan S. Szenasy is currently the Director of Design Innovation of **Metropolis**, the award-winning architecture and design magazine, and served as its editor-in-chief from 1986-2017. She is internationally recognized as an authority on sustainability and design, and holds four honorary doctorates.

CROSS COUNTRY

RR: I think our skills as architects are needed in much more radically diverse ways than simply producing buildings. I don't really ever focus solely on the building until I've thought about a much, much bigger picture. Good ideas become self-fulfilling sometimes. If you get the right situation set up and the right collection of events and people, then a project develops its own momentum. Engaging in key relationships and partnerships with land-scape architects and engineers in ways that are about the public space is important.

DAD'S GIN AND TONIC
By Toby Cecchini

3 oz. **Gin**
6 oz. **Chilled tonic water**
1 **Lime**
Garnish with the **lime fronds**

Cut the lime in half and juice, setting juice aside. Cut spent lime hulls into thin strips and muddle together with the gin in a large mixing tin or measuring cup for 20 or 30 seconds. Fill a tall highball glass halfway with ice and add the tonic water, pouring gently on a slant. Over the back of a spoon, strain the gin/lime mixture atop the tonic water to float it. Add a straw carefully and heap the left-over lime frond on top as the garnish.

Robert Rogers, like every architect, wanted a martini. His edict was: "Let's get together and talk gin!" So I took the abundant water present in his work as an invitation to, instead, do a gin highball, in fact my favorite one. In this version, you extract and incorporate the precious citrus oil in the lime's skin, which, as Robert Frost wrote, makes all the difference.

Growing up in Colorado, I went camping in the winter as much as I went camping in the summer. That **engagement with the elements** drives you to think about the world—that you want to be out in it, you want to be engaged, you want to participate, and you love it as much as the urban world.

I built a lot of projects in Wyoming, but that's a very different mountain landscape than where I grew up. Colorado is greener, steeper, wetter, more forested. And I have to say that to go back and to be able to do something in the mountains with authority and delicacy in a place that wanted a building, not some big lodge at a ski resort, but something that had a programmatic value and intent for being in and around the mountains, would be amazing.

When I first started school at Rice University, I took contract law courses as well as architecture, because I'd always been fascinated with the law. I actually used to take the bus to downtown Denver and watch a neighbor who was a trial lawyer try cases. I always thought that's what I was going to do, even though my father was an architect and, in fact, my mother as well. She was the second registered female architect in the State of Texas. My high school art teacher was so upset when I told her I was going to study law that she said, "Oh, you've got to do something else at the same time." So I ended up doing both, and after one semester of pre-law stuff, I was in love with Studio for the rest of my life.

SANDRIDGE COMMONS, OKLAHAMA CITY, OK

SANDRIDGE COMMONS, OKLAHAMA CITY, OK

Postmodernism and education in the early 1980s was a real soup, and there was a lot of that soup at Rice at the time. James Stirling had just completed a new building [School of Architecture's Anderson Hall]. I had had always been a bit frustrated with that as a direction. When I finished school, I decided: "**I'm an American architect and I'm going to know my country as if it was my own backyard.**" So I took my Datsun station wagon and drove around the United States, Canada, and Mexico for the summer. I went to pretty much every major city, almost never on an Interstate, sleeping in the back of the car or camping. I was a kid, so I could drive for 12, 15 hours and love it. That formed my love of the American landscape in all of its parts. A prairie is an exceptional thing, and Chicago is the quintessential American city.

CONSTITUTION GARDENS, NATIONAL MALL, WASHINGTON, DC

My sophomore class took a trip to Washington, DC. We walked around the Mall on a foggy, misty evening and came upon the East Wing of the National Gallery, which had just opened. There was a lot of postmodernist stuff going on at Rice. The East Wing blew me away. It was like, "Oh my God, this is another kind of architecture!" I didn't know it could be like this in terms of form and space, the materiality. That's when I decided that I wanted to work for I.M. Pei when I got out of school.

I kept a journal, of course, with sketches, and also made recordings describing what I was seeing. I've gone back a number of times to listen to them, and they bring back powerful visual images. My car didn't have air conditioning so the wind was howling. Willie Nelson was playing in the background. And I'm talking about my reaction to the temperature driving across Death Valley, or what it's like to arrive at the Grand Canyon.

When I moved to New York, I worked at I.M. Pei's office for seven years. From Day One, the conversations were: "How do you make things last? What is this going to look like in 25 years?" I was schooled in an attitude about responsibility that's wasn't: "Can I make this curved this week?" I think our work reflects that. It tries to be very thoughtful. I'm just as concerned about what it's going to be like 25 years from now as I am the day it opens, and sometimes it's better.

I took my portfolio everywhere, but when Pei's office invited me to come back, I decided that was the thing to do. It was interesting because it's not like you had a personal voice in the office. You could contribute to strategies and parts and pieces, but you didn't necessarily get to explore your own. So there was a delay while getting training and exposure before you were actually able to begin to explore your own vision and your own sets of ideas. For me, it began to coalesce that the stunning art of building came from the Pei experience, and my love for the American landscape and American cities came from the rest of my background. It's become this kind of reservoir for me in thinking about cities.

THE ELEVATED ACRE AT 55 WATER STREET, NEW YORK, NY

SS: I know firsthand that Oklahoma City has a great mayor. He's incredibly activist in terms of the physical environment and architecture. When there's something really interesting happening in a mid-size city, it usually means that there's political leadership and power, that there are programs that are really working for what the people actually need, that the mayor and the city council are completely engaged and are working within the American democratic system.

Here's a city that voted to tax themselves for urban improvements in what may be one of the reddest of red states that exists. This is an example where the motives are all the same, even if the politics are different. They're really making incredible strides and efforts to understand that **"Downtown" is the economic driver, and that you have to nurture it and care for it to make it happen.**

ATLANTA'S PARK OVER GA400, ATLANTA, GA

HENDERSON-HOPKINS HIGH SCHOOL, BALTIMORE, MD

We were invited to do a corporate headquarters for an energy company in Oklahoma City. There was a 50-story tower underway for another energy company. So we said that it was better to go horizontal to engage the city. Let's see how much ground we can cover. Land is so bloody cheap. Let's spread out and take on as much of the city as we can. **Instead of throwing a rock in the pond, let's throw a handful of gravel and watch the ripples** and the impact as the corporate headquarters grows. We programmed a series of opportunities to surround the main building with a restored building, and with new buildings and high-quality public spaces extending up and down the major avenues. Not only are you occupying horizontally in terms of program, buildings, and opportunities, but you're also taking on the impact of the ground plane, putting people back into the city.

4

24

TODD
SCHLIEMANN

Todd Schliemann is a design partner at **Ennead Architects**. His designs are recognized internationally for architectural excellence and have received numerous national AIA Honor Awards, New York State and New York Chapter AIA Awards and American Architecture Awards from the Chicago Athenaeum, among others.

CLIFFORD
PEARSON

Clifford Pearson is a contributing editor of *Architectural Record*. He is a director of Asia Design Forum and the former director of the University of Southern California's American Academy in China. He is the author of *Indonesia: Design and Culture*, published by Monacelli Press, and the editor of *Modern American Houses*, published by Harry N. Abrams.

LOSERS REVISITED

TS: The worst thing you can call someone is a loser. But I think if we embrace it and learn from it, there's a lot of positive stuff that we can get from it.

About Failure

Paula Scher: *"When you're working you make mistakes, particularly when you're young, you make discoveries, because you do things that are inappropriate and wrong-headed, but within the wrong-headedness, you find an unexpected way to go. These things are truly the breakthroughs. You have to fail in order to make the next discovery. You have to get bad in order to get good. You have to try a lot of things and fail in order to make the next discovery."*

Thomas Edison: *"Many of life's failures are people who did not realize how close they were to success when they gave up."*

John Wooden: *"Failure is not fatal, but failure to change might be."*

George Bernard Shaw: *"When I was young, I observed that nine out of 10 things I did were failures, so I did 10 times more work."*

John Burroughs: *"A man can fail many times, but he isn't a failure until he begins to blame somebody else."*

Oscar Wilde: *"Ambition is the last refuge of the failure."*

Truman Capote: *"Failure is the condiment that gives success its flavor."*

THE ESQUIRO
By Eben Klemm

Build in an ice-filled Collins glass:
1 1/2 oz. **Blended scotch**
1 oz. mix of:
   1 part **Lemon juice**
   1 part **Lime juice**
   1 part **Light agave nectar**
Fill 3/4 of the glass with **club soda** or **sparkling water**
Float on top: **carrot juice** spiced with **fresh ginger juice** to taste (I recommend 10 to 1)
Garnish with **candied ginger** and **lime wheel** cut slightly off axis.

My conversation with Todd Schliemann resulted in a cocktail that aimed to reference his love of sailing and taste for scotch. Since the Dark 'n' Stormy is a yachtsman's cocktail, I swapped whiskey for the rum and, wanting to re-create the effect I saw in sun playing across the mirrored façades of some of his buildings (or perhaps a sunset at sea), I floated carrot juice across the surface. I really like carrot and ginger as a combination in cocktails, especially with a sugar-like agave, which can conceal its vegetality.

All architects design a lot more than they ever get a chance to build. If you're young, it's a long haul to get anything built. When you're old, maybe, **for every 100 buildings you've designed, you get one built.**

If you believe that the ultimate destination of architecture is to build, that's a rough road. I want to talk about some of the projects that I did with others that never got built. We were never selected as the architect, but they had ideas in them that didn't go away, that we didn't let go and we reinvented for other projects that did get built. When I lose a project or competing for one that loses, I immediately let it go. I put it behind me and look to the next one. You don't get into the reasons why you lose. I think it's a good idea to look back every once in a while.

THE STANDARD, HIGH LINE, NEW YORK, NY

In the end, losers can win. **Failure begets success, as long as we learn from it.** I think the key question is: How do you learn from it? That's the difficult part, because you can tell someone, Okay, you failed, now figure out how to take that failure and create something successful. Sometimes you fail, not because the idea was bad, but because the developer didn't provide enough money, or the jury just picked the wrong scheme.

CP: When you realize that something is actually wrong with your design, how do you then take that next step and ask, "Okay, how do we turn it into something successful?"

When an architect makes a mistake, it lives for a long time, so you have to be very, very careful. The one thing you have to be is honest with yourself, and realize that what you did was wrong. Don't wonder what the circumstances were under which you could blame someone else or blame a circumstance, or bury it. We do have a tendency to bury our failures. You have to figure out a way to build on it, not to correct it necessarily, but to stand on it to move forward. Because if you don't, you're just going to repeat what you're doing now over and over and over, and progress won't be made. And sometimes you have to plant ivy on your building, as Frank Lloyd Wright said.

NATURAL HISTORY MUSEUM, SALT LAKE CITY, UT

NATURAL HISTORY MUSEUM, SALT LAKE CITY, UT

It's also important to look around, to understand the world and bring that to bear on the architecture. You can't create a meaningful thing without doing that, especially if you're working in the public realm.

For the Weill Cornell Greenberg Center, we designed a low-iron glass with a special frit pattern, which actually is really fabulous, because the faceting creates some of the most amazing shadows and colors, and reflects the sky. There are little round thumbprint-like things in the spandrel glass on the east side of that building. Every morning when the sun hits it, there's a moiré because the glass is not flat and the two patterns are not in registration. When we saw it, we were disappointed and felt that the glass was ruined. It wasn't ruined, but we pushed it out of proportion. At some point, I just said, "Yeah, but it's actually, it's kind of cool, look at it. Look at it closely." Get close to your mistake, really close to it, and accept it, **be honest with yourself.**

We grasped hold of this idea of the moiré and said, "Okay, great. So we'll make our entire building a moiré." So it became a kind of light ball for York College.

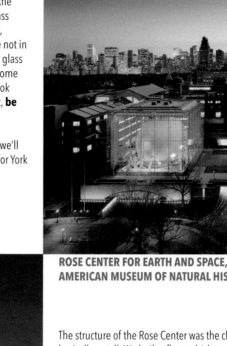

ROSE CENTER FOR EARTH AND SPACE, AMERICAN MUSEUM OF NATURAL HISTORY, NEW YORK, NY

The structure of the Rose Center was the cheapest you could do. It was basically a stall. We built a floor, which was a stable diaphragm that had three legs, big legs, and that was it. Then we built a dome on top and hung a dome on the bottom. It's just bent I-beams, sort of crude. I hated that. It was very painful to build such a beautiful thing with such a clumsy structure. Nobody sees that structure inside the sphere, but I do.

MARINA BAY INTEGRATED RESORT COMPETITION, SINGAPORE

CP: It's also interesting that you're dissecting and learning from a "success." The Rose Center got pretty good reviews; certainly, not too many people were criticizing it.

It's in the integrity of the entire project. It's like the Powers of 10 idea [reference to Charles and Ray Eames film]. I want to be able to create something that, at a distance, is an attraction. Then, when you leave, you take the memories. I want the whole thing. I want it to be built perfectly, beautifully, every little detail.

COCKRELL SCHOOL OF ENGINEERING EDUCATION & RESEARCH CENTER, UNIVERSITY OF TEXAS, AUSTIN, TX

BIOLOGICAL SCIENCE BUILDING, UNIVERSITY OF MICHIGAN, ANN ARBOR, MI

With our practice, Jim Polshek was a sort of impresario, always open to having a collaborative office where a lot of people had a lot of opportunities. I used to say that Jim was really good at creating **a killing field for design**. He would talk to a client and then give us this wide open place to design. He was brilliant at it. He still is. The transition to Ennead took about five years. It was a long process that nobody knew about until we created this really unusual name, which shocked everybody. The whole idea is that this entity could go and on and on and on.

CALVIN **TSAO**

Calvin Tsao, founder of **TsAO + McKOWN Architects**, draws from his experience with diverse cultures and a lively engagement with a variety of art forms. He serves on the board of The American Academy in Rome, and is an active board member and president emeritus of The Architectural League of New York.

KAREN **STEIN**

Karen Stein is an architectural advisor and executive director of the **George Nelson Foundation**. She serves on the board of The Architectural League of New York and the Chinati Foundation in Marfa, TX.

SLOW ARCHITECTURE

CT: Our architectural training allows us to do much more than brick-and-mortar architecture. Design thinking is extremely potent when it's applied outside of the architectural realm. How do we do something to perpetuate and advance the cause of The Human Condition? We want to make life better, not only our living conditions, but our spiritual condition. We are continually thinking and re-thinking our collective ethics and our personal responsibility towards the whole. Our own desire for expression is in that context. We believe that the whole world cannot possibly live in one ideology or one style, and that we should be continually exploring classicism, modernity, scale, emotions, history, memories…

THE URBAN INTRUSION
By Eben Klemm

2 oz. of **American rye whiskey**
1 oz. **Water**
1 oz. **Squash syrup**
2 dashes **aromatic bitters**
Strain into ice-filled rocks glass. Garnish with **long lemon horseneck**. Combine all ingredients in a shaker with ice and shake 20 times.

Squash Syrup: Oleo Saccharum:
Thin-slice two lemons and pack in tight container with two cups of white sugar. Toss to make sure slices are completely coated. Let sit for 1 to 2 days, tossing occasionally. Sugar should be completely or nearly liquid. Strain and remove lemons. Lemons may be lightly rinsed and water added to syrup. Steam one quartered and cleaned Kabocha squash in covered pot with 2 cups water until flesh is soft. Scoop flesh from skin and purée. Mix squash purée evenly with lemon syrup.

It was very important for Calvin Tsao that his cocktail—like his work—referenced organic and seasonal issues. The name itself references how we wanted to envision the drink, as a bit of nature forcing its way into a very urbane cocktail.

BHUTAN ELDER SANGHA SANCTUARY, BHUTAN

Our signature is not a visual one, but one of approach—where we place the end-user, whether it's someone's home, a civic entity, or every woman in the world who wants to use a lipstick. We design for them. They are our inspiration, and our cultures are our inspiration. It is that intersection that really makes our presence known.

We've always been interested in the phenomenology of nature and the man-made. Domestic architecture is something we continue to explore, whether a vernacular or a geography or climate, and how that's reflected in the way people live. We ask: What is domesticity for the 21st century? **How do we define identity? What is integration into the neighborhood fabric and cultural fabric?** We look at economy of means and culture, and use projects as a lab for the future.

Going large in scale, we are looking at transportation—the flow of cities, the pulse of cities—and asking what the anatomy of an urban figure is, and looking at its soul. On another scale, we are looking at a retirement community for a group of Buddhist monks in Bhutan.

BERKSHIRE MOUNTAIN HOUSE, ALFORD, MA

SAGAPONAC HOUSE, WAINSCOTT, NY

We are all tagged. We're all branded. When you cannot be described or refuse to be described, it's very frustrating. As a business, it's almost the kiss of death. But thank God that over the years we have had about a half-dozen champions, people who sought us out; one has been a client for 25 years.

It's very satisfying to pull together a group of like-minded people, whether they are our clients or our students. You feel you're not alone, and that's great currency. Who wants to be wealthy and lonely? I would much rather be poor and surrounded with love, which is very corny.

ASTRID HILL HOUSE, SINGAPORE

KS: Your work is hard to typecast. It's not just that you work in a wide array of scales, from furniture to million-square-foot city developments, but also there's no discernible signature style. Do you think there is a Tsao + McKown style?

The whole idea of **a signature style is grappling with personal expression and ambition.** I think, as an architect, we all believe that **it's a calling, not a business,** although we have to survive as a business. As a calling, you have to grapple with the self and the whole.

KS: Do you think that most of the clients you meet for the first time really understand what architects do?

No. I believe they think we're, at best, someone who makes a beautiful commodity. We can. But that's selling ourselves short and we're not looking at what we can offer. We can offer so much more, and I think we should claim, with great diplomacy, that we could do so much more.

When we get a client, we channel them, we inhabit them and we become them. It might be my background in the theater, but when you have the script, you're Hedda Gabler. When someone comes to you and says, "I want you to design my home," it has to be a home for them. You ask: What would I do if I were living in this house, if I were them? Inevitably, you can't have a style because you're someone else.

The search for universals that every culture can possibly agree on is to dig deep into our human psyche to find what the connections really are that make an Eskimo and a Samoan tick. There must be some common ground among all of us. I think that **design taps into the subconscious**, or at least we have to believe that. It's not just about the built, it's also about the content, the container and the content have to be considered at the same time.

WILLIAM BEAVER HOUSE, NEW YORK, NY

JIANFU PALACE MUSEUM, THE FORBIDDEN CITY, BEIJING, CHINA

KS: Is this a good time to be an architect?

This is a good time to be an architect. **We need good architects more than ever.** In times of confusion, people are looking for direction. This is when we can use our ability to "see" in the broad sense. We can use our global eye. When people talk about an architect, they mean that he or she is a mastermind, hopefully masterminding something really great and relevant. At the same time, we also trained to have the ability to take that big picture and bring it down to earth, piece by piece, brick by brick, and look at it bit by bit.

JIANFU PALACE MUSEUM, THE FORBIDDEN CITY, BEIJING, CHINA

To me, truth is the most beautiful thing in the world. It cuts you to the quick, but it also releases you and makes you grow and evolve. It's always between the lines that you see some kind of Truth, or Veritas, that has been overlooked because it's not a line, it's a space. I think it is a better use of the eye to see truth in things.

Really good environments are the ones to explore, revisit, and savor over time. We hope that all the hard work will last more than a few years; good environments have to continually reveal their qualities, so that generation upon generation can get something from them. Those are qualities that we're looking for. I'm not saying that we always succeed, but it is something that we aspire to do.

WILLIAM
PEDERSEN

William Pedersen is a founding partner of **Kohn Pedersen Fox Associates (KPF)**, started with A. Eugene Kohn and Sheldon Fox in 1976. He is interested in the development of the "fundamental building block of the modern city": the high-rise commercial office building. He connects his buildings to their neighbors.

CAROL
WILLIS

Carol Willis is the founder, director, and curator of **The Skyscraper Museum**. An architectural and urban historian, her focus is on the history of American city-building. She is the author of *Form Follows Finance: Skyscrapers and Skylines in New York and Chicago*, which received critical acclaim and an AIA book award.

BUDDHIST SMILE
By Toby Cecchini

2 oz. **Vodka**
1 oz. **St. Germain Elderflower Liqueur**
1 oz. **Lemon juice**
1 scant tsp. **Lemongrass juice**
2 strips of **Buddha's Hand citron zest**
4 oz. **Prosecco**

Combine first five ingredients and shake well over ice, then strain into a flute glass. Top with prosecco and garnish with a spear of lemongrass.

William Pedersen avowed that he drinks only wine, and is all about "the high-rise commercial office building and all the daily bustle therein." So my mandate was clear: tall and vinous. Invoking his many Asian projects, I went to fresh lemongrass juice and Buddha's Hand citron to inflect this take on a French 75, using vodka in place of cognac.

SCALE & THE CITY

WP: James Stirling said a long time ago that he knows a lot of chairs that have great, great presence. And that word, "presence," is possible at all scales. Size sometimes makes presence more difficult to achieve simply because of its lack of connectedness to anything around it. So when one is designing something of a scale, from a chair to a very tall building, one has to search tirelessly for a means of connecting to a place so it seems to flow naturally from it.

Why is it so important at this stage of my career to be interested in the design of a chair? Chairs are probably one of the more difficult design challenges. A lot of architects and designers have attempted them and a few have left milestones. And any architect, at some point in their career, probably wants to be able to test themselves against these milestones. The other reason is to find a way of creating something that would distill and represent my own visual sensibility, and is economical and comfortable.

I also make a lot of wire sculptures that allow me to think in a different way from the more pragmatic aspects of the large-scale work we do. In the process of making some of these, I came upon the possibility of creating, with a single gesture, the armature for a chair. That, then, became a process that took about three or four years, ultimately to a series of prototypes. The process was simply the creation of a single loop, with one end passed through the other. I call it the Loop de Loop, a term used by the old barnstorming flyers for one of their major aerial stunts. It attracted me because it was an extraordinarily simple idea.

The open-knit fabric is actually a tension member, and the frame is a compression member. It's the interaction between the two, when you stretch the fabric over the frame with tremendous tension, that they develop these extremely elegant, curvilinear shapes. These shapes are then further accentuated when a person sits in them. That is the essence of the chair.

10 & 30 HUDSON YARDS, NEW YORK, NY

Without experiences like that, KPF wouldn't have happened, to be perfectly honest. A lot of work came to us quickly, and there are two ways of dealing with it. One would be to try to supervise the work in a way so it can be totally delegated to others. But in the long run, it didn't seem like a satisfactory way. Everybody needs to be able to have a sense of their own accomplishment, so building a group of people who are able to contribute a lot of themselves to the process all the way along the line has always been the goal.

While I feel very committed to my projects, all of my partners have an equal body of work that they feel committed to in the same way. And that has created the dynamic of Kohn Pedersen Fox. There's a level of competition, obviously, but it's a competition that, over the years, has proven to be an extremely positive one.

GANNETT USA TODAY HEADQUARTERS, MCLEAN, VA

ONE JACKSON SQUARE, NEW YORK, NY

I had a mentor when I was going to the University of Minnesota. His name was Leonard Parker. He had worked for Eero Saarinen for 10 years, and eventually became a well-known architect himself. After school, I was his only employee. Then I came to New York. When I first interviewed with I.M. Pei, I came in with my portfolio and we had a wonderful conversation lasting about a half hour. Then his assistant came in and said, "I.M., you have a meeting with the National Institute of Arts and Letters in about 15 minutes." I.M. said, "That's not important," and we went on talking. So I had I.M. Pei as a mentor for five years as well.

A lot has to do with the interaction of the initial partners and the culture we were establishing. I can't go any further without talking about Gene Kohn and his role. The energy that he has instilled in the office, and the sense of pleasure and fun in every aspect, mediates the entire spectrum of activity here. It's always said of him that he's perhaps one of the greatest salesmen in architecture. Well, this does him a great disservice, frankly. Yes, he is a great salesman, because he loves people and he loves what he's selling. He's also very supportive of us. And Shelly Fox was the stability of it all. Gene, probably more than any of us, always wanted to go past the initial partners. He wanted the firm to be able to grow—we all wanted the office to become stronger and stronger as the years went on, and this is what's happened.

Almost **every client has a level of aspiration that can be discovered and then turned to architectural advantage.** I think that the desire to discover it is part of the game.

Minoru Mori, who commissioned us for several buildings including the Shanghai World Financial Center, was one of the best. He had a tremendous love for Le Corbusier's architecture and art. Everything he did as a developer was totally connected to the Japanese culture, to an idea about how to transform the city in a positive way, and how the components need to be placed in juxtaposition to each other to pull this off. Stephen Ross [Related Companies founder] is another great client. He wants Hudson Yards to be transformative for the city—a place of tremendous vitality. This is his aspiration.

333 WACKER, CHICAGO, IL

As an architect, to be honest, the aspect of ego was important only in its relationship to the problem. **The nature of a very tall building, from my perspective, is that it can't do the sort of things that one normally wants to do at more reduced scales—to make gestures and connections.** It tends to be insular. For me, the taller a building goes, the quieter it should be, the more serene it should be, and that was the basis of the design of the Shanghai World Financial Center. The relationship of earth and sky, the relationship of the symbolic nature of the earth and the manner in which the building met the sky was everything in the design. Whether it was 500 meters or 600 meters didn't really make any difference. From my perspective, the nobility of an object has nothing to do with its dimensions.

LOOP DE LOOP

SHANGHAI WORLD FINANCIAL CENTER, SHANGHAI, CHINA

CW: Could we talk about the world's tallest building? You didn't quite make that, and other people will always try to design one, build one, conceive one, float one, whatever. There seems to be an indelible fascination with that idea. For Minoru Mori again, the Shanghai World Financial Center aspired to be the world's tallest building. How did that figure in your design, in his? Was it an ego thing? A lot of my scholarship has been trying to deny the exceptionalism of "world's tallest building," arguing that the economics of very tall buildings increases once you get in the territory of competition for tallest. Can you illuminate the competition for the tallest of the late 20th century that you participated in?

HUGH HARDY

Hugh Hardy founded **H3 Hardy Collaboration Architecture** (2004) as the successor firm to Hardy Holzman Pfeiffer Associates (1967), which followed Hugh Hardy & Associates (1962). Through architecture, Hardy built and reshaped significant elements of America's cultural landscape. He died in 2017.

JAMES SANDERS

An architect, author, filmmaker, and the principal of **James Sanders + Associates** design and research studio, Sanders has garnered a Guggenheim Fellowship and Emmy Award for his work. His landmark study on the city and film, *Celluloid Skyline* (Knopf), was hailed by Jane Jacobs as a "marvelous, miraculous, book."

THEATER OF ARCHITECTURE

HH: Let me explain what it was like to be a student at Princeton. We were the students in the middle of all the change in architecture. Our professors were brilliant people in our own history because we were actually taught art history and taught about old buildings, while the other schools, the other fancy design schools, had abandoned all history because the past didn't exist.

I think they wanted to lock up the library. Incredible though it may seem today, you could go to some fancy school to get credentialed and not be taught the history of architecture. The whole curriculum was talk without color. There was no color in architecture, which was reinforced by the fact that all the publications didn't use color.

CONSIDER THE MARTINI: *The Development of a Classic Drink*
By Toby Cecchini

In honor of Hugh's exclusive preference for the martini, and given the wild variety of his projects over the decades, I decided to present a sort of brief history of the drink, beginning with its perhaps apocryphal forebear, the Martinez, proceeding to the Fitty-Fitty, the small, wet martini that fueled the 3-martini lunch for decades, and finishing with today's "vulgar" bone-dry vodka version with an olive.

MARTINEZ

2 oz. **Hayman's** or
    Anchor Distilling's Old Tom Gin
1 oz. **Carpano Antica Formula** OR
    Cinzano sweet vermouth
1/2 tsp. **Luxardo Maraschino liqueur**
2 dashes **Angostura orange bitters**
In a mixing glass filled with ice, combine ingredients and stir until well chilled. Strain into a chilled cocktail coupe and garnish with a twist of orange zest.

FITTY-FITTY

1 1/2 oz. **Plymouth gin**
1 1/2 oz. **Carpano Antica Formula** or
    Cinzano sweet vermouth
3 Dashes **Angostura orange bitters**
In a mixing glass filled with ice, combine ingredients and stir until well chilled, up to a minute. Strain into a chilled cocktail coupe and garnish with a twist of lemon zest.

DRY MARTINI

3 oz. **Absolut Elyx vodka**
1/4 oz. **Dolin dry vermouth**
Fill a mixing glass with ice and add vermouth. Swirl and strain off, then add vodka and stir until well chilled, up to a minute. Strain into chilled cocktail glass, and garnish with a Castelvetrano olive or a twist of lemon zest.

In 1970, there was an explosion in the basement of 18 West 11th Street. A group of Weathermen from the Students for a Democratic Society were making bombs to blow up the library at Columbia University, among other targets. Three of them died; two survived. It destroyed the house.

MARITIME AND SEAFOOD INDUSTRY MUSEUM, BILOXI, MS

At the first Landmarks Preservation Commission hearing, it looked like they might respond positively to my design, which was miraculous. The commissioner said it was such a poetic expression. The tilt and thrust of the wall says something about the blast, which is what makes this so beautiful.

JS: This is a fundamental issue that everybody is still wrestling with—modern interventions. That was certainly an answer, as it was for the theaters you restored.

LANGWORTHY HOUSE - 18 W 11TH ST, NEW YORK, NY

That building was, for me, a talisman in many ways because it was a part of two ideas. **When is history, history? I think history is very much a part of architecture. The past and the future join in the present.** The second thing is diversity. I've always believed it was a great thing in architecture and in life. For me, this work is something that could never be repeated. You could not do this now because of what preservation means today. It has taken on a completely different cast.

CLAIRE TOW THEATER ABOVE VIVIAN BEAUMONT THEATER AT LINCOLN CENTER, NEW YORK, NY

BRIDGEMARKET, NEW YORK, NY

There are many moments when you think what you do about that issue. In New York, there have always been two approaches. One, you should just put back what was there before, and the other is that you should try to do something contemporary. Now **the issue becomes what "contemporary" means; it is different for each generation.** Of course, those who thought the 11th Street building should be rebuilt the way it was had the problem that it had been many things over time. And it had already been a landmark. The Preservation Commission itself felt that this should not be a recreation. In fact, I was charged with producing something that they could approve as contemporary, and this was how it was resolved.

CENTRAL SYNAGOGUE RENOVATION, NEW YORK, NY

JS: There was a time when Radio City Music Hall was going to be demolished. Could anybody imagine New York City without Radio City? Could you imagine this community denied a place of that extravagance—the scale and extraordinary skill of its workmanship.

Whether this place is a public building or not, it is, for me, absolutely unbelievable. What you have to remember now is the era of 1932, when this gem came into being. At that time there had never been an architectural space like **Radio City's Great Hall**—such a room! Before then, all theaters were designed simply as walls and ceilings. But with just one big gesture, instead of being lit with chandeliers and all the usual equipment, it was designed to glow, and it all glowed in five colors of light. It was the first use of reflected artificial light. To come here in the 1930s was unbelievable.

JS: I do think that there has been a theme running through our conversation. It seems there was a high-low divide. For instance, scenic art and art direction for movies were not taken seriously by architects.

True, they were not making the kind of lush experiential quality as the interior of Radio City Music Hall. It was considered on a par with interior decorating. I can I remember when that revelation came to me, seeing those fantastic interiors. For those who didn't know you could expose a ceiling, it was fantastic.

Why does it have to be either old or new; why can't you have both; why can't you celebrate the contrast between old and new? When we began working on the Greenwich Village Townhouse building, the top 15 feet of it were missing. The windows were not those of the original house. The city had repossessed it for back taxes, and it was turned into a school with the public space divided into five classrooms. And there never was a canopy. So having to restore the façade is a story in and of itself. When the need came for a true canopy, **how on earth could you recreate something that never existed?** The answer was to make it as contemporary and as light-hearted as possible. It all comes together—a contemporary version of the past.

SCHUSTER HALL RENOVATION,
WRIGHT STATE UNIVERSITY, DAYTON, OH

TWO RIVER THEATER, RED BANK, NJ

I was stage struck. But, as it turned out, it wasn't about the performance, it was about the transformation of this dumb little brick box and the people in it—I mean the people who were performing. **In this city—the theaters and the streets and all that is going on here— to be a part of it has led to my affection for the city. The city is so magical— it's an amazing theater.**

BELMONT FREEMAN

Belmont Freeman is the founding principal of **Belmont Freeman Architects**. Monty is on the faculty at Columbia GSAPP and a columnist for *Places Journal.* For 10 years, he was the president of the board of Storefront for Art and Architecture. He is a leading expert on Cuban architecture, about which he writes and lectures, and leads tours of Cuba.

CATHLEEN MCGUIGAN

Cathleen McGuigan is the editor-in-chief of **Architectural Record**, and former architecture critic and arts editor of *Newsweek*. She has taught at Columbia's Graduate School of Journalism and has been a Poynter Fellow at Yale and a Loeb Fellow at Harvard. Under her leadership, *Record* won the Grand Neal award in 2012.

THE LONG VIEW

BF: My advice to young people who are thinking that they want to go into architecture is to make sure that this is what you really, really want to do, because it's a long haul and it's a difficult way to make a living. On the other hand, the rewards can be tremendous.

THE MONTY DAISY

By Eben Klemm

2 oz. **Plymouth gin**
1/4 oz. **Orgeat**
1/2 oz. **Orange Curaçao** or high quality **Triple Sec**
1/2 oz. **Aperol**
1/2 oz. **Fresh lime juice**
1 oz. **Grapefruit juice**
Add ice and shake 20 times. Strain over fresh ice and garnish with lime wedge.

Mr. Freeman was among the most specific collaborators in terms of his favorite alcohols and flavors. I presented the Monty Daisy as a mash-up of influences, referencing his Cuban roots and how that, in turn, led to Latin architecture informing his own practice.

My office has always done a lot of residential work, which in New York means apartments, lofts, townhouses, and small apartment buildings. We also have a long history of institutional work for a roster of universities, including Columbia and the University of Pennsylvania.

The Gertrude Ederle Recreation Center was the first commission awarded by the New York City Parks and Recreation Department under its then-new Design Excellence Program. We were honored to get that commission with Bargmann Hendrie + Archetype. The complex consists of a 1906 bath house and a new 10,000–square-foot addition. We used the classic trope of putting a glass spine between the old and new. **I cannot say enough good things about the Design Excellence Program.** The funds the program put into public sector construction over the last several years got my firm through some very tough years. During the recession this stimulus worked for me and I'm grateful for it.

KOWALEWSKI RESIDENCE, ATLANTIC BEACH, NY

My ultimate experience with preserving a landmark modernist work of architecture came when I was hired to restore the Four Seasons Restaurant in the Seagram Building. It was a little-by-little restoration project. Honestly, **I never thought I would be channeling Philip Johnson**, but I have.

Philip Johnson ate lunch there every day. He watched the place closely. Whenever a new carpet had to be installed, he would design it. If the furniture needed to be rearranged, he would oversee it. If light fixtures needed adjustments, his office would take care of it.

RIVERSIDE DRIVE PENTHOUSE, NEW YORK, NY

We renovated Wesleyan University's Zilkha Gallery in the 1973 Kevin Roche John Dinkeloo and Associates' Center for the Arts, a beautiful minimalist modern structure. It was a wonderful exercise in the **preservation of a modern masterpiece**. I don't consider myself a preservation architect per se. I think that **design is design**, and when you're dealing with a project that involves a 1906 bath house or a 1973 modernist building, it is about how to gracefully incorporate all the preservation components as part of the larger design goal.

SUSHI YASUDA, NEW YORK, NY

URIS HALL, COLUMBIA BUSINESS SCHOOL, NEW YORK, NY

But Philip had died about eight years earlier, and since then, the restaurant owners realized it needed constant attention, which it hadn't received. When I went there for the first time in broad daylight and sober, I saw a lot. We created an action plan, with one of the requirements being that all work had be done in small increments and without closing down the restaurant. So the project extended over several sequential phases. Starting with the ladies lounge in 2011, we worked on the restaurant until it closed in 2016.

My mother was from Cuba. We last were there as a family in 1956, and then I went back in 1998 on an architectural tour. Since then I have travelled to Cuba many times. There's a lot of interest in preserving the colonial architecture, but the modernist legacy in Havana has been neglected. Some of the best modern architecture in Latin America in the 1950s was in Havana. The work from the 1960s, the first years after the Revolution, is just as eye-popping.

After the Revolution, when the architectural old guard in Cuba left the island along with their clients, a very young, politically committed, well-educated group of architects did amazing avant-garde work, which in those early years had political support. We had an exhibition of this remarkable body of work at the Storefront for Art and Architecture.

THE CARRIAGE HOUSE, UNIVERSITY OF PENNSYLVANIA, PHILADELPHIA, PA

THE FOUR SEASONS RESTORATION, NEW YORK, NY

How does a young professional commence his or her own career? I stayed at my first job for nine and a half years, and then started my own practice [initially with partner Max Pizer]. It's probably healthier to move around a bit. **If you aspire to have your own practice, don't jump off too early.** Don't attempt practice solo prematurely. When I was still working at Davis, Brody & Associates, I had lots of friends who started their own practices right out of architecture school. Some of them got stuck in a lower-level, small-scale practice. They had not learned enough during their internships to know how to design a real building.

I would advise someone in high school to go to a liberal arts college and study everything and anything except architecture as an undergraduate. You should get the broadest possible background. I am fortunate that I got that advice my freshman year at Yale. Then go to graduate school and concentrate on professional education, because if you think about it, when you're out there and practicing, who are your clients going to be? They will be doctors, lawyers, and financial people, and you need to be able to understand their language. **Get the broadest possible education you can when you're young—that will make you a better architect.**

EZRA AND CECILE ZILKHA GALLERY RENOVATION, WESLEYAN UNIVERSITY, MIDDLETOWN, CT

GERTRUDE EDERLE RECREATION CENTER, NEW YORK, NY

Architecture is not for anyone who needs immediate gratification. You face such a long, slow progression, both with the gestation of the art and the establishment of a career. **You have to take the long view, because making buildings is fun—terrific fun!**

ENRIQUE **NORTEN**

Enrique Norten was born in Mexico City, where he graduated from the Universidad Iberoamericana with a degree in architecture in 1978. He obtained a Master of Architecture from Cornell University in 1980. He founded **TEN Arquitectos** (Taller de Enrique Norten Arquitectos) in Mexico City in 1986, and opened a New York office in 2001.

PEDRO **GADANHO**

Architect, curator, and writer Pedro Gadanho is the director of **MAAT: The Museum of Art, Architecture and Technology** in Lisbon. He was the curator of the Department of Architecture and Design at **MoMA**, and the editor-in-chief of *Beyond, Short Stories on the Post-Contemporary*, a bookazine started in 2009.

A TALE OF TWO CITIES

EN: I should very proudly say, if you will permit me, that now I'm a man of two cities. Mexico City's my city by birth, where my heart was formed, and New York is my city of choice. I could have selected any city in the world, but I'm very proud to have selected New York. The energy, the intellectual quality of the city, is very, very high; you cannot find it elsewhere. It's like this: I have the enormous privilege of sitting with one of the great thinkers of the world, having a conversation in front of all of you, because I'm in New York. Because we both happen to be in New York. That's what New York is for us.

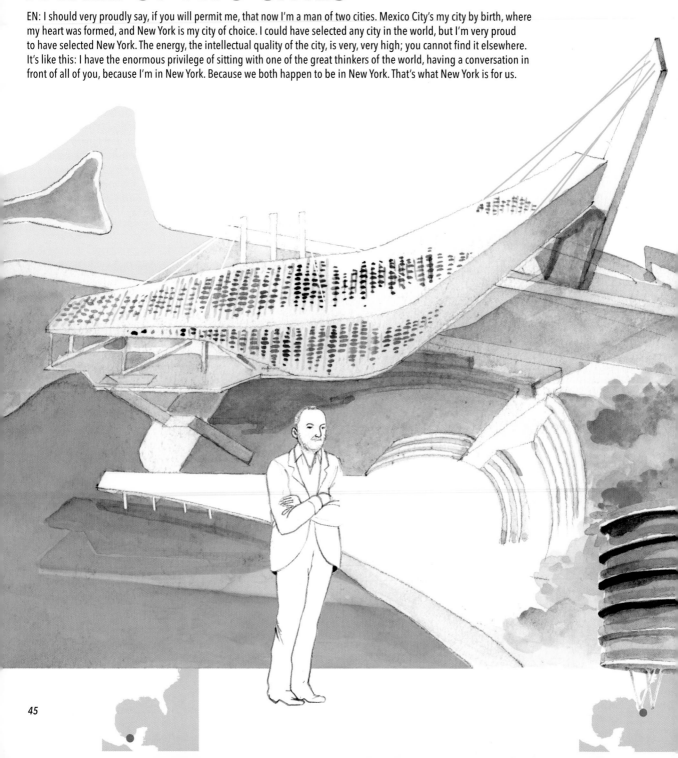

FORGOTTEN CONVERSATION
By Eben Klemm

1 1/2 oz. **Silver tequila**
1/2 oz. **Silver mezcal**
1/4 oz. **Amontillado sherry**
1/4 oz. **Pineapple syrup**
1/8 oz. **Fresh lemon juice**
Dash of **bitters**
Combine all ingredients in a shaker with ice and shake 20 times. Strain over fresh ice or large ice cube.

Pineapple syrup:
Dissolve an equal amount of sugar in fresh pineapple juice.

I sprang this one on the architect. By sheer kismet, I met Enrique years earlier at a dinner party in a restaurant on the Lower East Side. We had an extensive conversation about tequila, but the only part that I remember was his favorite brand.

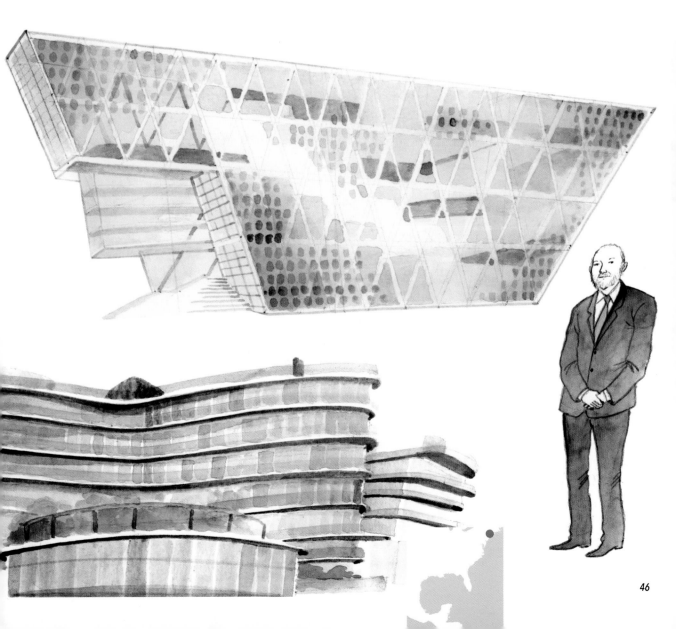

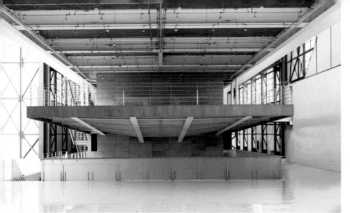

CHOPO MUSEUM, MEXICO CITY, MEXICO

I don't think there are two neighboring countries in the whole world that contrast more than Mexico and the United States. It's the harshest border ever. I cannot imagine any other place in the world where there is one line that defines two geographies and two cultures in a stronger way than that line between Mexico and the United States. The Anglo-Saxon culture is such a litigating culture.

PG: I call this **the terror of liability.**

MUSEVI, TABASCO, MEXICO

PG: I share this condition of being a foreigner in New York, embedded in its culture, and I'm fascinated by this condition. Let's call it **a tale of two cities**. *People can move between two cities, two cultures, two different situations, and then enjoy a specific quality in their work because of the permanent confrontation of two cultures. How does moving from Mexico City to New York influence your architecture? What influences you in living between two different cities and moving from one to the other?*

MERCEDES HOUSE, NEW YORK, NY

Bureaucracy is bad everywhere, in different ways. The problems are different. Here, this probably comes back to the issue of democracy. I just came from a meeting with a community board—a very direct democracy. Anybody, without any knowledge, has the right to tell you you're an idiot. In our countries [Portugal and Mexico], we elect our governors, we elect our officers, then they elect their advisors and they make the decisions. They've also been difficult, but you don't need to convince every person on the street of what you're doing. So that also creates a different way of achieving architecture. These are our political processes. They are super interesting, and super important to the creation of architecture.

THE NEW YORK PUBLIC LIBRARY 53RD ST, NEW YORK, NY

One of the reasons I decided to establish myself in New York is because I've always believed very strongly that we were moving into a condition of globalization. That is what characterizes our generation, and I don't speak for myself, I speak for many of my colleagues—we grew into this moment of globalization. On the one hand, there is the desire to be part of a global discourse; on the other hand, and probably what distinguishes our work, is the importance of understanding the particularities of the poetry of the location.

CASITA, SOUTH BRONX, NY

I think one of the huge privileges of our profession is that every opportunity allows us to learn a lot. Obviously, we listen to people. We bring our expertise, which is about creating space and form—to use all of that knowledge, that very special condition that we call architecture, as a means of giving life to the social texture. This is where we really see architecture breaking through.

Part of our role is to question and to push the envelope.

There's another equation that is very interesting in very sophisticated cities and societies like New York and Europe. Labor is very expensive and technology is very inexpensive. In other parts of the world, like Asia and Africa, labor is very inexpensive and technology is hugely expensive. That changes the challenges in a very, very important manner. It's impossible to get a very nicely poured concrete wall in the U.S., for instance. In my country, it's completely the opposite.

MUSEO AMPARO, PUEBLA, MEXICO

RUTGERS BUSINESS SCHOOL, PISCATAWAY, NJ

I hope that my next project will allow me to step into territories that are completely unknown to me. **There's nothing more fascinating than working on project of a type that I've never even dreamed of**—it's so fascinating because I know nothing about it. That allows me to question everything and reinvent everything from many directions—the site, the client, political conditions. You end up dealing with this amazing palette of characters, of interests, of rules and regulations. I think that's what's beautiful about architecture.

I've always been very interested in technology, all kinds of technology. From new materials, new processes, to new ways of representing architecture, from the digital to the material. It has always been an interest of mine, because I'm a true believer in the future. I really believe that we need to always be looking forward. I'm always very, very ready to experiment with things.

When we're doing a project here, people will ask me who we call to be the landscaper. I say, we're the landscaper. Who's the planner? We're the planners. What do you mean? Where's that differentiation? Here, there is lot of specialization. **Specialization is about formulas. It's about predetermined solutions.**

CENTRO, MEXICO CITY, MEXICO

JOEL
SANDERS

Joel Sanders is the principal of **Joel Sanders Architect** and a professor at Yale School of Architecture, where he is the director of the M.Arch II Program. Editor of *STUD: Architectures of Masculinity* and co-author of *Groundwork: Between Landscape and Architecture*, his work explores the relationship between culture and social space.

BARRY
BERGDOLL

Barry Bergdoll is the Meyer Schapiro Professor of Modern Architectural History at **Columbia University**, and a curator in the Department of Architecture & Design at the **Museum of Modern Art**. He has also served as president of the Society of Architectural Historians, and was the 2010-11 Slade Professor of Fine Art at Cambridge University.

ARCHITECTURE AS A CULTURAL PRACTICE

JS: Both of us, both Barry and I, share a commitment to the pursuit of architecture as a cultural practice, one that registers the impact of changing cultural, and particularly historical, forces. We have pursued this common preoccupation through common practices, including teaching, writing, exhibition design, and activities that actually speak to the overlap between curation and architecture.

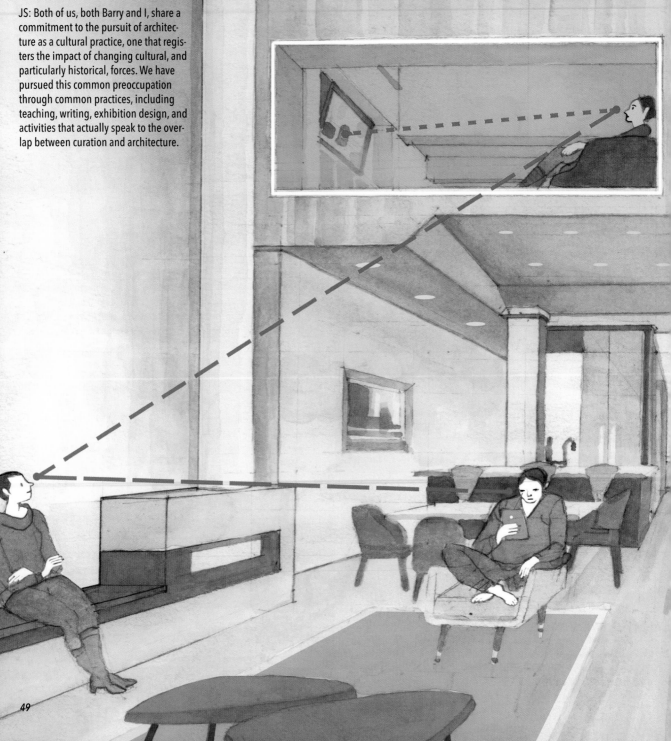

BRAMBLE REDUX
By Eben Klemm

2 oz. **Beefeater gin**
1 oz. **Lemon cordial**
1/2 oz. **Fresh lemon juice**
1/2 oz. **Blackberry/raspberry syrup**

Combine first 3 ingredients in a shaker with ice and shake 20 times. Strain into rocks glass filled with ice, crushed if possible. Float syrup over the top and garnish with a lemon wheel, a blackberry, and a raspberry.

Blackberry/raspberry syrup:

Mix 2 cups sugar with just enough water to give it the consistency of wet sand in a saucepan and bring to a boil. Add 1 cup each raspberries and blackberries and stir rapidly, crushing berries with a wooden spoon. Remove from heat and strain through a fine sieve.

Some argue that the Bramble is to British cocktails what the Cosmopolitan is to American: a simple to make, well-balanced cocktail that refocused bars' attention to fresh and quality ingredients. Our only alteration here was to lighten the weight of the blackberry cordial with the acidity of raspberry.

NEW CANAAN RESIDENCE, NEW CANAAN, CT

The second theme that informs my work and my teaching I refer to as **interface**, and it's championed in my recent book, *Groundwork: Between Landscape and Architecture*, co-edited with Diana Balmori. The book is an urgent appeal for designers to pursue a design approach that overcomes what is still the false professional dichotomy between architecture and landscape. I am a product of an architectural education, which I think largely persists today in most curriculums, where we tend to fixate and focus on buildings as objects that are completely indifferent to their sites.

Working with my students and with my staff, we've begun to look at the way digital technologies can be deployed in every-day, site-specific contexts with the objective of instigating face-to-face, embodied interactions.

In the same way that Labrouste embraced new structural technologies to invent the first public library, today, digital technologies are equally transformative, possessing great sensory implications for the way in which people interact in public space.

CAPSULE LOFT, NEW YORK, NY

Diana opened my eyes to this completely other world that I was unaware of. I would say that the exposure to the discipline of landscape architecture completely changed the way I think about architecture. Rather than consider landscape as an afterthought in the design process, which architects are often prone to do, *Groundwork* encourages cross-disciplinary design teams to come together from a project's very inception. Unified design concepts tap into the formal and programmatic potential of sustainable design principles that will create robust spaces that are provocative and integrate people, buildings, and sites.

BROADWAY PENTHOUSE, NEW YORK, NY

Architects have mined the rich potential of digital technologies to revolutionize our discipline, making possible new formal vocabularies, new modes of representation, and new fabrication techniques. While I'm interested in these areas, I'm particularly interested in another aspect of the digital revolution, and that is the profound, but often overlooked, impact of information technologies on the spaces of our daily lives—places like our homes, offices, and, in particular, libraries.

WOODSTOCK LIBRARY ANNEX, WOODSTOCK, NY

25 COLUMBUS CIRCLE, NEW YORK, NY

BB: You said you don't want to join the diagnosticians who study the loss of attention in a society of ultimate distraction—you want to adopt a more optimistic view. Have your feelings evolved on this issue of attention and distraction? **How do you get from voyeurism to optimism about distraction?**

In my early work, I was preoccupied with **ocularcentrism**, but also **voyeurism** and **spectatorship**.

HOUSE ON MT. MERINO, HUDSON, NY

Luckily, these projects have now moved from being internalized and protected and guarded to being much more expansive and open to the landscape.

I've forced myself to think about an unrealized aspect of our discipline—the untapped potential of buildings to be **multisensory and immersive**, which is clearly an important idea in contemporary practice. The challenge is: How can we use new media in urban spaces, in homes, and environments to produce more productive engagements?

A lot of my work offered opportunities to reverse traditional ideas of one-sided spectatorship and drew from queer theory, allowing both men and women to be subject and object of the gaze. I was accused, rightly so, of being fixated on the look, which I probably still am.

The Seongbukdong Residences in Seoul, South Korea, is an enclave of 12 houses. It employs energy-efficient green roofs to integrate the housing complex within its steeply sloping historic site. Here, we were updating the principle of the borrowed view, a technique employed by 18th-century European and Asian gardeners to compose landscapes by merging natural features in the distance with private gardens in the foreground.

SEONGBUKDONG RESIDENCES, SEOUL, SOUTH KOREA

PRINCETON JULIAN STREET LIBRARY, PRINCETON, NJ

BB: Not only is there a renaissance and interest in the library, it's completely counterintuitive to what we were told 20 years ago. Why is it that people still want to build libraries when there is absolutely no need to go to a physical place to use most of the resources that a general public would need from a library? And I suddenly thought that the library is not always so much about books; it's about a resource to be shared.

There is something interesting about an Ivy League school like Princeton getting rid of its books and embracing social media platforms to transform its libraries into 24/7 places of community.

Here, the staggered arrangement of the L-shaped houses ensures that everyone enjoys an unobstructed southern view framed in the foreground by the neighbor's green roof below.

Our early bachelor houses were about trying to construct a protected environment that would be literally shielded from the disapproving eyes of neighbors. When we were doing those projects, the social acceptance of LGBTQ people was completely different.

BOBST LIBRARY PIXEL VEIL, NEW YORK UNIVERSITY, NEW YORK, NY

UNIVERSITY OF PENNSYLVANIA INSTITUTE OF CONTEMPORARY ART CONCEPT STUDY, PHILADELPHIA, PA

Working with this notion of visual and climatic porosity at NYU's Bobst Library, we came up with this solution: The pattern—we call it the pixel matrix—references the grid that is expressed in Philip Johnson's original building, in the structural bays, the coffered ceiling, the reading room's square lighting. But we thought it would also refer to the contemporary language of digital information, the pixel language on our screens, or the contemporary barcodes that we see every day. The gradient was not only meant to be functional and performative, but also contextual.

MASSIMILIANO FUKSAS

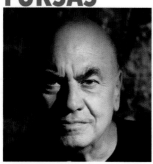

Massimiliano Fuksas is the co- founder of **Studio Fuksas**. He graduated in Architecture from the Sapienza University of Rome. Over the past 40 years the studio has developed innovative approaches through a strikingly wide variety of projects. Fuksas has been a visiting professor at a number of universities.

GREGG PASQUARELLI

Gregg Pasquarelli is a founding principal of **SHoP Architects**. He received his architecture degree from Columbia University and a Bachelors of Science from Villanova's School of Business. He has taught at Yale, Columbia Graduate School of Architecture, Planning & Preservation, and the University of Virginia.

FINDING COMMON GROUND
TECHNOLOGY IN ARCHITECTURE

PG: I thought when the two of you were put together, that it would be a challenge finding common ground, because your work is very different, but in fact, your work is not very different in a lot of ways. You're after very similar things, it seems to me, which is trying to create systems that use the most advanced technology to make possible a lot of forms that would not have been possible at all. Or, if possible, would not have been economical before. I see you're both doing that in slightly different ways, but ways that seem very consistent with each other.

PAUL GOLDBERGER

Paul Goldberger, who The Huffington Post called "the leading figure in architecture criticism," won a Pulitzer Prize for his writing in **The New York Times**. The author of several books, he has also served as architecture critic for *The New Yorker* and *Vanity Fair*, and holds the Joseph Urban Chair in Design & Architecture at The New School.

THE ERIN
By Toby Cecchini

2 oz. **Bourbon or rye**
1/2 oz. **Sweet vermouth**
1/2 oz. **Bigallet China-China Amer bitter liqueur**
1/2 oz. **Suze**
2 Dashes **St. Elizabeth's Allspice Dram**
Stir, strain into double old fashioned glass with one large ice cube, garnish with a large twist each of lemon and orange.

Creating a drink for Gregg was a straight layup. Not only is he a good friend, but his mandate was simple and direct: "Just use Barclays: dirty, brown, urban, and sexy." For that, I cobbled what we in the industry call a "brown-and-stirred," a dark, boozy bourbon (or rye) lowball nudged this way and that with various strong-headed characters wandering in and out: gentian, allspice, orange, but none taking away the supporting structure of the whiskey.

GP: We wanted to be a "both/and" firm that could think and write and explore and do capital "A" design. But we also wanted to be a firm that could execute really complicated, very large-scale projects, especially in New York, which is such a tough place to design and build. When we looked at what performance-based architecture might be, we saw a lot of it, obviously, in nature, the purest form of performance-based design. We started looking at the history of technology and the way that technology had impacted building and art. Every time a new material was developed or there was a new way of putting something together, we also saw a kind of aesthetic correlation to them.

BARCLAYS CENTER, BROOKLYN, NY

We began to realize that the traditional notion of plan, section, and elevation was actually not a very good way for us to communicate, and that, in fact, as architects, we say we build buildings. We built this building, we built that building. But the truth of the matter is, that's not what we do. **What we do is make instruction sets for other people to build buildings**, and while we are very good at thinking about things in 3D, 4D, 5D, if you will, we convert everything down to this two-dimensional system of plan, section, and elevation, and then hand it to people who have to bring it into a more complicated reality.

Drawing became an incredibly important thing for us, as we started to think about how to execute these complicated buildings, so that they would be easy to build, and our projects wouldn't get value engineered as we put them out into the world.

For Porter House in the Meatpacking District, the 4,000 unique pieces of zinc that make up the façade were actually executed without any drawings. We figured out a way to just feed all the information into a spreadsheet that would go directly to the laser cutters that cut out the parts.

111 WEST 57TH STREET, NEW YORK, NY

That was what really began to get us excited about architecture and about design and the way we wanted to work. While ornament and beauty are incredibly important to the way that we think about things, equally important is the way that something is actually rationalized, understood, fabricated, and assembled. It's that duality of trying to master both of those things that really can help push design forward.

PIER 17, NEW YORK, NY

GREGG **PASQUARELLI**

111 WEST 57TH STREET, NEW YORK, NY

Barclays was originally a Frank Gehry project of phenomenal design: four towers with large foundations that basically held the bowl of the arena in the middle. What was so brilliant about it was that 80% of the arena itself was embedded in the base of the buildings. While I think the press often erroneously says that the Gehry project was too expensive, it wasn't; he had designed it right on budget. The issue was that in 2009, when [developer Forest City Ratner] tried to build, the four towers were not financeable because of the global economic crisis. They had to try to redesign the building. The problem was that, because of tax laws changes, if they didn't get it in the ground by December 31, 2009, the stadium bond financing would no longer be tax-deductible. This would have been a $400 million hit to the project.

While Bruce Ratner adores Frank and the work that he did, obviously—they did 8 Spruce Street together—they had to think of another way to do it. So they went to Hunt Construction, the largest design-build contractor for arenas. The developer asked, "How do we get in the ground on a new arena in seven months?" And Hunt said, "There's no way to do it, unless you find one of the buildings that we've already built, and it fits on the site in Brooklyn. We order the steel tomorrow, and you have a shot at maybe getting it done."

So, they picked the Conseco Fieldhouse in Indianapolis, and dropped it onto the Brooklyn site. It got some people very upset—they felt that it was a bit of a bait-and-switch. So Forest City Ratner came to us and said, "Can you take this existing steel, strip it down, and think of a way to rebuild with what we already have ordered in a completely new way that would engage the city in a very different manner?"

THE PORTER HOUSE, NEW YORK, NY

Forest City Ratner liked the drawing we sent, and gave us seven weeks to redesign the entire building, detail it, and cost it. We had a $40 million delta on the budget that we had to be within to redesign the building. I never want to live through that summer again. We had every single piece figured out. It was 12,000 different shaped panels of weathered steel with a cantilever, and 30 months later the building was done.

Another client, Michael Stern of JDS, purchased Steinway Hall, a landmark building on West 57th Street. Then he bought the empty lot next to it, and purchased basically every available air right on the block. We only had a 60-foot-wide lot to build on, but when you got up above 22 stories, the views were unbelievable. You're literally dead center on Central Park to the north, and almost dead center looking south to Midtown.

It was going to be a very tall building. The idea was to pack as much of the structure as possible behind the east and west façades to open up the north and south for those views.

AMERICAN COPPER BUILDINGS, NEW YORK, NY

One of the things that I think is so difficult about a sports facility is that it really turns its back on the community. It's got these big walls, so we sank the building and the court below grade. With the front, we made a grand civic gesture—what we were calling "arms of Bernini, hip hop style," and put in an oculus. For the aesthetics, we thought about post-industrial Brooklyn, and the idea that **technology and gritty materials could be executed in a seductive way.**

MIDTOWN CENTER, WASHINGTON, DC

UBER HEADQUARTERS, MISSION BAY, CA

There's a five-story retail base, and then 21 stories of nothing—21 stories of just atrium and mechanical space, because it's valuable enough to build 21 stories of nothing to get the first apartment to have the view of the park. Then we asked: What should this building be? **As New Yorkers, we really wanted to push what makes a New York building a New York building.** It's the tower. It's the setback and the texture of the façades. The building is 1,400 feet tall and 60 feet wide, a 24.5-to-one ratio, making it the most slender building in the world when it is done, by a lot.

An airport is a place where you go inside, and you never come back, you never go out. You disappear. It's a strange place. You enter, check in, security, you buy, you see, you drink, some gates and some doors. You go there, finito. You don't see the people who leave. You see only the people coming in. It's a big mouth. It's a monster.

The Shenzhen Bao'an International Airport is a double-skin building based on a hexagonal grid of folded paper. You can see the inner skin. The project is like a fish, a manta. The manta becomes a bird and the bird becomes other things. This was the idea. We considered: What is Shenzhen, the city? It's one hour away from Hong Kong. It was a village of 25,000 fishermen in the 1970s. Now, it's 20 million.

MASSIMILIANO **FUKSAS**

SHENZHEN BAO'AN INTERNATIONAL AIRPORT–TERMINAL 3,
SHENZHEN, GUANGDONG, CHINA

MS: For the past 15 years, I have had a column in the Italian magazine *L'Espresso*. I speak about this only for one reason: I published the Barclays Arena in a column last year. Why? Because I felt, finally, New York is a little bit more courageous, more brave, after a very long period. I love architecture, but not only my architecture, as most architects do. I think that **when you love architecture, you love good architecture.**

We had a very, very strange and very bad adventure in China in 1992. They asked the French government to organize a team of European architects to study the Pudong area of Shanghai, and then invited Richard Rogers, Dominique Perrault, Toyo Ito, and me. What we discovered was a city, Shanghai, of seven million bikes—without brakes. They stop with their feet. I saw for the first time in my life an accident between two bikes.

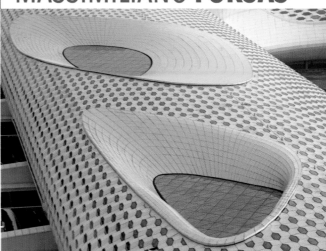

SHENZHEN BAO'AN INTERNATIONAL AIRPORT–TERMINAL 3,
SHENZHEN, GUANGDONG, CHINA

They built the city with the idea of competing with Hong Kong. People arrived from all of China. They didn't know each other. They spoke a lot of different dialects. But it's a fantastic place. For me, it's much better than Beijing. Our project was built exactly as we designed it. We cannot say there is one piece that we did not design.

When you do a very large building, you don't understand if the scale is right. You have to finish. You say, "Yes, it works," but you wait, and after time, you can say, "Yes, it's okay," or, "It doesn't work." It is always like this.

TBILISI PUBLIC SERVICE HALL, TBILISI, GEORGIA

We started the project. They said, "Thank you very much"—then changed everything. Where we put a garden, they put buildings. Where we put a tower, they put gardens. Then, I heard nothing more about China until one day someone sent us a letter. It said, "Do you want to do an airport?"

I had never done an airport before. We asked if it was a competition. It was, and we said, "Yes, we will do it." Afterwards, we discovered the way in which the jury judged our project. When the jury saw the projects, my project was thrown out. But there was one man, Mr. Jung, who said it was not so bad. And the jury paid attention. Then, they brought us back a second time, and said, "This, no." This happened three times. Finally, we won the competition.

RHIKE PARK, MUSIC THEATRE AND EXHIBITION HALL, TBILISI, GEORGIA

GP: Could you have ever built that airport in Rome?

MF: Oh, don't speak about Rome, please.

PG: *Do not dare speak about Rome in your presence?*

MF: You know why? Because 16 years ago, I won a competition. We are still building.

PG: *Architecture is such a long game, and the arc of a career is usually very, very long. It's rare that somebody has the degree of success at large projects that you've had, Gregg, before 50, let's say. It's quite unusual. Is there a risk when you reach that point where, as you've just put it very articulately, the same age as the decision makers, that you lose a sort of quality of being a prodigy? Architecture's not used to prodigies because careers in architecture happen so slowly. I was thinking about that the other day. There are very, very few people who have done important work before they were...*

GP: In their 60s. Massimiliano, you said something that I thought was so great, about never having done an airport. It's where we are still in our careers—that we were completely unqualified for every project we've ever done.

MF: Me, too.

GP: I find that to be a terrible business model, that as soon as we become an expert at something, we don't want to do it anymore. But it is a wonderful way to live life—we want to constantly challenge ourselves. I think if you're willing to do that, you stay forever young.

NEW NATIONAL ARCHIVES OF FRANCE, PIERREFITTE SUR SEINE–SAINT DENIS, PARIS, FRANCE

GP: My point about now being the same age as the decision makers is that you can talk to someone who has taken risks in their lives to get where they are. They have a connection to the creative spirit in a way that most people don't. That's where we've started to see the most interesting thing: We haven't done an airport, we haven't done a stadium, we haven't done this or that, but we're going to look at it with fresh eyes, just the way you founded your company or your institution, with fresh eyes. It's that symbiosis that makes good architecture.

MF: **If you have no passion, you cannot do architecture.**

NEW ROME-EUR CONVENTION CENTRE "THE CLOUD", ROME, ITALY

NEW ROME-EUR CONVENTION CENTRE "THE CLOUD", ROME, ITALY

PG: *A lot of very bad architecture has been produced by people who became so experienced at certain building types that they began to just churn them out without thinking. If you look at the people who control the hospital world or control much of the sports stadium world, and so forth, they use their knowledge of certain technical and programmatic requirements as a way of basically locking out all other things, claiming that this is a unique expertise.*

GP: What happens is that the people who you often interview with or who you're trying to get a project from are not at the top of their firm. They want to be safe. They want to protect their jobs by saying, "I picked the architect who's done 20 of these projects or 30 of those projects." That's exactly when creativity starts to dwindle.

MORRIS ADJMI

Morris Adjmi Architects is known for contemporary architecture and interior spaces, innovative use of materials and technology, and inspired by context and history. Adjmi's passion for the aesthetic of industrial architecture has revitalized old industrial buildings and restored meaning to historic neighborhoods.

WILLIAM HIGGINS

William Higgins founded **Higgins Quasebarth & Partners**, a historic preservation consulting firm that advises private, corporate, government, and institutional clients in the preservation and rehabilitation of historic properties. He works to integrate every project's unique combination of issues.

BUILDING ON HISTORY

MA: There were two sites that were virtually identical on Laight Street in New York. It occurred to me: Why do something that approximates or looks similar to the building if I could do something that's exactly like the building? The Ise Shrine in Japan occupies two sites, and every 20 years they take a piece of the building and move it to the other site. What I find really amazing is that there's a continuity of history from the beginning, when it was originally constructed, to now. They don't always use the same piece, but there's that history of reuse and the continuation of the lineage of the original structure. The idea is that the new construction is fresh and special and pure. Then they dismantle the old building after they've constructed the new.

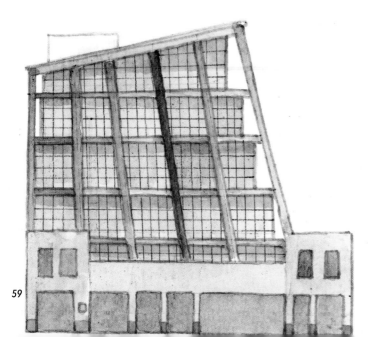

THE ADJMI (NON-TRADITIONAL) SAZERAC
By Toby Cecchini

1oz. **Cognac**
1oz. **Rye**
1oz. **Laird's Bonded Straight Apple Brandy**
1 barspoon (7 ml.) **Demerara simple syrup** (equal parts demerara sugar and water)
3 dashes **Peychaud's bitters**
Rinse of **Absinthe**

Stir together the first four ingredients in a mixing glass. Rinse a double rocks glass with absinthe and pour off. Strain drink into rinsed double rocks glass with one large ice cube and garnish with a large twist of lemon.

Pegging Morris's staunchly classical, historically drawn, ur-American structures to a cocktail, and taking into account his Cajun upbringing, led me to a slight updating of the classic Sazerac, a bedrock of New Orleans' lexicon, here lightened with cognac and a very old American apple brandy.

520 WEST 20TH STREET, NEW YORK, NY

WH: Aldo, at least to me, was primarily not an architect. He was a man of culture. He was an artist, a lover of history and of cities and of movies. He was a Renaissance man who was about culture as a complete and total thing, and out of that, somehow, his architecture blossomed.

Aldo entered architecture from a different place. I think that he used writing and sketching as fundamentals for his work. He looked at architecture as a way to test his writings, to test his drawings. Many times, he would do a sketch and then say, "I'm done. You guys go figure out how to build it." He didn't want to get bogged down with the details of how something was built, but if it didn't look like it was built architectonically, then it wasn't right to him. He taught me to think about how structure and materials relate to each other. He hated cantilevers. He thought that one of the worst things that could happen in a building was a cantilever.

WH: I first got to know Morris and Aldo Rossi as the Scholastic headquarters project was starting. It's been my pleasure and my privilege to not only witness, but to participate in the continuity of an architectural practice, an architectural style and attitude, and to see how somebody creates under the influence of a really powerful mind and a powerful creative force, a cultural force, which is what Aldo was.

Then, that force dies. Morris had to figure out where to go from there. This was a sped-up version of what happens with a lot of architectural firms, where the founder is a big name and a powerful influence. Then the founder retires, and the partners are left to figure out who they are and what is their style. When that really works, it seems to me that what happens is that an architecture evolves in which you can clearly read the influence and the continuing presence of the founder, but the architecture continues on. It's not, just as Morris says, Aldo's greatest hits over and over again. It is a new architecture that is familially connected to the old.

WYTHE HOTEL, NEW YORK, NY

WYTHE HOTEL, NEW YORK, NY

WH: You are really not about creating individual, stand-alone, star-type buildings. **What you are about is creating buildings that are pieces of a city.** It's the city that is the work, the great work of architecture. It's been around for a long time, and with help, will be around for a long time. You're creating a piece of something bigger. You're not creating primarily your own world.

It may sound limiting, but I like to start with a grid. For me, it's the departure point, and it gives my ideas a place to start. You can see that in all the projects, but it doesn't always look the same. Historical context plays a similar role. Like the grid, the history doesn't limit you. They are starting points that give us opportunities to transcend what was done before while honoring the DNA of the architecture.

I think that's it's okay to be quiet. **Sometimes it's better to be quiet than to make a lot of noise about nothing.**

A lot of people, developers or architects, dread the whole idea of going through the Landmarks process, but I've completely embraced it. I've found that it forces you to make really great architecture. The additional scrutiny and attention that you have to put into the project yields a much better product.

520 WEST 20TH STREET, NEW YORK, NY

WH: One of the things that makes 837 Washington Street such a good building is that it is responding to a multilayered site in a multilayered way. The site is in a landmark district at the weird point where the grids collide, it's an old building, next to the High Line. As Morris said, it's not a rooftop addition. It's a new building whose immediate site is an old building. This building really rises, or more accurately, rises and twists, to that oddity of site.

*WH: It takes a really good architect to demonstrate that **really good architecture is both individual and rooted in a tradition**. It's so hard to pull off without doing something that is either totally individual and pretends that it comes from nowhere, or something that slavishly copies the old or something that is a pastiche or a cartoon of the old. But where it really succeeds is when there is this really organic relationship between where the design comes from and its originality.*

Every landmark, literally or figuratively, is an odd place where the grid twists, and you can either look upon that as a pain in the ass, or you can look upon it as another inspiration that's going to push you to create a more interesting building.

837 WASHINGTON STREET, NEW YORK, NY

837 WASHINGTON STREET, NEW YORK, NY

We had a lot of fun working on 837 together. When Taconic, the developer, first contacted me, they asked how much we thought could be added to the building, with the lower two floors of the existing structure contributing to the district. Typically, visible additions in historic districts are one-and-a-half or maybe two stories, but Taconic really wanted to push the envelope and asked if I thought we could do something more. I said that we would certainly give it a try. We were able to add four stories.

The building sits at the point in the city where the Greenwich Village street geometry and the orthogonal grid of the Commissioners' Plan of 1811 come together and create these really interesting openings and vistas that you don't typically see in the standard city grid. This was something very important to us from the beginning of the project, and I think the building embodies that transformation.

I thought that we could do something that would allow the two buildings to coexist on the site. By shifting the new structure, the existing building presents itself as part of the overall composition.

KEN SMITH

Ken Smith established New York City-based **Ken Smith WORKSHOP** in 1992. Trained in both design and the fine arts, he explores the relationship between art, contemporary culture, and landscape. He is committed to creating landscapes and other public spaces as a way of improving the quality of urban life.

ALAN G. BRAKE

Alan G. Brake is a writer and critic based in New York. He is the former executive editor of ***The Architect's Newspaper***, and has written about architecture, design, and urbanism for *Architect, Architectural Record, Azure, Art in America, Dezeen, Landscape Architecture, Metropolis* and *The New York Times*, among other publications.

CRAFT - SOCIAL SPACE - ECOLOGY

KS: I always say, "Architects are my best friends," which is true. I am kind of an architect myself. As one gets a little older, it's a little easier to put the egos in check and work with people when you've become a little more comfortable in your own skin, your own talents. I think that we can collaborate. We don't always agree on everything, but it works both ways. I've seen in my career a kind of breaking down of professional boundaries. It's happened between the art world and the design world. All the boundaries are much more fluid than they used to be. It produces hybrid circumstances that are actually kind of interesting. I think that is a very contemporary notion.

THE GARDEN VARIETY
By Toby Cecchini and David Moo

1 oz. **Ford's Gin**
3/4 oz. **Chartreuse**
3/4 oz. **Lime**
1/2 oz. **Lavender simple syrup** (1:1 ratio by volume of lavender tisane and white sugar)
12 **Mint leaves**, plus top sprig for garnish
1 **Persian cucumber**
4 oz. **Soda**

Chop cucumber into small pieces, reserving one long slice for garnish. Muddle pieces along with the mint leaves in a shaker, then add gin, simple syrup, lime, and Chartreuse. Add ice and shake well. Double-strain into a large rocks glass half-filled with ice. Top with soda and garnish with cucumber slice, a lime wheel, and the mint sprig.

Ken Smith was our second landscape architect, and August in New York called for something directly in line with what he suggested as well: light, bright, and frothy. Chartreuse gave this highball a firm structure along with that beguiling green, perfectly reflecting someone whose life is spent in verdant pursuit.

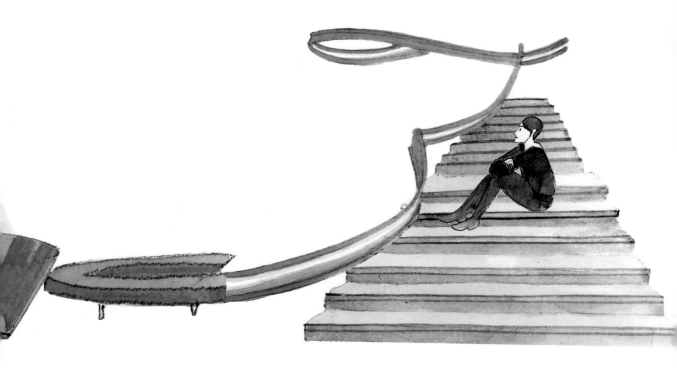

After graduating from Harvard Graduate School of Design I went to work for Peter Walker and Martha Schwartz. Technically, Martha hired me—they were a partnership but they each had their own staff. So I was on Martha's side of the office, which Pete's side referred to as the playpen.

What I learned in that office was **rigor of craft**. And I learned how to put things together, which I bring with me today: a preoccupation with craft. I was also seriously interested in modern music, and listened to John Cage and Steve Reich and people like that. I became interested in systems, systems as they were articulated through art as opposed to science. We're still doing art-oriented projects, but I would say that they're now increasingly in the service of a social or environmental program.

I took my first bonus check and went to France in the winter, and visited all the André Le Nôtre gardens. I am a big Le Nôtre fan because of his use of perspective, and creating different kinds of dimensions and effects in the landscape with simple means of topography and grade changes and space. Soon after, I went to Japan—all the Zen gardens, which were also doing interesting things with scale manipulation, taking exceedingly small spaces and making them feel bigger than they actually were.

BAM CULTURAL DISTRICT TFANA ARTS PLAZA, BROOKLYN, NY

WALLFLOWERS, COOPER HEWITT, SMITHSONIAN DESIGN MUSEUM, NEW YORK, NY

I always liked that big old elevator at the Whitney Museum. Normally, you get on an elevator and everybody looks at their feet or their personal device. But there's something about the social circumstance that's scaled differently or functions differently and makes people operate differently. I always found that the Whitney elevator had a social life. You get on and people start talking to each other.

COWLES COMMONS, DES MOINES, IA

I think a lot of ecology gets reduced down to being green or being low-impact, but there's a cultural dimension to it that's interesting.

I'm interested in social spaces in cities, metropolitan spaces, and how you create places that bring people together. It strikes me that we live in a world of Fox News and MSNBC, where nobody ever talks to each other. But in public spaces, there is the chance that people might actually rub shoulders, or meet somebody who's actually not like them, or not from their neighborhood. So for me, it's a question of **how you create spaces that foster some kind of social interaction.**

CROTON WATER FILTRATION PLANT, BRONX, NY

AB: It seems that what we expect a landscape to be has changed a bit in recent years, and, if anything, has gotten more complex. We expect our landscapes to do more and more for us. Has that, in your mind, tipped the balance in any particular direction, and has that impacted your work in any way?

In the 1980s, when I was starting out, there was an art orientation to what a lot of the landscape profession was doing at that time, and it was sort of art for art's sake. I think **now there's a much stronger emphasis on program, and landscapes providing service in some way.** The service could be cleaning storm water, or providing space for this or that use. It could be in service of fostering revitalization of a neighborhood. There's a much greater emphasis on the programmatic use of outdoor space.

I'm clearly interested in irony and secondary meanings, layered meanings. I think that **in the art world, abstraction is really important.** And it always occurred to me that in cities, where you're dealing with multiple cultures and a diversity of people, abstraction is very useful. People can read their own meaning into a place, and I find that interesting. But most sites have a fair amount of contradictions in their program, or there's something at odds between the context and the program, or this site and the next site. I find contradictions in a site interesting. That's what, for me, generates the irony or the whimsy. It's playing with a subtext in the site that I'm trying to express in some way.

AB: I think your strategy—and that's maybe where this idea of abstraction comes in—is that you're able to still play with these ideas of meaning and a layered, contradictory sense of things. But in this abstract language, you're able to transcend some of what we have come to see as a kind of calcified idea of what postmodernism is.

SILVERSTEIN FAMILY PARK, 7 WORLD TRADE CENTER, NEW YORK, NY

PACIFIC COAST RESIDENCE HAND RAIL, LAGUNA BEACH, CA

AB: We've seen an expansion of the role of landscape architects, particularly as it relates to the infrastructure realm. Have you seen the profession of landscape architecture take on a more active, civic role, and being more involved in some of these larger urban and ecological questions?

Landscape architects are generalists, so I think they're oftentimes in a position where they can assume a leadership role on the team, and deal with organizing different groups and ideas together in a way that deals with the complexities of urban sites and scales of urban sites. I also think that schools are taking a stronger interest in training people for leadership roles, and certainly group dynamics, and the sort of things that are necessary for public projects.

EAST RIVER WATERFRONT ESPLANADE AND PIERS, NEW YORK, NY

AB: Does the idea of play still function in your work? I see a playfulness that often crops up in your work in way that I think is delightful.

When you're on the riverfront—**when you're doing a $160 million project, it's more difficult to be overtly whimsical.**

Although we did an interesting dog run that is pretty funny.

FRANCES HALSBAND

Frances Halsband is a founding partner of **Kliment Halsband Architects**, winner of the AIA Firm Award and AIANY Medal of Honor. She was the first woman president of the AIANY Chapter and The Architectural League. She served as dean of the School of Architecture at Pratt, and is a former commissioner of the NYC Landmarks Preservation Commission.

MICHAEL J. CROSBIE

Michael J. Crosbie is a professor of architecture at the **University of Hartford.** He has made significant contributions in the fields of architectural journalism, research, teaching, and practice. He is editor-in-chief of *Faith & Form* magazine, and has served as an editor at *Architecture: The AIA Journal*, *Progressive Architecture*, and ArchitectureWeek.com.

ICE CUBES & GLASS BOXES

FH: I was thinking about cocktail glasses, which brought me to an architectural image of glass boxes, and I thought, Eureka that's it (refined, as Mike Crosbie brilliantly observed, into ice cubes). So this is an essay about transformations of historic buildings by adding tiny glass boxes, which completely change what's there. These are small interventions that transform an old building into something modern and useful. Thinking back on that image, I see that the power of one small ice cube to permeate and transform a drink is exactly how I was describing a series of buildings.

THE FRANCES SMASH
By Eben Klemm

2 oz. **Woodford Reserve bourbon**
1/2 oz. **Lemon juice**
Dash **Orange bitters**
1/4 oz. **Maple syrup**
Mint sprig

Mildly crush a mint spring in a rocks glass. Shake the remaining ingredients 20 times in an ice-filled shaker. Strain into rocks glass and add large ice cube. Garnish with mint sprig.

This cocktail was inspired by the collection of projects Halsband has built for university campuses, and how, in my mind, there's a tension between the bucolic and the urban. Smashes are a family of drinks that combine the herbaciousness and strength of juleps with the refreshing nature of sours.

FDR PRESIDENTIAL VISITOR & EDUCATION CENTER, HYDE PARK, NY

"Preservation creates relevance without new forms. Newness, in other words, is not a reliable index of cultural significance. Context is no longer thought of as only the physical environment of a historic building, but also the aesthetic, cultural, and intellectual framework within which it holds currency and value." —Jorge Otero-Pailos

What I do is not preservation. It is transformation of the past into forms that are relevant for today.

There are 10 projects, and there's a lot that can be said about them. But what I'm really talking about is **how you can add one little dot and everything changes.**

MJC: I spend a lot of time with students who are constantly asking questions about what the world is really like when they get out of school. "Have I really made the right decision about my future? What was it like after the Civil War for you?" This will be a wonderful opportunity to talk about where you come from and where you're going and why you became an architect.

I don't have a linear life plan. I was going to be a musician first. It was in the '60s. I never really understood if I was having any impact as a musician. I wasn't connecting with the culture. Then I was an art major at Swarthmore. I had some friends who were in architecture school. Some of them were in Louis Kahn's classes. At the University of Pennsylvania at that time, people were talking about really important things. Men in suits would talk about what was happening in the world. I wanted to be part of that because it was very exciting.

FDR PRESIDENTIAL VISITOR & EDUCATION CENTER, HYDE PARK, NY

AMBULATORY SURGICAL FACILITY, KYABIRWA, UGANDA

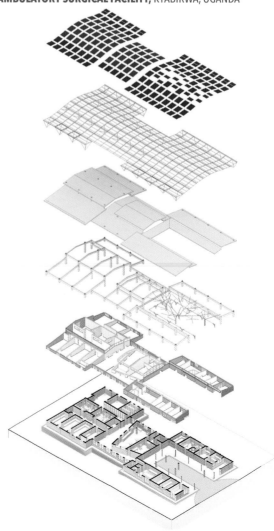

For Edward Durell Stone's enormous SUNY Albany campus, the dot was a 600-square-foot glass pavilion containing a stair that connects the classrooms buried below the podium to the faculty offices upstairs. It made it possible for people to get to and appreciate the campus in a way they could not have done before. This was a subversive act. Stone would probably not have been pleased. But it was a positive one for student culture.

At Columbia, the problem with the renovation of Hamilton Hall was that the McKim, Mead & White plan seemed to be counterintuitive to the culturally accessible spirit of the Admissions Office. We got the idea of entering through a giant piece of stonework from the College Gates. From College Walk you can now enter at grade. That made it possible to bring the public into the building. The intent was to **examine what's worth keeping and what's preventing modern life from taking place in this building.**

In the course of renovating Welch Hall at Rockefeller University we realized that the only way it could be code compliant is if it had a second stair. A glass cube sitting on top of stonework makes the whole thing possible. Of course, the building was also beautifully restored. A huge amount of effort went into **making it look like nothing had ever happened to it over its lifetime.**

Gilman Hall was the oldest building on the Johns Hopkins University campus; the entire school was in one building. It was a sensational plan. But it was a shambles. We recognized that the center of the building should be the center of the academic enterprise. So we made a glass box at the center, in the heart of the building.

MJC: What was your dream in entering architecture?

I am not a dreamer. I can't even remember my dreams the next morning. I am completely inspired by what's right here. It's fabulous when you get into a problem and go with it. You don't really know who your clients are going to be. The fun of it for me is that you really don't know what comes next.

NEUBAUER COLLEGIUM FOR CULTURE & SOCIETY, UNIVERSITY OF CHICAGO, CHICAGO, IL

WELCH HALL LIBRARY, ROCKEFELLER UNIVERSITY, NEW YORK, NY

In working with a team or a committee or a group, it is critically important to be open to new ideas. You can't put a lot of energy into thinking about yourself. Learn about things outside of yourself. The real fun of teaching, for instance, is to put a problem out there and get 15 or 20 different responses, just like that. To be able to see that many different approaches is tremendously exciting.

MJC: Do you ever get intimidated by the architects whose work you added to, like Ed Stone, McKim, Mead & White? Because some people say, "Oh my God," and start trembling.

No, never. It's just there. It's all the material you're dealing with.

You don't know that a private school in New York is going to engage you and involve you in the whole life of that school. You don't know that a federal judge is going to explain to you why he's a judge and what that means. We want to know everything that's there, and how do we tinker with it to come up with something that's right for them. **The excitement for me is seeing a culture through someone else's eyes.** You can realize other people's dreams.

MJC: It seems like you're a terrific listener. So you listen to what people's dreams are and to what is there already. You've discovered that the solution to a problem is in the problem itself, and it's up to you to channel it.

We also spend a huge amount of time looking at the site. In fact, we really want to know everything about the history of the building. Not knowing what I am going to hear or see or invent that day is what gets me out of bed in the morning. **You never really know where a good idea will come from and you have to be open.**

GILMAN HALL, JOHNS HOPKINS UNIVERSITY, BALTIMORE, MD

GILMAN HALL, JOHNS HOPKINS UNIVERSITY, BALTIMORE, MD

Probably the visitor center for the Franklin D. Roosevelt Presidential Library in Hyde Park is my favorite project. The history of the site was intense: The Dutch colonial heritage of the Hudson Valley was FDR's heritage, and he designed his library in that style. Sixty years later, we designed the visitor center in that same style, transformed. FDR's porches became glass roofs to let in light while sheltering visitors. The sloping roof forms define individual pavilions and activities. The courtyard provides an entrance to the grand estate beyond.

The Ambulatory Surgical Facility in Kyabirwa, Uganda, now under construction, is my current favorite. It brings modern medicine to an underserved off-the-grid small town in Uganda. The history here is native brick-making tradition, reinterpreted in modern ways. The solar roof shades the structure, much as the local banana trees gather sun and provide shade. 70

DANIEL
LIBESKIND

Daniel Libeskind established his studio in Berlin in 1989, after winning the competition to design the Jewish Museum Berlin. **Studio Libeskind** moved its headquarters to New York City in 2003 to oversee, as master planner, the redevelopment of the World Trade Center in Lower Manhattan.

BRETT
LITTMAN

Brett Littman is the director of the **Isamu Noguchi Museum and Garden** in Long Island City, New York. His interests are multidisciplinary. Over the last decade, he has curated more than 20 and overseen more than 75 exhibitions. He was formerly the director of The Drawing Center for more than 10 years.

ON DRAWING

BL: When I talk about design with architects, I like to hear from them about the haptic spatial, sound, and light qualities of their structures. I want to know how the building lives and breathes, rather than how it was built.

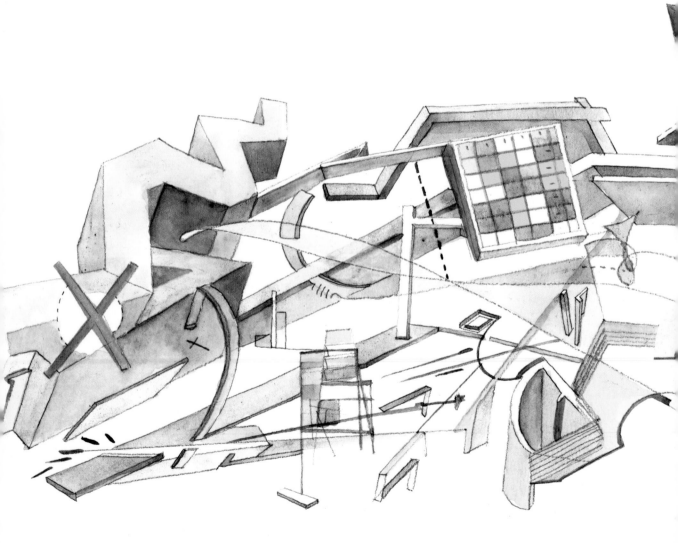

THE WEDGE
By Toby Cecchini and David Moo

Absolute Elyx vodka
Fresh shiso leaf
Pomelo peel

Infuse Absolut Elyx vodka with fresh shiso leaf and pomelo peel, then spin for 30 minutes in a commercial medical centrifuge, and re-distill in a rotary evaporator. Served in a double old fashioned glass with one hand-carved wedge of sculptural ice.

At the process's finish, 3 oz. of the completed cocktail is added to a double old fashioned glass with one doorstop-shaped, hand-carved wedge of ice fashioned by Hundredweight Ice of Long Island City.

For Daniel Libeskind, I wanted to push myself to create the purest iteration of a cocktail I could imagine: a clear, unadorned drink that incorporates all the elements of a full-fledged cocktail. For this, I took vodka and blended it with fresh shiso leaf and pomelo peels. I put that mixture through first a medical centrifuge and then a rotary evaporator, emerging with a powerful tincture that made for a cocktail that looked like a glass half-filled with water, but blew up the senses: no citrus, no sugar, but every element of a cocktail rendered. To garnish, we had Hundredweight Ice make us hand-carved wedges of pure sculptural ice that emerged from the glass like a monolith.

BL: I want to focus on Daniel Libeskind's use of drawing, rather than his built projects, to better elucidate his architectural ideas.

Libeskind, from early in his career, employed drawing as a way to emancipate and challenge the orthodoxy that had settled over the application of drawing in architectural practice. Projects like Micromegas in 1979, Chamber Works in 1983, and Theatrum Mundi in 1985, and most recently the drawing/sculpture/sound installation Sonnets in Babylon for the 2014 Venice Architecture Biennale, all point to different strategies towards understanding what I would call the projective nature of drawing. That is, something beyond engineering, description, and technique, something that is perhaps more deeply engaged with and questioning of the world at large.

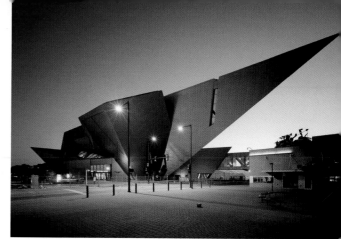

DENVER ART MUSEUM EXTENSION, DENVER, CO

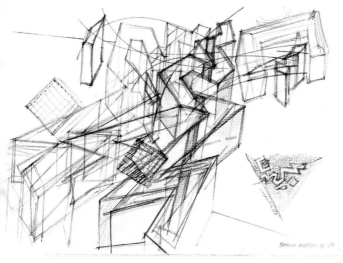

JEWISH MUSEUM BERLIN SKETCH

I love to draw. Everything I've done and have been lucky to build came from drawing. I didn't start by apprenticing myself in an office. I never even worked in an office before, so I actually apprenticed to drawings, and **drawings are a mystical thing**. How did I get involved in drawing? Well, I was a musician and, as you know, music is based on musical notation, which is a kind of a code which anyone studying music universally understands and can perform. Of course, the performance doesn't just depend on the code; it depends on how you interpret and how you are able to respond to the instructions of a score. For me, architecture is very musical. Architecture is a musical operation because whether you're drawing a building, a representational drawing of a building or of a plan, or even if you're just meditating through drawing, it has the power to infuse one's mind with a path. I always think that the **drawing is the soul of a building**, because no building just starts with a building. It has to start with an idea and something that is graphic, because that's how we communicate in the tradition of architecture.

I didn't start to draw for any expedient reasons. It was just a force of nature, and the drawings came out the way they did. At that time I drew them, they seemed to be crazy to many people. I remember people would say, "Oh, did you take LSD?" or **"What kind of drugs do you take?"** But the drug I took was architecture.

I understood that **drawing is something more than just some physical operation, that it's a way to think, and it's a discipline.** I don't say that it's a discipline just in of the immediate context of my schooling, but it's a tradition of architecture.

A drawing doesn't come from doodling, and it doesn't come from some theoretical meditations. It comes from attempting to deal with what you know about the history of drawing, but also what you experience in incredible spaces, like the atrium at the Metropolitan Museum of Art.

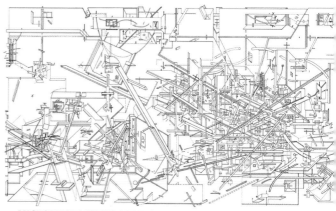

MICROMEGAS SERIES, LEAKAGE

JEWISH MUSEUM BERLIN, BERLIN, GERMANY

The Jewish Museum Berlin was influenced by two drawing series: Micromegas and Chamber Works. I never really succeeded in doing a pure building based on Micromegas. Chamber Works is much easier to instrumentalize than Micromegas. I've used it because they've helped me to analyze geometries, analyze requirements of program, and they're a little bit like an index.

The drawing, if it is the soul of something, like the human soul, it's not really there. You can't find the soul even if you cut into the brain. It's not to be found in the physical slicing of the hippocampus. It's something that haunts you, that you want to do, and that you construct in order to escape from the desire to do such a thing again. But you can't.

Drawing is also a quantitative phenomena; it's how many lines it has. The *Chamber Works* drawings have thousands of lines, and each line is related to other things. When I saw them at the end, I thought, "It's possible to use these drawings." Actually, they are not as silly as they look from the outside. They can actually be considered plans for cities or views of cities, or even views of certain kinds of spaces and buildings.

WORLD TRADE CENTER MASTER PLAN CONCEPT SKETCH

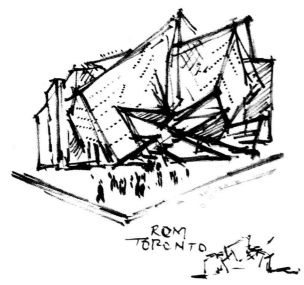

ROYAL ONTARIO MUSEUM CONCEPT SKETCH

To do a drawing, I think you have to have an accident of some sort. You can't ask for it. It's some sort of accident that befalls you, then a certain drawing happens, and it's an event. It's not really something that you set up aesthetically. I never thought of my drawings aesthetically anyway. I didn't think how they fit into an aesthetic regime or aesthetic sense, and I didn't even care if they were ugly. Some of the *Chamber Works* are very dark, almost not visible, and I didn't like them personally when I finished them. But they were what I really wanted to do, and they led me into completely different realms.

Drawing is, in a way, a text, because it's not just something visual. It's a deep longing. **A drawing represents a certain desire which is imminent in the lines of drawings itself**.

But loving to draw is the whole thing about drawing. It's some sort of ritual. It doesn't mean you have to have nice paper or good ink or anything like that. It's a means of doing something that is not very clear to you, and I don't think it's very rational either.

BL: There're two ways of looking at drawing. One could be more traditional: you're rendering something to shine light on it, so in your mind you're looking for that thing, you're going closer. And then there's the other idea that maybe the act of drawing itself, the black dot on the page, is an explosion of darkness, and that you're moving further away from the object.

Drawing is also a form of cutting. You might not be cutting stone, but you're cutting through space.

CHAMBERWORKS SERIES, III-H

WORLD TRADE CENTER MASTER PLAN SITE, NEW YORK, NY

I admire artists because they have total freedom. Architects don't. Architects aren't really artists in that sense. They are different because architecture has limits. It has to do with foundations, making a building, or creating a space. It's very different from the scope of an artist. I think they're two different worlds, even though sometimes an architectural drawing can sometimes look like an artistic drawing and an artistic drawing can look like an architectural drawing.

DEBORAH BERKE

Deborah Berke is the founder of **Deborah Berke Partners**, and the dean of the Yale School of Architecture. She was the recipient of the inaugural Berkeley-Rupp Prize awarded to an architect who has advanced the position of women in the profession. The firm also received a National Design Award from Cooper Hewitt, Smithsonian Design Museum

CATHLEEN MCGUIGAN

Cathleen McGuigan is the editor-in-chief of **Architectural Record**, and former architecture critic and arts editor of *Newsweek*. She has taught at Columbia's Graduate School of Journalism and has been a Poynter Fellow at Yale and a Loeb Fellow at Harvard. Under her leadership, *Record* won the Grand Neal award in 2012.

FOREGROUND / BACKGROUND

DB: We take clues from what's around us because none of our work is what we call spatula architecture—the kind of building that you can slide a spatula under, lift up, and put somewhere else. That is profoundly what we don't do. Obviously with adaptive reuse, one cannot do spatula architecture, but in new buildings we get our initial creative inspiration from the things around us—whether it's a built or natural context or the story or the smell of the place.

THE PERFECT LOBBY
By Eben Klemm

2 oz. **Bourbon**
1/2 oz. **Sweet vermouth**
1/2 oz. **Manhattan Milk Punch**
Combine all ingredients in a shaker with ice and stir 20 times. Strain and serve, garnish with lemon twist.

Manhattan Milk Punch:
Combine 2 cups bourbon, 1 cup sweet vermouth, 2 cups lemon juice. Bring 2 cups milk to a simmer. Remove from heat and let sit 2 minutes, then add to punch. Stir briefly and let sit for 30 minutes. Strain through fine sieve and then a coffee filter until clear.

Coincidentally, I've designed a lot of cocktails served in bars built in projects designed by Deborah Berke, so on some level she is one of the most influential architects in my career. I wanted to experiment here with the texture of a Manhattan, Ms. Burke's favorite cocktail. Milk Punches are difficult to make, and there was no way I could make enough for a large group, but they have a marvelous velvety texture impossible to recreate with any other cocktail. I wanted to use that texture to influence how we might taste this old warhorse of a cocktail.

21C MUSEUM HOTEL, BENTONVILLE, AR

The Yale School of Art is less about the presentation of art and more about both the making of it and teaching the making of it. That's where I think it's so important that the architecture becomes background rather than foreground, because there are two things that need to be in the foreground. One is teaching about the creative process, which is very different from second-grade teaching. One builds a dialogue with the teacher as the thing is made. I don't think you want the building to get in the way of that. I think you want the building to support that dynamic relationship by disappearing as much as possible. In the purpose of that building is the art itself. The rooms and spaces you've created should not impede an individual's creativity.

We intentionally, and happily and gratefully, find inspiration from what is around us. So the use of site context makes seemingly very different kinds of projects actually quite similar because **there is no place where you're going to build that is contextless.**

When we go to a site to do a freestanding building, we are looking at a number of things that are similar: What's the experience like to get there, how do you approach it, what dominates your initial experience of the place?

21C MUSEUM HOTEL, BENTONVILLE, AR

One year it's going to be somebody who works on canvas; another year a sculptor will occupy that room. Arts education buildings must meet programmatic requirements and technical requirements first. How do you do the light? How do you get the clay in and out? How do you keep music from this room from interfering with music from that room? Other than that, you simply want all of these gifted teachers and students to do their work.

CM: Who were your biggest influences?

My favorite architect when I was in school was Eero Saarinen. He was not popular then. What I found in his work was, in fact, much about what we've been discussing—buildings that are about site-specific programming. They're less about a type of sameness that gets placed anywhere. **That's the signature of site**. It's the opposite of sameness. The signature comes from responding to the place, the program, the client. That's consistent with what we do.

ROCKEFELLER ARTS CENTER, SUNY FREDONIA, FREDONIA, NY

Ninety percent is vision, but not all is vision—so is it the tree? Is it the slope of the road? Not all the things have to be beautiful. Beauty is nice, but if there's an endless repetitive row of telephone poles, perhaps their rhythm gets you thinking about how you're going to create rhythm in what you're making. You draw from the context. **We are consumers, in a positive way, of contemporary culture**, reading, listening, looking; we bring that to the work as well. I get a lot of inspiration from fashion and from regular stuff.

ROCKEFELLER ARTS CENTER, SUNY FREDONIA, FREDONIA, NY

In my early 20s, I don't think I could have remotely articulated why I was drawn to his work, but Saarinen was far and away my favorite architect. A distant second, with no reflection of the quality of the work, but simply in terms of my interest, was Louis Kahn. I think that's too easy to say now.

CM: You once said that one of your favorite modern buildings in New York when you were teenager was the Pepsi-Cola building because you learned it had actually been designed by a woman, Natalie DuBois.

The Pepsi-Cola building is a very, very beautiful building because the proportions of the verticals and the horizontals are perfect, and the scale is different from its surroundings on the street in just enough of a way that you think, "Ooh … Nice." It's highly crafted and perfectly envisioned, but somehow, on that street, it becomes quite an exquisite, neutral thing. Yet the exquisite background thing leads to the foreground because it's better than anything near it.

The women's issue has risen to the forefront again, thanks to the work of the women who argued strenuously for Denise Scott Brown to receive the National AIA Honor Award, which was a great thing. I think the low number of women in architecture is more likely diminished by a thousand cuts of little insults and minor difficulties, and more complicated insults and more profound difficulties, as opposed to a single issue being a gigantic roadblock to being a woman in architecture.

21C MUSEUM HOTEL, NASHVILLE, TN

We do a lot of work in the Midwest. All of the projects we're working on really have to do with the revitalization of the smaller city, and that feels fantastic. The enthusiasm of the politicians and our clients, our local consultants, and the people we encounter in restaurants is unanimous in their faith in the revival, in the revitalization of their city. And that, as an urbanist, is really heartwarming. The people are incredibly nice and the food is getting better. It is mostly easier to work there.

In New York, you go through endless regulatory bodies with projects that slide from one approval process to the next and then the next, which complicates building. Some of this we lay on ourselves, while others are very real because every site in New York is dense, compressed, and hard to get to. It's hard to build here, but it is extremely satisfying.

CUMMINS INDY DISTRIBUTION HEADQUARTERS, INDIANAPOLIS, IN

MARIANNE BOESKY GALLERY, NEW YORK, NY

Things will be better in architecture when one no longer has to say "woman architect." I think architecture faces perhaps an even bigger problem in terms of underrepresented populations in this country and in architecture, whether it be race, economic background, religion, educational background.

78

SCOTT
MARBLE

Scott Marble is a founding partner of **Marble Fairbanks**, and William H. Harrison Chair and professor at **Georgia Tech School of Architecture**. The firm's work focuses on cultural and institutional projects, including the NY Public Library, Queens Library, Brooklyn Public Library, Hunter College, Columbia University, NYU, and MoMA.

DAVID
BENJAMIN

David Benjamin is the founding principal of **The Living** and assistant professor at **Columbia University GSAPP**. Work focuses on expanding the definition of environmental sustainability through the frameworks of biology, computation, and a circular economy. Clients include the City of New York, Airbus, 3M, and Björk.

DESIGN RESEARCH

SM: We're colleagues at Columbia and we actually spend a lot of time together. What I am interested in is that we represent three generations of thinking about technology. I look at Ken's work as a historian and the influence it has had on me—understanding the history of architecture not only through technology and its role in production, but also in the kinds of social structure of practice and the social structure of society. Technology plays a critical role. For me, David's work is probably some of the most advanced work by taking technology to another level. He almost transcends technology in some way to get to the biological. This is what I think ties the three of us together. What we're trying to do is explore ways of bringing other information into the process of building, into the process of design.

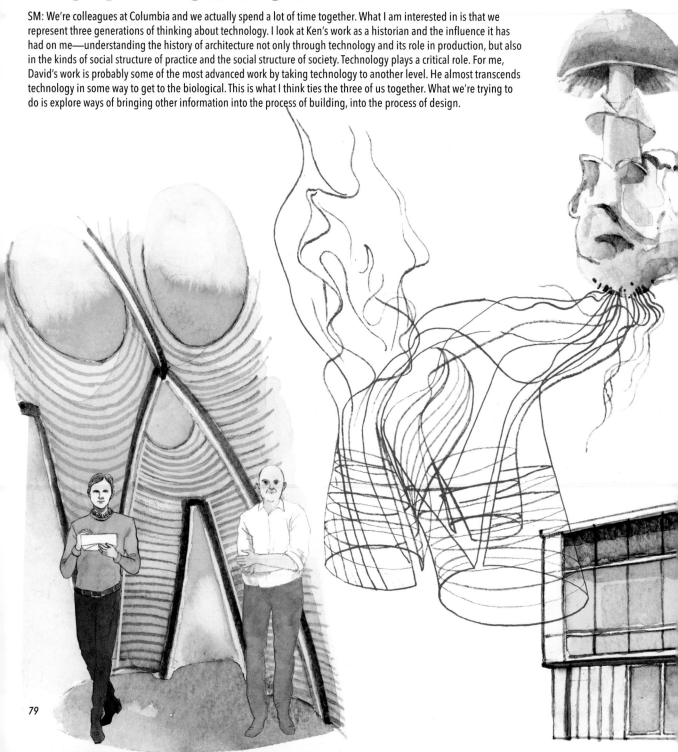

KENNETH FRAMPTON

Kenneth Frampton is the Ware Professor of Architecture at **Columbia University GSAPP**. He was born in the U.K. and trained as an architect at the Architectural Association School of Architecture, London. After practicing for a number of years in the U.K. and Israel, he served as the editor of the British magazine *Architectural Design*.

NEW YORK CHRISTMAS SOUR
By Toby Cecchini and David Moo

2 oz. **Wild Turkey 101 Bourbon**
1/2 oz. **Fresh lime juice**
1/2 oz. **Fresh lemon juice**
1 oz. **Ginger syrup** (2:1 sugar to fresh ginger juice)
1 oz. **Red wine mulled with winter spices** (allspice, star anise, clove, black pepper, cardamom, cinnamon, grains of paradise)
Shake first four ingredients together over ice and strain into a double old fashioned glass filled with ice. Float the mulled wine on the top and garnish with a slice of orange and a slice of lemon, pinned together with five cloves and a stick of cinnamon run through the center.

Given the presence of not one but three architectural eminences, we simply punted here and decided to do a seasonal cocktail, acknowledging the New York-based trio by conjuring a New York Sour that employed a heavily mulled red wine as a float, fresh ginger syrup as a sweetener, and a citrus element, split half, each of lemon and lime.

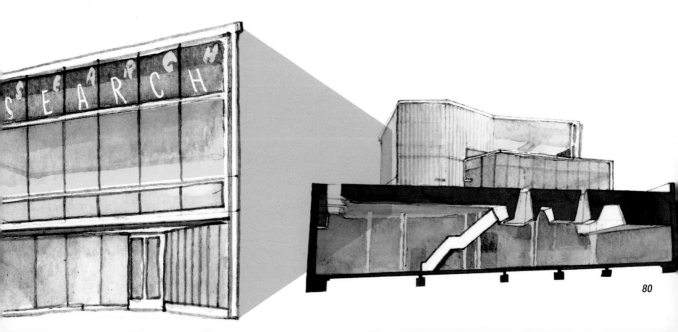

SM: We're a small practice, so we don't have a huge R+D budget. In each project we look for an opportunity to explore something that is completely beyond the brief. So in an extreme way, you could say that, **for us, projects are an excuse to do research.** We satisfy the client's needs, and our research is in the interest of the client, too. It's not something we're doing as an esoteric side thing. It's something that we feel strongly about, as important for us to be thinking about as architects in terms of our profession, and also for a particular project.

GLEN OAKS BRANCH LIBRARY, QUEENS LIBRARY, QUEENS, NY

SCOTT MARBLE

GLEN OAKS BRANCH LIBRARY, QUEENS LIBRARY, QUEENS, NY

We wanted the front of the building to have a civic presence. We have a large picture window in the upper level, where the children are. We came up with this idea of having a word that would move across the façade using the trajectory of the sun.

There are no lights here, no moving parts, no machines; it's simply the sun tracking across the sky that projects the word **"SEARCH"** onto the side. It was accomplished with a double parapet system. The word itself was highly controversial with the Queens Library. At one point they asked us, "Why don't you do the word 'find' instead of 'search'?"

Another part of the story about the project is the demographics. Thirty languages are spoken. We translated "search" into all of them and used it as a design driver to develop a frit pattern which, from a distance, has a sense of books on a shelf. Each language has a bar which appears on the façade in proportion to the percentage the language is spoken in the community.

The Glen Oaks Branch Library was one of the first projects in New York City's Design Excellence Program in 2005. It was finished in 2013. A building should not take this long to build.

The program that we were given was twice what was allowed on the site. We had a 20,000-square-foot program, and only 10,000 square feet could legally be built on the site. This was one of the challenges, and led to one of the major moves, which was to basically bury half the building. If you put space underground, it doesn't count toward the allowable square footage. There wasn't really a lot of play in where we put the program because there were three main parts: the adult reading room, the teen area, and the children's area, each on a different level. We used a series of different sized skylights to make the below-grade main reading room feel like an anti-basement and let in light.

GLEN OAKS BRANCH LIBRARY, QUEENS LIBRARY, QUEENS, NY

GLEN OAKS BRANCH LIBRARY, QUEENS LIBRARY, QUEENS, NY

The economy crashed when we finished the construction documents and the library was put on hold. We used this as an opportunity to research BIM, building information modeling, and to solve coordinating the construction process when there are multiple contractors who have to work together. BIM was an incredible tool. In some ways, it's a kind of social dynamic, a team problem. How do you coordinate the efforts of people who are working together when they've never worked together, they don't know each other? How can you coordinate all that work, which is a big challenge in a project like this. This project was the last one we did in AutoCAD. As an exercise, we took our two-dimensional CAD drawings and used them to build a three-dimensional model. We basically built a BIM model of our project from our own drawings to an extreme level of detail.

We developed this very detailed model, then got input from the contractor. They had never even heard of BIM. We asked, What will be helpful for you? They wanted to be able to go into the model and just click on an object and get information relative to the specification. That was useful for them.

Once a project is built, how do you judge the success of its architecture?

It's a simple question with a very complex answer. There's the easy answer that in a project like the library, which was probably the greatest success for us, it is the way that it is used.

GREENPOINT LIBRARY AND ENVIRONMENTAL EDUCATION CENTER, BROOKLYN, NY

GREENPOINT LIBRARY AND ENVIRONMENTAL EDUCATION CENTER, BROOKLYN, NY

DB: There are two ways that I can think about success for Hy-Fi, our MoMA PS1 project: if the product can resonate on technical and the atmospheric levels, then that's interesting to me. Also, in this case, the project was selected for a LafargeHolcim Sustainability Award. To be recognized in that forum as having contributed to the conversation about sustainability is a success.

KF: Let's talk about the issue of bricks. Architecture is a funny field because brick has a traditional dimension about it, which is an anachronism. Making buildings is somehow anachronistic. When you put a building in the ground, you cut a hole in the ground. Thus, the techniques used to put a building in the ground today are the same techniques that the Romans used. The chaos of placing a building in the ground is a mess. So, in a way, nothing much changes.

The attendance went from 45th in the system's 60 libraries before we built the building to sixth. That **the project actually created a kind of social change, a social interest, curiosity, if nothing else, is the success.**

In a practice like ours, there are other dimensions for success. **Success also means that we can do something new, and it might be completely unrelated to the client's brief.** This is where research comes in; sometimes you have to do things in the background. There is a lot of practical stuff you have to go through to get a project completed. But **to also have the ability to test new technologies, new ideas, and to advance not only your own practice, but architecture in general, is success.** Those are kind of the book ends of what I would consider the success of a project.

GREENPOINT LIBRARY AND ENVIRONMENTAL EDUCATION CENTER, BROOKLYN, NY

THE SCHOMBURG CENTER FOR RESEARCH IN BLACK CULTURE, NEW YORK, NY

There are aspects of the art of making buildings that are still anchored in the past. I remember Cesar Pelli saying, when talking about the course of rocketry and of the cutting edges of techno-sciences, "High-tech architecture is a ridiculous term because architecture is not high tech by definition and practice." I do admire what is called high-tech architecture. Yet the question of building techniques pertaining to different time periods and being combined in the making of a building, I think, is interesting.

DB: We're thinking a lot about **design as an ecosystem with interconnected loops of things** like ideas, technology, culture, street life, humans, non-humans, the natural environment, all kinds of interacting and mixing together. For our project called Hy-Fi, for the Museum of Modern Art and MoMA PS1, the idea was basically to do two things. The first was to create an exciting, interesting space for people to be in, both for the weekly summer parties and just as a museum visitor. And the second was **to explore what we thought could possibly be a new paradigm for design and manufacturing, with almost no waste, no energy, and no carbon emissions.**

DAVID BENJAMIN

HY-FI AT MOMA PS1, LONG ISLAND CITY, NY

More specifically, we started with the Earth's carbon cycle—the normal kind of endless loop of growth and decay, and then re-growth and renewal. We had on our mind the way most buildings get made in a pretty linear way, which basically involves taking high-value, raw materials out of the carbon cycle, and spending a lot of energy to convert those raw materials into building elements.

We wanted to experiment with **taking low-value raw materials, and spending almost no energy to convert the raw materials into building elements.** Create a building that was functional. And then, at the end of its life, take all that material and return it to the earth in a usable way within 60 days, instead of sitting in landfills for hundreds or thousands of years. **How do we do this?**

Through a living organism called mycelium, which is basically the root-like a structure in mushrooms. It turns out that you can combine agricultural waste, such as chopped-up corn stalks, with mycelium, and pack it into a mold of almost any shape. In about five days, the mycelium grows, binds together the agricultural waste, and creates a solid object, which can be used in a variety of ways.

We were experimenting with making a building element out of this process. In the end, we created a lightweight, low-cost brick that essentially was entirely biodegradable and compostable.

HY-FI AT MOMA PS1, LONG ISLAND CITY, NY

HY-FI AT MOMA PS1, LONG ISLAND CITY, NY

So, unlike most architecture, this project was designed to disappear as much as it was designed to appear. We were very interested in the **material life cycle** of the project and what would happen once this temporary installation went away.

We had to do a lot of testing. **This was a new material that had never been used in architecture before.** We took one of our lightweight bricks to a universal testing machine at Columbia University. We applied 100,000 pounds of pressure, which, of course, it would never have to resist in a building, and observed what it did. A single brick could be tested to a load of 50 cars—that was interesting. Yet the material was 20,000 times softer than steel. It's a really soft material, but can you imagine what happened with this brick? It started out at four inches and compressed to about three-quarters of an inch, but it never really failed. It never cracked. It never lost its ability to transfer the load, which was fascinating to the structural engineer.

EMBODIED COMPUTATION LAB, PRINCETON UNIVERSITY, PRINCETON, NJ

How could we possibly make this thing? We ended up using computation just to solve the immediate problem of constructing the 40-foot-tall structure. The issues we were solving, in many ways, became very technical—the testing, the computer model, solving how to lay out the bricks. But, at the same time, we wanted to test the kind of atmospheric or creative capacity of the material. What would be the effects of light and shadow? What would be the effects of texture, pattern in the building? What would it be like to stand within an enclosure made out of this material? How would it frame the natural environment?

EMBODIED COMPUTATION LAB, PRINCETON UNIVERSITY, PRINCETON, NJ

Then we tested an assembly. We found a compostable mortar and were able to build a brick-and-mortar structure.

We were able to see that we can take individual bricks, put them together into an assembly, and each still behaves similarly to a single brick. Therefore, we could advance to a structural model, which allows us to continue testing on a computer. The important thing was to be able to make a series of assumptions so that we knew how to model a surface.

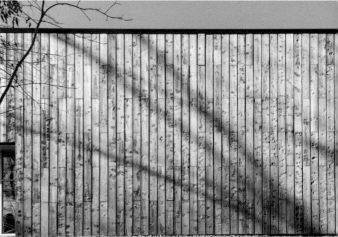

EMBODIED COMPUTATION LAB, PRINCETON UNIVERSITY, PRINCETON, NJ

We installed a second version of the project in the lobby of the Museum of Modern Art. This allowed us to experiment with other forms and other colors and material treatment, because the project is really more about an approach than about a singular form. Return to the idea that, in many ways, the project was designed to disappear. It was about the material's life cycle. We like the idea that the building came from nothing but earth, and then returned to nothing but earth.

BIONIC PARTITION, HAMBURG, GERMANY

PIER 35 ECOPARK, NEW YORK, NY

It was really an interesting project for us. We were engaging this cycle of physical testing, digital testing, analysis, and then going all the way back to the ingredients of the building block to work with a new version of the design.

The next challenge was to create a tall structure. Because it would be a terrible idea to cut this material, to cut this brick on site. We had to figure out a way to create a design so that we would **never have to cut a brick, but would still be able to make a complex form**.

DAVID
ADJAYE

Born in Tanzania to Ghanaian parents, David Adjaye's influences range from contemporary art, music, and science, to African art forms and the civic life of cities. Since **Adjaye Associates** started in 2000, his ingenious use of materials and sculptural ability established him as an architect with an artist's sensibility.

THOMAS
CAMPBELL

The second recipient of the **Getty Rothschild Fellowship** (2017/18), which supports scholarship in art history, Thomas Campbell was formerly the director and CEO of **The Metropolitan Museum of Art**. Prior to that, he was a curator in the Department of European Sculpture and Decorative Arts, specializing in tapestries.

ARCHITECTURE BETWEEN CULTURES

DA: I'm interested in Africa not because I'm African, but because it's this very particular continent with very unique geographies and extraordinary cultures. It's the birthplace of humanity. It has this incredible precedent that is only referred to in terms of the Northern Hemisphere in critical architectural discussion, mostly because colonialism wiped out most of the architecture in the Southern Hemisphere. There are so many fragments in its art and its cultures that are incredibly instructive in dealing with a hybridized, globalized world. I started going back to Africa on my own and doing research on my own. It took me 11 years to visit every single country on the continent.

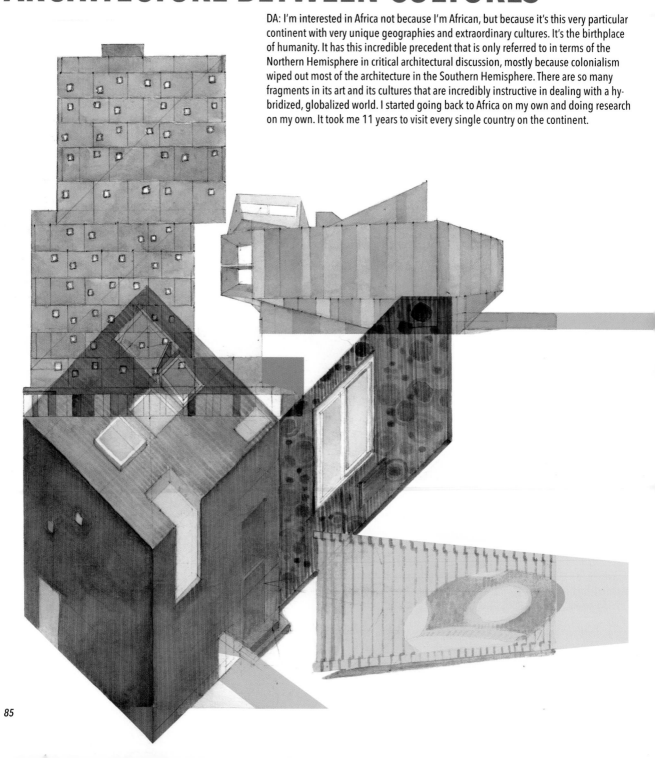

THE ADJAYE SWITCHEL
By Toby Cecchini and David Moo

2 oz. **Roasted banana-infused Plantation 5-year Barbados Grande Réserve Rum**
3 oz. **Switchel**
1/2 oz. **Fresh ginger syrup**
Shake, strain into an ice-filled double old fashioned glass, no garnish.

Switchel:
2 tbsp. **Bragg Apple Cider Vinegar**
2 tbsp. **Honey**
2 tbsp. **Molasses**
1/4 tsp. **Ginger powder**
1 cup **Water**
Mix together ingredients and shake well. Let stand for at least one day.

Banana-infused rum:
Lay four bananas flat on a silicone-padded baking tray and roast, in skins, for 20 minutes at 450-500 degrees. Allow to cool and peel. Crush with hands into a large sealable container and pour in 1 liter of rum. Allow to macerate at room temperature for 36 hours, then strain off the rum and filter out particles.

Fresh ginger syrup:
Juice fresh, peeled ginger with an extraction juicer. Add 2 cups white cane sugar to each cup of ginger juice and mix well until sugar is dissolved. Refrigerate.

Taking as our obvious inspiration David's Museum of African American Culture and History for the Smithsonian, David Moo and I came up with a drink based on a Switchel, the vinegar-based pre-Colonial-era thirst quencher that emigrated with the diaspora of slavery from the Caribbean to the mid-Atlantic and Northeast, taking on various ingredients along the way. Goosed with a roasted banana-infused aged rum, this was a pointedly thematic study in one glass.

TC: You began by working with artists on houses.

There was a young generation of artists (YBA – Young British Artists) who suddenly came into a lot of money and were able to commission architects to collaborate with them. I was teaching at the Royal College of Art then. My first projects were their studios and homes, always hybrid projects that were work-home scenarios.

They definitely wanted to make a mark in the city. There was a sense that London, being an old city, felt very full and they wanted to scribe themselves into its history. There was a move to the east, which was bombed during the war. It became the go-to place for artists and designers because we could actually explore what "contemporaneous" could be in London at that time.

IDEA STORE WHITECHAPEL, LONDON, UK

GWANGJU PAVILION, GWANGJU, SOUTH KOREA

I talked to my clients; we said no. The fact that it had this kind of deformed quality was something that we wanted to speak to, and what you'd normally call ugly was what we wanted to transform. **Contemporary is not about trying to find the latest material, but actually reimagining the past in a new future.**

I found that I didn't want to practice an architecture that didn't have a dialogue with contemporary culture, and I found artists very articulate about contemporary culture and contemporary ideas. I wanted to immediately wrestle with that group.

TC: How did the Dirty House fit into that early trajectory?

The Dirty House was really the seminal house I did in London. It was for two artists, a couple. It was about looking at what I call the ordinariness of the city, being excited about that ordinariness and wanting to elevate it. It was an old piano factory that had been fragmented beyond recognition with lots of additions. The city said, Please tear it down and build a shiny new building.

DIRTY HOUSE, LONDON, UK

SUGAR HILL, NEW YORK, NY

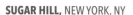

TC: Do you enjoy the process of public debate, explaining the concept, pushing it through the planning process?

It's what I was trained to do in England. That's the baptism for every U.K. architect, and you rise or fall depending on the strength of your arguments. It's not about what you can and can't do, it's about what you believe is right.

In America, you have zoning, but in the U.K. you have planning. Planning is about you debating the merits of your project. There is no as-of-right, there is no height limit. It's all the debate, the discussion, and it's about your ability to engage the conversation. It frames the way in which you approach work and, conceptually, it also frames the way in which you always present work, because it's very much about being clear about the arguments, especially in sensitive areas.

MOSCOW SCHOOL OF MANAGEMENT SKOLKOVO, RUSSIA

SMITHSONIAN MUSEUM OF AFRICAN AMERICAN
HISTORY AND CULTURE, WASHINGTON, DC

Architecture has to enable the greatest opportunity for the least fortunate. The whole purpose was to lift up the conversation, and to create a project that not only housing architects should do. Young firms should team up with more established firms to bring their design visions to the sector, which it badly needs. It's really underserved, and it's actually the greatest amount of housing going on in the city.

If you want to see the quality of New York improve, it's not about the high-end stuff, which is about 5-10%. It's actually the social housing projects that will bring the greatest amount of beauty, which we will all reciprocally enjoy.

SMITHSONIAN MUSEUM OF AFRICAN AMERICAN HISTORY AND CULTURE, WASHINGTON, DC

TC: How did you segue from bespoke houses into larger, socially-conscious projects?

It was a national competition run by the council, and I won. That started my first discussion with public bodies and communities. I was no longer working with artists. We had to go into an inner city community where 15 languages are spoken. We had to talk about this idea of making a new library, which was no longer going to be called a library. It was going to be called an **Idea Store**, with a mix of yoga, teaching spaces, cafes, exhibition spaces. It was about **looking at the small local library and transforming it to be relevant in the 21st century**. That led to other cultural projects. The Idea Store has been the most successful program for the transformation of libraries that the U.K. has seen. Lots of European countries came to see it. The mayor of Washington, DC, came to see it, which is why we were brought to Washington to work on libraries almost a decade later.

TC: The Sugar Hill project in Harlem is a social housing project that has a kindergarten and a children's museum built into it. There are 125 units and hopefully an urban farm on the roof.

When we found out about this project, I was very excited. Here was a project at a time in New York when the discussion was all about the next luxury tower on the High Line by the next starchitect. Here was a conversation happening about how we deal with housing for the homeless, and how we deal with the lowest economic ladder of the community. I was excited as I thought we really needed to have that discussion. I entered the competition. I was very passionate about it. We won. Something that is now a fundamental for me is the belief that all strata of society have a right to share in the fruits of the city and to improve their lives.

LOUISA HUTTON

In 1989 Louisa Hutton co-founded **Sauerbruch Hutton** in Berlin. She has taught at the Architectural Association and Harvard. She is a member of the Curatorial Board of the Schelling Architecture Foundation, and was a commissioner at CABE as well as a member of the first Steering Committee for Germany's Bundesstiftung Baukultur.

BARRY BERGDOLL

Barry Bergdoll is the Meyer Schapiro Professor of Modern Architectural History at **Columbia University**, and a curator in the Department of Architecture & Design at the **Museum of Modern Art**. He has also served as president of the Society of Architectural Historians, and was the 2010-11 Slade Professor of Fine Art at Cambridge University.

SENSE AND SENSIBILITY

LH: Three of the themes that have nourished us through our career: The way a building sits in the city—its relationship to site and to place, ideas of sustainability, and, in particular, the use of color.

DEVIL AND THE DETAILS
By Eben Klemm

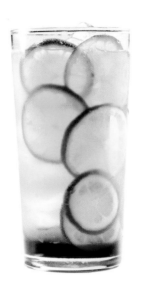

Build in an ice-filled rocks glass:
1 1/2 oz. **Silver tequila**
1/2 oz. **Cassis juice**
1/2 oz. **Ginger malt syrup**
1/2 oz. **Lime juice**
Top with Soda and stir. Garnish with lime wheel.

Ginger malt syrup:
Mix 12 oz. malt and 4 oz. ginger juice and combine with 16 oz. white sugar.

I love the buoyant coloration of Louisa's buildings and how it is an intrinsic part of her deeply environmentally-conscious practice, integrating the buildings with their surroundings. This cocktail is based on a classic tequila cocktail, with Ribena replacing cassis (because I think that everyone in Europe drinks it), and adding malt to the flavoring syrup for some earthiness.

My partner Matthias Sauerbruch and I began our careers taking part in competitions and, luckily, occasionally winning them. Most of the locations happened to be unloved, edge-of-city sites that were areas of post-industrial neglect. We tried to put into practice what we had learned from the English landscape garden (as well as from architects like Hans Scharoun), which is: **how to work positively with the existing situation, how to see the poetry in it, and how to transform it.**

When working on the design of a project we always have, from the outset, an idea about the materiality of the building, both outside and inside, as well as the interaction of materials and color. Our approach to the use of color draws on the development of painting in the early 20th century, when color had been freed from form (in the work of Ferdinand Leger, for example). For us it is this liberated use of color that is of interest and relevance to architecture.

Josef Albers remains a particular influence, with his research into what he called the difference between *the actual fact and the factual fact*, as well as **the deception of color—the way that colors can and do create space.** We take inspiration from painters, like Bridget Riley, who are working very much with one's corporeal as well as one's visual perception of color.

JESSOP WEST BUILDING, UNIVERSITY OF SHEFFIELD, UK

Another project that has become a benchmark for sustainable design is the Federal Environment Agency in Dessau. While we are particularly concerned with the design of low-energy buildings engineered to minimize their detrimental impact on the environment, we view sustainable design as a holistic imperative—not just the fulfillment of various quantifiable criteria. For us, sustainability operates on many scales, including that of the well-being of the individual. Aiming to give pleasure-in-use, we work with space and material to stimulate the senses and the imagination. For example, the atrium of the FEA, with its abundant landscaping as well as its many bridges for social exchange and circulation, offers a particular and welcoming character for all users and visitors.

GSW HEADQUARTERS, BERLIN, GERMANY

IMMANUEL CHURCH AND PARISH CENTER, COLOGNE, GERMANY

GSW Headquarters is a building that came into being in the euphoric period of the early 1990s, following the fall of the Berlin Wall. We were asked to deal with an existing tower from 1957 in an area that had been almost completely bombed out during the war. We proposed a composition of five buildings that address many layers of history and paradigms of the city that include a "landscape" order that transcends that of the 18th-century grid.

We wanted to bring in a lot of light. We also wanted to ventilate the building naturally, although this is difficult with a tower. The west façade with its double-skin produces a chimney effect that drives the natural ventilation of the office spaces; a wing-like canopy on the roof supports this airflow. Protection from glare as well as heat from the sun is provided by multi-colored panels. **In their ever-changing arrangement, the west façade becomes a dynamic composition that illustrates the way the users are inhabiting the building at any one time.**

BB: So on one level, your buildings seem to offer some inspiration that we might escape the banality and the austerity of the every-day surroundings, even though they have such a loving relationship to bland buildings that they sometimes incorporate. And on the other hand, they seem to reactivate the whole history of color in modernism.

The further away you are from the Brandhorst Museum, the more the individual colors blur and the façades become very similar to the context—say with sand- or ochre-colored buildings. Then the closer you get, the more apparent the individual glazed ceramic rods become. As you view the building head-on, you understand more of the layering and the horizontal nature of the striated sheet-metal skin behind the rods, whereas when you approach the building anamorphically, you get a blurring of color of just the rods themselves. And when you get even closer, you see—and even feel—the layered glazes on the rods, and can appreciate the transparency, for example, of a blue glaze laid over red clay.

We're aware of working simultaneously with flatness and depth. With sustainability in mind, one often can work with a thick façade that incorporates the additional depth of louvers, and this enables a play between flat surfaces and recession. Some colors recede while others come forward, according to the actual tonal and hue values being employed. We like to work with these techniques because of the simple desire to create spaces—even, and most particularly, everyday ones—that lift the spirit. Our aim is to directly engage people with the building, giving them some sort of bodily, emotional relationship with it.

BRANDHORST MUSEUM, MUNICH, GERMANY

I think that, **as an architect, you're never working in isolation. You're somehow aware, or should be aware, of the history of architecture, and of modern architecture in particular.**

What we're trying to do is to work simultaneously with the space and the form so that, in a way, the pressure is coming from the space and it's producing the form, rather than the other way around.

FEDERAL ENVIRONMENT AGENCY, DESSAU, GERMANY

FEDERAL ENVIRONMENT AGENCY, DESSAU, GERMANY

BB: The colors are localized per project? There are Sauerbruch and Hutton favorites. But the actual approach to color is not a theory of color that's brought to each project. It is actually more an interest in color that develops.

I still like our early conceptual sketches for GSW—even if they may seem unconventional or unversed, I dare to say that they bring the message across in a bold, fresh way. And when looking around among young colleagues today, I invariably admire the fantastic naïveté with which they draw things. If there's anybody young in the audience, just carry on. Don't worry, just draw your ideas. We had these sort of flying floor plates in our perspective drawings, with no respect or understanding of fire safety regulations and such.

Part of me regrets that we don't have such naïveté and bravura anymore. I mean, I hope we still have the bravura, but with experience, you drop the naïveté. I hope that we nevertheless retain a sort of childish enjoyment of place, of spaces, animated by light, color, and texture.

92

ANDREA LEERS

Andrea Leers is principal and co-founder of **Leers Weinzapfel Associates**. She was the director of the Master in Urban Design Program at the Harvard Graduate School of Design. She has taught at Yale and Penn. She currently serves on the Boston Civic Design Commission and on the University of Washington Architectural Commission.

JANE WEINZAPFEL

Jane Weinzapfel is principal and co-founder of **Leers Weinzapfel Associates**. She has taught at MIT and the University of Arizona. She is a former president of the Boston Society of Architects, and was a trustee and board chair of Boston by Foot, and a former trustee and current overseer of the Boston Architectural College.

MADE TO MEASURE

AL: The idea of "making" is very important to us. We care about the detail of things—what they feel like, their durability, their cost, their availability, and the joy of experiencing them. All of that making is in service of providing spaces for human activities and social interaction, tailored to a very specific moment and aspiration.

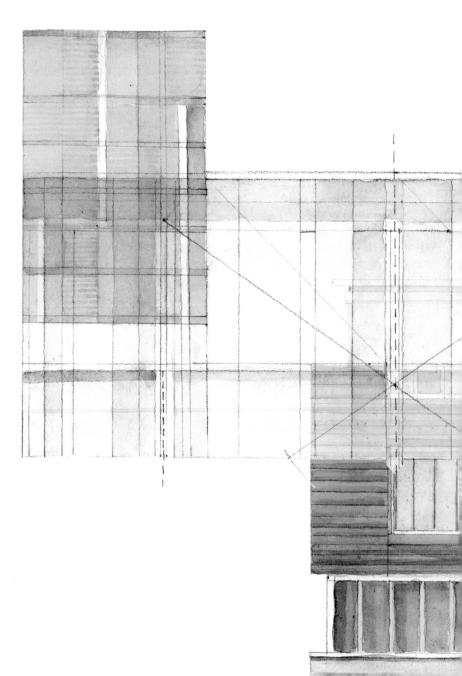

SUSAN S. SZENASY

Susan S. Szenasy is currently the Director of Design Innovation of **Metropolis**, the award-winning architecture and design magazine, and served as its editor-in-chief from 1986-2017. She is internationally recognized as an authority on sustainability and design, and holds four honorary doctorates.

THE HARTFORD
By Eben Klemm

2 oz. **El Dorado 8-year-old rum**
1/4 oz. **Averna**
3/4 oz. **Coffee vermouth**
1/4 oz. **Mint syrup**

Stir together in a mixing glass full of ice. Strain into ice-filled rocks glass and garnish with twist of lime.

Coffee vermouth:
Infuse 750 ml. bottle of red vermouth with 2 oz. whole dark roasted coffee beans for 4 to 6 hours. Strain out beans.

Mint syrup:
Place 1/2 liter of 1:1 simple syrup in freezer for 2 hours. Flash blend with 1/2 cup of mint, then strain.

The thirsty reader might detect the heavily mutated genetics of a Manhattan here, and deduce the name as a reference to a city in between New York and Boston. For the service, liquid nitrogen was used in both the chilling and the manufacture of the mint syrup. I've eliminated that for the home.

AL: The ideas that are common for us are the ideas of social and public realms. We are kids of the '60s, Jane and I, and that's how we learned architecture. That's what we believed in. And we're really delighted to see young people returning to **a focus on the wellbeing of the world as we make it.**

JW: One of our most delightful projects is encouraging young people. We have had a terrific opportunity to work with a number of young people who go on to form their own firms. This is a real chance to celebrate the opportunity to work with people, and let them do as much as they can as part of our studio experience.

PAUL S. RUSSELL, MD MUSEUM OF MEDICAL HISTORY AND INNOVATION, MASS. GENERAL HOSPITAL, BOSTON, MA

FRANKLIN COUNTY COURTHOUSE, GREENFIELD, MA

AL: Both Jane and I really, really enjoy the fabric of building, exploring new materials, looking at details, all because it adds up to the experience of building. It means that **buildings have an emotive force** and we enjoy that aspect. We've come to be very dedicated to the notion of building in the ensemble, **a building is always part of its urban setting, its landscape, not an isolated event.**

We are looking for the fit between a place, a purpose, and a space that we're making. It is like tailoring: you take measurements, you choose materials very carefully, you fit it over and over, you adjust it.

JW: Because we were friends before we were architects running a firm together, we very much did not want to have our practice disturb our friendship. So we said if something gets in the way of our friendship, friendship comes first. **It's wonderful working with such a friend.**

JW: I would say that very often we share the values of our clients. We're looking for clients who have aspirations, who are committed to their communities, who are often professional clients, and who see the value in the long term. **Making to measure, then, is to serve the highest aspirations and the most functional performance.**

AL: When we visit a place, when we see the site, when we see things around it, we have a sense of what ought to be there in terms of mass, in terms of material, in terms of color. This is a very intuitive reading.

Our buildings are different from each other because they really are inspired by the sensibility of the place and the purpose.

HARVARD SCIENCE CENTER EXPANSION, CAMBRIDGE, MA

UNIVERSITY OF PENNSYLVANIA GATEWAY COMPLEX, PHILADELPHIA, PA

SS: You were a woman-owned firm at a time when that was rather unusual. Who were your first clients? Who came to you? Who did you go after? How did you convince them that you were just as great as the men who were practicing?

AL: We had a good piece of advice from Joan Goody, who was one step ahead of us and one of the very few people whom we could look to for this experience. She counseled us to do some public work, to do some work for the Commonwealth of Massachusetts. Any kind of work at all. She said, "Repair roofs, fix a mechanical system. Just let them know that you're responsible and clever people." And that was really good advice. So we started applying for all these public projects. The first one we got was a tiny garage.

AL: The Design Building for the University of Massachusetts gathers architecture, landscape, and building technology under one roof. The building technology department was investigating mass timber. This was really exciting for us, because they went to the state legislature and managed to get special funding to make this **a demonstration building** for mass timber for large, multi-story buildings in terms of sustainability, quality, and durability.

SS: *Mass timber buildings are everywhere now: Scandinavia, Germany. Canadian architects are doing TED Talks on this. This is a movement, and yours seems to be the only one in the U.S. So how do you get rid of the prejudices against using timber in a large building? And what hurdles did you have to jump?*

DUDLEY SQUARE NEIGHBORHOOD POLICE STATION, BOSTON, MA

OHIO STATE UNIVERSITY EAST REGIONAL CHILLED WATER PLANT, COLUMBUS, OH

AL: **It's definitely not enough to make a better mouse trap.** We really need to think bigger—build what we need, not what we don't. We need to use fewer resources. We used to need to use less of everything. That's the foundation of what it is to be sustainable.

JW: **Who funds the research? We do. We make it part of the project.** Sometimes we are able to persuade our clients to add additional funds, as was the case in the mass wood building. But usually it's part and parcel for us in whatever we're doing. Many times we do projects that are studies or competitions. We do them to do research. That's a good way.

JW: Hurdle number one is how to weave through the codes, and make it a clear to the jurisdiction that needs to approve it that this is a suitable and safe technology. In addition to the codes is the cost. The prejudice against it has been that wood has historically, in this country, been light wood framing for homes and small structures and barns, and not thought of as a material for large buildings. We've had some horrific fires from Boston to San Francisco. Out of that grew our very cautious codes.

AL: But I think it's really the impetus of it as a renewable resource that has given it legs again. I think we will see more of it.

SS: *Are we getting there with sustainability, or are we just fooling ourselves that we're checking off LEED points? We're fine, we're so happy with ourselves, and then we can just say, "It's okay, we're doing our bit"? I don't see you being satisfied with that.*

UNIVERSITY OF MASSACHUSETTS, JOHN W. OLIVER DESIGN BUILDING, AMHERST, MA

UNIVERSITY OF CONNECTICUT SOCIAL SCIENCES AND CLASSROOM BUILDING, OAK HALL STORRS, CT

JW: In terms of my background, I was taught by some professors who were taught by Louis Khan. This was at the University of Arizona in the very early days of the architecture department, certainly early days of women in that department. The open space of Arizona had a huge influence on me, quite different than the rooms of New England.

AL: Louis Kahn was the spiritual head at Penn. I had been an art history student. I thought architecture was like big sculpture, but I looked at the work and it really moved me. So I took myself there. He only taught second degree candidates. But the rest of us baby architects hovered around the desks when he gave crits, and went to all his reviews and really absorbed it. I came away with a profound sense of Kahn's modernity, his commitment to exploring materials, the expression of systems, and philosophical inquiry.

96

MARION
WEISS

MICHAEL
MANFREDI

Marion Weiss and Michael Manfredi are co-founders of **WEISS/ MANFREDI** Architecture/Landscape/Urbanism, a New York-based firm at the forefront of redefining the relationship between architecture, landscape, infrastructure, and art. Their work creates connections between natural and built environments to craft settings that are distinctly public in nature. The firm was named one of North America's Emerging Voices by the Architectural League of New York, and received the AIA New York Chapter Medal of Honor. The firm was honored with the 2018 National Design Award in Architecture by the Cooper Hewitt, Smithsonian Design Museum.

CULTURAL COCKTAILS

MW: The idea of "unfolding" is a preoccupation in our work. Unfolding the liminal space between landscape and architecture, infrastructure and ecology.

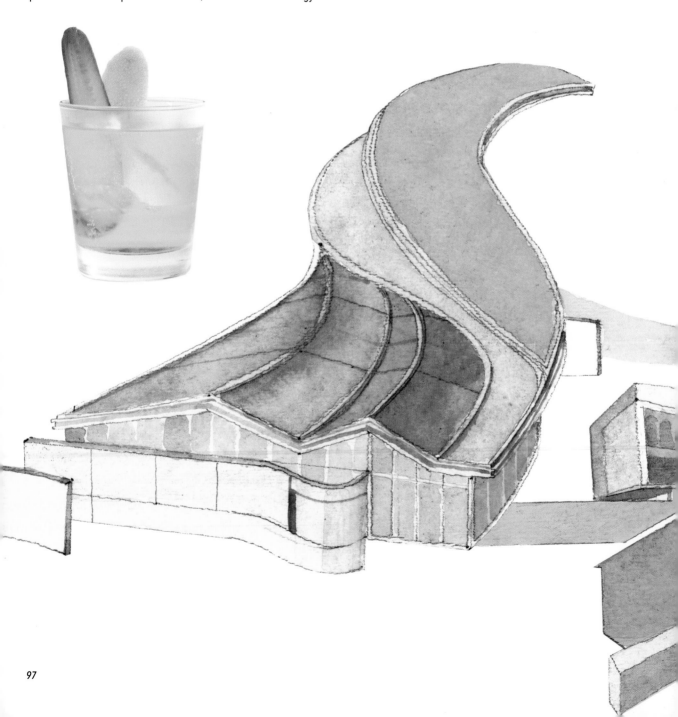

JULIAN ZUGAZAGOITIA

Director and CEO of **The Nelson-Atkins Museum of Art**, Julian Zugazagoitia discovered his passion for art and architecture one summer in New York, a teenager stranded with little money and a great deal of time. Trying to make sense of the galleries, he began developing narratives to explain what he was seeing and experiencing.

NEGRONI SBAGLIATO BIANCO OR WHITE MISTAKEN NEGRONI

By Toby Cecchini and David Moo

1 oz. **Suze gentian liqueur**
1 oz. **Carpano Bianco vermouth**
3-4 oz. **Prosecco**

In a double old fashioned glass pour, in order, over a large ice cube. Garnish with a long, thin slice of **Persian cucumbe**r and a **grapefruit peel**.

As Marion and Michael had just released the book *Public Natures*, relating architecture to landscape, and had recently completed the redo of the Brooklyn Botanic Garden buildings, I wanted something referencing green. Michael grew up in Italy and loved the Negroni, while Marion cleaves almost uniquely to prosecco. That led naturally to a Negroni Sbagliato, clarified and with one tiny aromatic embellishment from cucumber.

MM: I think Marion and I have always believed that **the clarity of the diagram** can help galvanize a number of different constituencies, particularity in a very complex urban situation. It's a way to connect the breadcrumbs that are there.

If the diagram is strong enough and grows out of existing institutions, we can start to galvanize the different dots and create a memorable district. Kansas City had this incredibly rich history of philanthropy, innovation, and optimism. We were excited to be help plan its cultural district.

NELSON-ATKINS CULTURAL ARTS DISTRICT, KANSAS CITY, MO

SEATTLE ART MUSEUM OLYMPIC SCULPTURE PARK, SEATTLE, WA

MW: The first person who raised his hand, and we knew him by name, said, "But who's gonna pay for this?" That was a way of saying there cannot be public money for a project like this. But we said, No no no, it will cost nothing. First of all, creating this cultural district has already been paid for. Why? Because we have two universities that exist. There are two museums, an art institute, two foundations, and a hospital that exist. So everything's already paid for. We don't put numbers on it because there's no point in putting numbers. And that changed the whole conversation.

MW: What was really striking in our first conversations with Julián and with members of the community was that everybody knew about each other. The Nelson-Atkins Museum, the Kaufman Foundation, the university, every one of these places was a wonderful heterotopia, aware of themselves, aware of each other, and completely oblivious to how close they were to one another. So one aspect of the genesis of our thinking was to say, Can we free up the idea of Kansas City as a collective of cultural destinations that might have things in common with each other?

HUNTER'S POINT SOUTH WATERFRONT PARK, LONG ISLAND CITY, NY

WOMEN'S MEMORIAL AND EDUCATION CENTER, ARLINGTON, VA

MM: Hunter's Point uses the idea of not creating a singular piece, but creating something that is very much a network. It incorporated ideas that, at the time, were extremely radical, such as soft shorelines absorbing water. Letting water become part of the composition of an urban setting—we think about living on the water's edge rather than it being something purely armored.

KENT STATE CENTER FOR ARCHITECTURE & ENVIRONMENTAL DESIGN, KENT, OH

JZ: We started a citywide effort of bringing people together around certain ideas about the cultural district, then they could react to them. There are a lot of people who want to kill any idea. The mayor has a name for them: The Cavemen.

MW: Kill all visionary, enlightened ideas.

MW: So, to the extent that a view doesn't exist until it's framed, we took it upon ourselves to frame what's surely one of the most magical views, I think, in the world. When Michael and I started collaborating, the one thing we discovered that we had in common was that we grew up in places where the whole idea of topography and territory was central to our experience. I grew up in Los Altos, California, where I was a distance runner. It was a terrain where I covered six miles every morning. Michael grew up with the Villa Giulia in Rome as his backyard.

BARNARD COLLEGE DIANA CENTER, NEW YORK, NY

BROOKLYN BOTANIC GARDEN VISITOR CENTER, NEW YORK, NY

MW: This issue of constraints is the inversion of what the real word means. The idea of the pure object on the ground—think of Villa Savoye for instance, the unobstructed object on the perfect plinth—is terribly uninteresting. What we like is the fact that there are systems far larger than what architecture typically engages—infrastructure, ecology, highways, cultural territories, and unconnected districts. Something larger unfolds that actually feels inevitable and connective in its identity. So those constraints, in fact, become leveraging opportunities. The Seattle Art Museum had this amazing vision. The museum was viewed as exclusive and excluding.

MW: One of the things that's really advantageous about coming to a city with fresh eyes is that, to us, it looks as if every institution and every organization should, of course, have things in common. When we have had the opportunity to meet with these communities and make presentations, we're beginning with, perhaps, a spirit of naïve optimism, but also with some insight about potential collaborative agendas that might be shared. So, for us to listen with fresh ears, but with a scaffold of possibilities, takes the heat off of neighborly tensions.

I think that the innocence of the outsider is actually a gift to the designer in this case—**being able to see the possible as opposed to being over-weaned and warned about the improbable.**

THE TATA INNOVATION CENTER, NEW YORK, NY

MW: There was this moment when Mimi Gates, the director, was in a helicopter with a number of trustees. They crash-landed.

MM: And survived.

MW: One of the board members was with the Trust for Public Land. They all wondered: If they could get out of there alive, what would they do? And, as a group, they decided that the most amazing thing would be to create a sculpture park that was free and open to the public in downtown Seattle.

KRISHNA P. SINGH CENTER FOR NANOTECHNOLOGY, UNIVERSITY OF PENNSYLVANIA, PHILADELPHIA, PA

NOVARTIS VISITOR RECEPTION PAVILION, EAST HANOVER, NJ

MM: Even an artist confronted with a painting thinks about the frame and the flatness of the work. And out of that comes a kind of friction. I think **any art, whether it's an applied art or a pure art, a social art, or like architecture, full of friction, relies on constraints.**

Mahomet
Public Library

100

TOM BALSLEY

Tom Balsley is the lead designer at **SWA/Balsley** (formerly Thomas Balsley Associates), an urban landscape architecture firm whose work has had a profound impact on the built environment and the quality of life in cities across the U.S. His unique fusion of creativity and innovation with the public process has produced extraordinary spaces.

MATT SHAW

Matt Shaw is the senior editor of *The Architect's Newspaper*. He is also the founder and co-editor of Mockitecture, a half-manifesto/half-satire collection of architectural debauchery. He has worked for the Columbia Laboratory for Architectural Broadcasting (C-Lab), Storefront for Art and Architecture, and *Architizer*.

BEYOND THE BENCH

TB: Public seating is critical to the success of our public spaces. In the '70s, NYC parks and plazas were in crisis—to the point of demands for the removal of seating! We've come a long way. The new culture of recreation demands that we design public furniture that moves, swivels, and fosters socializing—a fresh alternative to the path-lined, sole-purpose benches of the 19th-century parks. My next book will be titled *Beyond the Bench*. With Gantry Plaza State Park, Hunter's Point South, and Riverside Park South, we have been at the forefront of resiliency strategies in New York. Superstorm Sandy came…and went, leaving these parks unscathed and models for future designers.

THE UNCOMMON COCKTAIL
By Eben Klemm

In a rocks glass:
1 1/2 oz. **Gin**
1/2 oz. **Applejack**
1/4 oz. **Ginger syrup**
1/4 oz. **Lemon juice**
Add ice and top with soda. Stir. Garnish with lemon, orange, apple slices, and a sprig of rosemary.

Ginger syrup:
Simmer 1/2 cup grated fresh ginger in 2 cups water for 5 minutes. Add 2 cups white sugar, remove from heat and strain.

Rarely do I make a drink that's led by its garnishes, but I felt Balsley's bold shapes in the landscape of New York City left me no choice. I love the way the laying out of bold curves and sharp lines helps reclaim nature in these public spaces.

In the '60s, New York City looked around and said: You know what? We need more open space in Manhattan. But they didn't have the dollars to buy half a block in Manhattan and build a park, so they created **incentive zoning**. If you own a parcel of land, you are allowed to build so much FAR [Floor Area Ratio]—if you squeeze the building back away from the street and create a privately-owned public space, or POPS. A public and private bonus! It resulted in almost 90 acres of open space in Manhattan—90 acres!

I've done more than 60 of them, but that's just a small dent in the amount of public space that landscape architects should have had their hands in, because **a small public space within a block or two of where you work or live is going to touch your daily life very differently than your weekend destinations.**

BALSLEY PARK, NEW YORK, NY

CAPITOL PLAZA, NEW YORK, NY

Madison Square Park was designed for a culture of recreation from the mid-19th century. Benches are lined up for watching the promenade. We decided that these small spaces should be designed for our current culture of recreation, which is very different. A group of coworkers want to sit outside and work on a project together. You can't do that with this linear bench arrangement. You can't socialize or collaborate. You'll break your back talking to each other.

Our intent for Capitol Plaza was to let it be a different kind of a park space. We've got the NoMad wig shop owners, we've got the creative class. We've got luxury millennial housing along Sixth Avenue. I wanted Capitol Plaza to be a reflection of the neighborhood, and touch it, part of which means understanding how important the furnishings are that we provide. It's really a small urban space. It should celebrate the city, and people socializing and meeting and greeting, just like they do in the great plazas we visit in Europe.

With Gantry Plaza State Park, we were interested in a new urban waterfront paradigm, an alternative to the Battery Park landfill model. We wanted to celebrate the diverse shoreline and its industrial history with details and materials that were very rugged: thick stainless steel and heavy stone blocks, part of expressing the heritage of the site. We were also thinking about resiliency—it had to be able to withstand storms as well.

CURTIS HIXON WATERFRONT PARK, TAMPA, FL

GANTRY PLAZA STATE PARK, LONG ISLAND CITY, NY

I was always a modernist. My heroes of the time, in the 1970s and even the '80s, were Lawrence Halprin, Dan Kiley, and M. Paul Friedberg. We all loved what they preached, but they didn't always practice a public process that would have created a meaningful park. We've transformed failed spaces from each and learned lessons along the way. But they were my heroes. They were breaking away from everything that was traditional about open space design. I came to the city with that same attitude, but it was a desert. Nobody was really interested in contemporary landscape architecture, so we had to just keep scratching and looking for opportunity wherever we could find it.

At Main Street Garden Park in Dallas, we created "study shelters." You can enter at night and the light turns on automatically. It's just you, two chairs, and one table, and you can sit and look at the street or into the park. As part of the garden café, we created a "mountain stream" fountain, which has a rushing skim of water with big marble slabs to sit on. Take your shoes off on a hot Dallas summer day, cool your feet, and have lunch on a slab with friends.

MAIN STREET GARDEN PARK, DALLAS, TX

MACOMBS DAM PARK AT YANKEE STADIUM, BRONX, NY

I came to New York from school and said: I'm here! Boy, was that a shock! But I had great designs and great drawings from school, and I would peddle them around to whom? Architects. So I would get in the door. I would show my drawings and they'd be seduced by them. And they'd say, "Yeah, we've got to work together. This would be great." Just based on the drawings, I think.

Early on it was a subconsultant role as opposed to real collaboration. At some point I started expanding further into the public realm with prime contract commissions that offered more independence.

A developer said, "This is your turf." And he told the architect, "You stay in the lobby, and Tom is going to do the plaza, and you guys are going to respect each other." **I never would do anything that wouldn't complement the architecture**. My design voice found an audience in those plazas.

Now I'm collaborating with all my architectural friends because I have more credentials, and there's an equity relationship that we enjoy. People finish school and think they have earned that level of trust with their fellow professionals, but you really have to work for it. It doesn't come automatically. **Landscape architects have to work harder to earn the respect of our architectural peers.**

INTERCONTINENTAL HOTEL COURTYARD, NEW YORK, NY

HUNTER'S POINT SOUTH WATERFRONT PARK, LONG ISLAND CITY, NY

Our urban parks should celebrate the city and its people.

BING
THOM

Bing Thom was the principal of **Bing Thom Architects** (now Revery Architecture), a Vancouver-based firm he founded in 1982. His work has impacted cities and communities around the world. With each project he sought ways to make a positive contribution to the community through his architecture.

MICHAEL
HEENEY

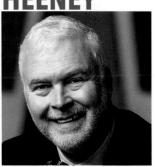

A nationally and internationally recognized city builder, architect, and urban strategist, Michael Heeney was a principal with Bing Thom Architects for 28 years prior to joining **Surrey City Development Corporation** as president and CEO in 2017. He holds degrees from the University of British Columbia and the University of Toronto.

FROM NORTH AMERICA TO HONG KONG

BT: The problem with global architecture is that we are still craftsmen. So yes, you can import a modernist office building and it doesn't matter where it is. The question is, how do you retain your authenticity when we are all now living in a global world? I have to learn how to bring my particular way of working to another place. We did a building in Spain. Before I even started designing, I travelled the country for a few weeks just to understand Spanish craftsmanship so that when I design a building, the Spanish craftsmen can build it.

GINA POLLARA

As the former executive director of the **Franklin D. Roosevelt Four Freedoms Park**, Gina Pollara was instrumental in its construction. She is a graduate of the Cooper Union Irwin S. Chanin School of Architecture. At the time of this conversation, she was the president of The Municipal Art Society of New York.

THE RAMOS GIN FIZZ
By Toby Cecchini and David Moo

The Classic Recipe from New Orleans:
2 oz. **Gin**
1/2 oz. **Lime**
1/2 oz. **Lemon**
1 oz. **Egg white**
1/2 oz. **Simple syrup**
1 oz. **Heavy cream**
3 drops **Orange flower water**
Seltzer

Shake long and hard, at least one minute. Strain into a chilled highball glass and let stand for 30 seconds before adding very cold seltzer to lift the meringue and separate the drink. No garnish.

Bing Thom was such a sweet fellow, and his predominantly white, airy, soufflé-like constructions called for a drink of exactly those same qualities. Though the Ramos Gin Fizz, another old New Orleans drink, is revered and despised in equal measures by bartenders for its labor-intensive build, we knew we had to fit it to Bing's lecture.

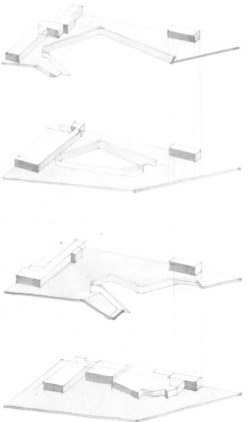

Since I'm in New York I want to tell a New York story. We work with Robert Heintges as a glass consultant. We had a project in Vancouver, so he flew to Vancouver. I'm trying to do this glass screen for a house. He said, "Well, Bing, I'm not sure." So I called up this guy and said, "I've got Mr. Heintges here. We want to see you. Do you think you can come down in 45 minutes?" He said okay, and shows up half an hour later, and I explained the project. I said, "It's never been done before." He said, "No, I've never done it before." I said, "Well, can I get a sample next week to see if it works?" He said he would do a sample, and leaves. Bob said to me, "This is amazing. It just never happens in New York, where you can call somebody to come in 45 minutes, ask him to do something for you that has never done before by next week, with no money, and he says yes."

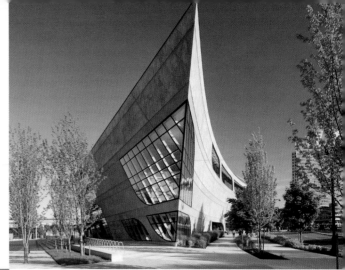

SURREY CITY CENTRE LIBRARY, SURREY, BC

SURREY CITY CENTRE LIBRARY, SURREY, BC

Our own office is a humble little thing. We built our own building from a series of joined warehouses. We come from 16 countries and speak 22 languages. Most of us have double degrees, like architect/planner; one was even an architect/physiotherapist. When my design partner Venelin Kokalov came to the office, he was self-educated Bulgarian and he didn't speak any English. But I looked at his drawings and said it didn't matter. Architecture is an international language—it's like the cocktail. It is a mixture. We have three offices: Vancouver, Hong Kong, and Washington, DC. Vancouver is the new Venice—10 hours to Beijing and 10 hours to London, time zones that work well in this economy.

I had two mentors: Arthur Erickson and Fumihiko Maki.

Arthur Erickson served in Asia during the war, and he was a Canadian who actually wished he was Japanese or Chinese. Fumihiko Maki is Japanese who wished he was more Western. So, working for the two of them was very interesting, and I am a so-called banana as I am in between. I drew inspiration from both by working with them.

I said, "Well, that's Vancouver." But **we are a city of hippies, a city full of vice presidents who don't want to be presidents because they want to live in Vancouver.** The reason I tell this story is because it's been increasingly difficult for me to bring the craftsmen from where I live to where I'm working all over the world. We tried it with the wood structure for the Arena Stage in Washington, DC. We had to essentially rewrite the building code for that one building, making it the first heavy timber building in DC.

GUILDFORD AQUATIC CENTRE, SURREY, BC

GUILDFORD AQUATIC CENTRE, SURREY, BC

They are both very different. Arthur was a form-maker, much more exuberant. He was much more wedded to the landscape—everything is more horizontal and everything grew from the earth, history and culture, glass and concrete. Maki is much more about layering of spaces, the ethereal aspect of Japanese cultural architecture. **You have to grow past your masters to become yourself.**

I have this theory that there is a regional sense of color that is very different depending on where you are. When you are making a form, the way you read the form varies under the light. Vancouver, climate-wise, is similar to Japan not only because we are on the Pacific, but we have a lot of moisture in the air and it is always a little bit foggy. Everything is a little bit grey. The sky is grey because of the moisture. There are no strong colors; everything has a grey tone.

Whereas in Texas you have the strong sun and the blue sky. We once spent three days on an interview, and everyone was drawing like crazy. I wanted to talk to an artist. I didn't draw anything. I asked the artist, "What is the color of Fort Worth?" It is burnt umber and sienna. The sun is so strong it burns the chlorophyll out of plants, so tree bark is very dark and the green of the leaves is very dark.

THE BUTTERFLY, VANCOUVER, BC

XIQU CENTRE, HONG KONG

You come from a mother and father, which are the two big theaters. I didn't want the baby to be dwarfed by the mother and father, so I had this idea of Richard Serra's *Torqued Ellipse*. Joshua Dachs, the theater consultant, said, "Bing, you are crazy! Why do you want them to walk all the way around?" I said, "Because I want them to lose the memory of the big space."

And when you look in the distance, all you see is dust, so there is a kind of redness to it. But there is the blue sky. When I was doing a plan, I was capturing that feeling, not literally, but figuratively…

The Arena Stage was originally done by Harry Weese in the '70s. It got its name when they went to get the building permit and the city didn't know how to classify it, so the commissioner said, "Oh, it's a boxing arena! Oh, no problem!"

XIQU CENTRE, HONG KONG

If we can make that circular walk something fantastic, you can get a glimpse of what you are coming into. You can bring sound, you can heighten the excitement, then you turn the corner and discover the theater. The wooden basket-weave walls are good for acoustics and a wonderful texture. There is no money in a black box for scenery—you could be in a boat, in a forest, in a study, in a fortress—it's only your imagination when you are in the Cradle's space. It has its own character, its own patina.

ARENA STAGE, WASHINGTON, DC

The theater had a very good proscenium stage, but had problems with the acoustics and traffic. We shrink-wrapped the building with a wall of glass and added a third building. We are from Vancouver—we love to use wood. We made these huge columns that hold up the roof and the glazing at the same time. There is the Cradle, the third theater. We kept talking about cradling new work, but we didn't want to do a standard black box.

ARENA STAGE, WASHINGTON, DC

FRANK
HARMON

Frank Harmon, founder of **Frank Harmon Architect** in Raleigh, NC, is also an educator and author of *Native Places*. He has designed sustainable modern buildings across the Southeast for 30 years. His work engages pressing contemporary issues, such as placelessness, sustainability, and restoring cities and nature.

SUZANNE
STEPHENS

Suzanne Stephens, deputy editor of *Architectural Record*, has been a writer, editor, and critic in the field of architecture for several decades. She has a Ph.D. in architectural history from Cornell University, and teaches a seminar on the history of architectural criticism in the architecture programs at Barnard and Columbia Colleges.

DRAWING AS A WAY TO SEE

FH: I'm an architect, but I've been drawing most of my life. I draw because when I studied the works of Le Corbusier, I learned that from the time he was 18 years old, he always had a sketchbook in his pocket. So, from the time I was 20, I've kept a sketchbook in my pocket. I would submit to you that to this day, in our world of digital technology and computer-aided drafting and all the marvels that we love, still, the single most effective way to generate an idea and to puzzle over it is with a pencil and a piece of paper. And underneath the drafting table is a trash basket, which is also a very important part of the relationship.

HARMON'S TI PUNCH
By Eben Klemm

Build in a rocks glass:
Squeeze in half a **lime** and drop in **husk**.
Add 1/2 oz. **Demara sugar** and muddle to paste; let sit.
Add 1 1/2 oz. Cold **rum** and two sprigs each **mint** and **arugula**.
Store **Rum Agricole Blanc** in freezer. Gently remuddle.

This drink was inspired less by Mr. Harmon's buildings and more by his nature sketches I found in his online journal nativeplaces.org, and this quote he emailed me: "Architecture is not unlike the ingredients in a cocktail : it's all about proportion : get the proportions wrong and it's dog food, get the proportions right and it's beautiful."

JC RAULSTON ARBORETUM LATH HOUSE, RALEIGH, NC

Virginia Woolf said, "It was important to write every day, because **how else could we clamp the net over the butterfly of life, but by capturing the moment?**" Which is the value of sketching.

About three years ago, I decided to make a sketch and combine it with a text. I love good writing, and so I started doing these little pieces, which I call "Native Places." I make a sketch and write no more than 200 words about it.

I've been drawing most of my life. As I travel, I make sketches. I often sketch barns. I find barns fascinating. I believe that **a barn is one of the best indicators of a society, of a culture.** If you look at a barn, you can tell what people grow, how they grow it, how they treat the land. In fact, what's important to them. If you look at barns, if you know what you're looking at, you can tell which way is north. The farmer certainly knew that when he built his barn. Barns were typically built by people who didn't know they were architects. They were farmers, so I've always studied them and learned a lot from them.

AIANC CENTER FOR ARCHITECTURE AND DESIGN, RALEIGH, NC

JC RAULSTON ARBORETUM LATH HOUSE, RALEIGH, NC

A sketch takes about five minutes, but writing 200 words takes about three hours. It's a lot easier to write 1,000 words. Abraham Lincoln, many people say, once wrote that he apologized for writing such a long letter because he didn't have time to write a short one. It's a wonderful discipline to be able to write and to draw.

People ask me, "What is North Carolina architecture?" I tell them it's very down-to-earth. It's practical, it's straightforward. It's a simple roof. It does the job.

NORTH CAROLINA MODERNIST HOUSE, RALEIGH, NC

We study art history and we learn from our professors that artists like Rembrandt were making sketches to think about a painting or trying to gather ideas that they might put together in some kind of mural. What I think Rembrandt was doing was trying to understand the world. That's why he was making his sketches. He caught the moment, and he was making sense of it.

WALNUT CREEK WETLAND CENTER, RALEIGH, NC

Students would meet with a teacher, Alvin Boyarsky, for example, and we would say, "Alvin, we've got this great idea," and we'd start drawing it on the wall. It was a common thing. The AA was repainted every summer, so that **in the fall the walls would be ready for sketching again. It was a form of communication.**

I then worked in New York for Richard Meier, who was a great influence on me because I learned what it took to do something really good. He had a passion. He had a fire that whatever he did, he was going to do it in the best way possible. We would design something, then, all of a sudden, the building code would come down on us, and the building inspector would say we couldn't build it.

SKETCH OF CHARLESTON, BY FRANK HARMON

SS: It is very good to talk to you tonight about drawing because we at Architectural Record are also interested in drawing. Especially in the digital age when a lot of students, we fear, do not have enough drawing lessons or classes or anything along those lines. We fear there is a generation of architects who might be maturing without knowing how to sketch or draw by hand or understand what drawing does. Can you talk about two types of drawings? One is the sketch of something you admire and analyze. The other is the concept sketch, where you're designing something for yourself as an architect. I'd like you to speak about the difference or talk about the creativity that occurs between the analytical drawing of something built and the concept sketch.

Richard was determined to find a way, whether it took a lawyer or a writer or something else. He was going to find a way to get around it. I learned then what it took. Hunger, I would call it. **There's a lot of talent out there, but if you can combine talent with hunger, like Richard did, it is remarkable.**

UNITED THERAPEUTICS FIELD HOUSE, DURHAM, NC

TAYLOR HOUSE, SCOTLAND CAY, BAHAMAS

There are two kinds of sketches. One is trying to understand what you see. Making sense of it. That's what Rembrandt was doing. These are quite spontaneous.

The other kind of sketch is a conceptual sketch for an actual project, but what I would say about the nature of that sketch is that it's still indeterminate. It doesn't set the design, but it suggests a direction and has many possibilities. It's neither a solution nor is it a speculation. It's a very interesting kind of drawing.

One of our classes at the Architectural Association was drawing, taught by Paul Oliver, who was a very fine artist and also an expert on American jazz. We all learned how to draw. The AA had all these white walls, but by the end of the semester the walls were completely covered with drawings.

SHOHEI
SHIGEMATSU

Shohei Shigematsu is a Partner at **OMA** and Director of the New York office. Since joining the firm in 1998, he has been a driving force behind many of OMA's projects, leading the firm's diverse portfolio in the Americas for the past decade with emphasis on maximum specificity and process-oriented design

AMANDA
DAMERON

Amanda Dameron is a design journalist and producer. She served as editor-in-chief of *Dwell* magazine from 2011 to 2017, and now leads Home and Design for **Tastemade**, a digital-first media company with a global audience of 200 million. She has held editorial positions at *Architectural Digest* and *Western Interiors and Design.*

PROCESS, PROGRESS, AND EVOLUTION

SS: OMA is a design-oriented firm with a global reach. It is no longer capable of being curated by a single mind. The partnership structure lends itself to independence and individuality within the firm. At the same time, the office and its organizational centers share a way of thinking. By orienting towards a process that observes changes in society, the architecture incorporates these changes. At OMA New York, we engage clients with specificity, narratives, and a collaborative spirit that allows us, in turn, to push the boundaries of known typologies.

BROWN DERBY
By Eben Klemm

2 oz. **Bourbon**
1 oz. **Grapefruit juice**
1/2 oz. **Rosemary honey syrup**
Add ice and shake 20 times. Strain over fresh ice into a rocks glass and garnish with a rosemary sprig.

Rosemary honey syrup:
Simmer 5 fresh rosemary sprigs in 1/2 liter water for 5 minutes. Dissolve in 1 liter honey.

The Brown Derby, an unlikely successful combination of bourbon, grapefruit, and honey, is one of the few cocktails actually named after a bit of architecture. The Brown Derby, a restaurant for 1940s Hollywood swells, was shaped like the hat, and the drink itself, interestingly, wasn't served there.

AD: You allude to community presentations. An essential part of building is listening to the inevitable feedback that comes. I'm wondering, as part of your practice, do you attempt to insulate yourself from such critical feedback as you know it will come no matter what you put out there, or is it helpful to you as part of your practice?

MILSTEIN HALL, CORNELL UNIVERSITY AAP, ITHACA, NY

PIERRE LASSONDE PAVILION, MUSÉE NATIONAL DES BEAUX-ARTS DU QUÉBEC, QUÉBEC, CANADA

AD: It's almost as if you anticipate this feedback—you position yourselves in a practice arena so that you are ready, like the presidential candidates do to prepare for a debate. Often it's said that, as part of the architectural curriculum, it's important to maintain a tough skin. Criticism is such an important part of a curriculum.

You have chosen to work with artists and as part of collaborating with them, it's acknowledging performance.

At OMA, we are **self-critical**. By constantly interrogating ourselves throughout the design process, we develop a robust way of explaining and defending our concepts. Architectural moves are, at times, difficult to communicate to people, especially to a larger audience. **We try to convey our concepts and schemes as boldly as possible through diagrams, books, and narratives.** When doing so, we are conscious of absorbing critical comments and responding in the most engaging way, encouraging collaboration whenever possible.

AUDREY IRMAS PAVILION, LOS ANGELES, CA

121 EAST 22ND STREET, NEW YORK, NY

The great thing about working with an artist is the unexpected framework that would not be possible as architects alone. There are also different kinds of challenges that come with working with artists, as opposed to other clients. In a way, the same rigor and creative processes that artists go through, in turn, push us to redefine typologies and boundaries of tradition. What is a theater? What is a museum? How are these typologies responding to our changing environments, and how should architecture be a conduit for manifesting these changes?

For the Marina Abramovic Institute in Hudson, New York, our design was very much driven by the artist's mission to cultivate new kinds of performance. The building would be dedicated to radical explorations of time-based and immaterial art, and the design aims to expand on the educational and institutional typologies. We proposed a new type of theater, surrounded by auxiliary program spaces. The new space provides a monastic ground that is both highly flexible and controlled. Three areas around the theater allow it to expand or be reconfigured.

FAENA FORUM, MIAMI BEACH, FL

MANUS X MACHINA, METROPOLITAN MUSEUM OF ART, NEW YORK, NY

There was a time when great architects had to have a manifesto. Today, I think it's not about one big idea, but more about observation of societal changes and reflecting those changes in architecture. OMA is hyper-aware of the environment around us and, in turn, we do not have a homogenous design language. We appreciate cultural knowledge and sensitivity, and encourage design to be derived from specificity—site, budget, client, program, and climate—and not to be stylistic.

It was a very refreshing experience to collaborate with Taryn Simon on "An Occupation of Loss" at Park Avenue Armory [in 2016]. She brought an intense and meticulous rigor to the project that resonated with us. The project was the culmination of three years of research and thought. Dealing with grief and representing loss was an interesting challenge for us. Not only was it a challenge to respond to an emotionally charged topic, but grief is also carried at diverse scales. As we discussed the scale of representation, we wanted to avoid "installation" as an "architectural exercise," but rather as a sonic exercise. Putting aside the aesthetic nature of architectural installations, we devised a concept that was at once monumental and intimate. It was also an interesting challenge to create something functionless, with no rules. In this instance, our installation was a vessel for the mourners.

AN OCCUPATION OF LOSS, WITH TARYN SIMON,
PARK AVENUE ARMORY, NEW YORK, NY

7 SCREEN PAVILION, CANNES, FRANCE

When I came to New York 10 years ago, I tried to establish a new culture inspired by the firm's Rotterdam office, but acting independently. Being in New York and away from Rotterdam enables me to pursue my own ambition while continuing the culture and practice of the firm. The firm is no longer capable of being curated by a single mind, but we still carry on the rigor and process that started in OMA Rotterdam.

My ambition is to capture conditions specific to our generation, and through those observations, create new architectural typologies. I want to immerse myself in key moments and turning points of institutions and other clients, and design buildings that will reflect their beliefs, contributing to their evolution.

116

MICHAEL MURPHY

Michael Murphy is co-founder and executive director of **MASS Design Group**, an architecture and design collaborative with offices in Boston and Kigali, Rwanda. As a designer, writer, and teacher, his work investigates the social and political consequences of the built world. He focuses on how environments shape behavior.

MICHAEL SORKIN

Michael Sorkin is the principal of **Michael Sorkin Studio**, a global design practice, and president of **Terreform**, a collaborative group of designers, social scientists, and urban researchers. He is a Distinguished Professor of Architecture and director of the Graduate Program in Urban Design at CCNY, and author or editor of 20 books.

ARCHITECTURE IS NEVER NEUTRAL: ON POLITICS, SPACE & JUSTICE

This program was held shortly after Donald Trump was elected President. After AIA National issued a statement that took all of us by surprise, including the executive directors of every AIA chapter, the board of AIANY issued a letter in response. Michael Murphy and Michael Sorkin got in touch with me and said they wanted to be critical and raise some issues. This Cocktails and Conversations provided a forum to discuss architecture and politics and the election results in 2016. —Ben Prosky, Assoc. AIA, Executive Director, AIANY

November 18, 2016

THE (IMPROVED) LIBERAL COCKTAIL
By Toby Cecchini and David Moo

2 oz. **Ragtime Rye, New York Distilling**
1/2 oz. **Sweet vermouth**
1/4 oz. **Bigallet China-China Amer**
3 dashes **Pernod Absinthe**
Stir all ingredients in a mixing glass over ice and strain into a double old fashioned glass with one large ice cube. Garnish with a twist of lemon.

As Michael has tried to emphasize using local sources in his constructions, he very much wanted me to incorporate that premise into his cocktail. So I turned to New York Distilling's Brooklyn-made rye to reboot a version of the old Liberal cocktail.

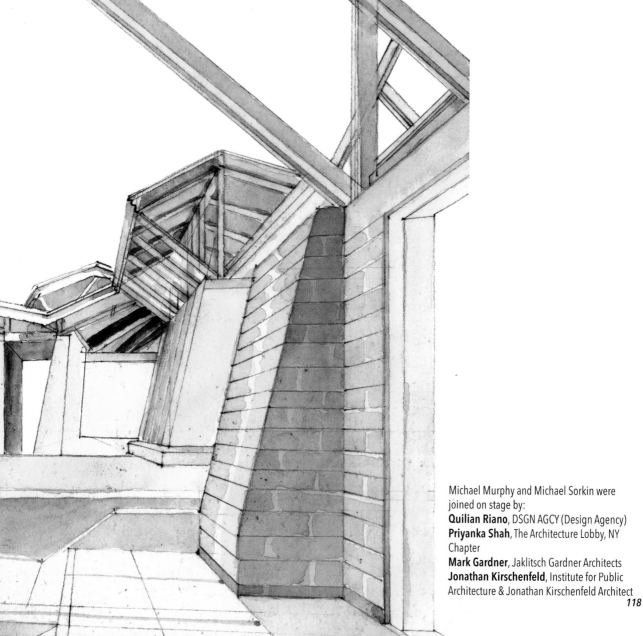

Michael Murphy and Michael Sorkin were joined on stage by:
Quilian Riano, DSGN AGCY (Design Agency)
Priyanka Shah, The Architecture Lobby, NY Chapter
Mark Gardner, Jaklitsch Gardner Architects
Jonathan Kirschenfeld, Institute for Public Architecture & Jonathan Kirschenfeld Architect

Excerpts from an open letter written by Michael Sorkin to Robert Ivy, Executive Vice President and CEO of the AIA. ARCHITECTURE AGAINST TRUMP: We are dismayed at the temperate, agreeable, indeed feckless, statement that the director of the AIA has issued on behalf of—although clearly without any consultation with—its membership on the election of Donald Trump. While his words appear anodyne and reflect the judicious position and celebration of America's history of peaceful transitions of power articulated by both President Obama and Hillary Clinton, they are an embarrassment to those of us who feel that the Trump presidency represents a clear and present danger to many values that are fundamental to both our nation and our profession.

HOTEL JELLYFISH, TIANJIN, CHINA

We certainly need to repair lots of roadways and bridges and, especially, to repair crumbling sewer and water systems. But is that the best we can do? We also need to think about the infrastructures of the future, those that will reduce our reliance on the automobile, i.e. public transit, and reduce sprawl and other increasingly unsustainable urban forms, like reconfiguring our imperiled coastlines, a circular system of conservation and re-use, fair wages, good work, and environmentally just material extraction, production, and use. All of this is the ethical purview of the architect.

4. In order to secure a sustainable future, we need enormous investment in research and education to create generations of citizens who have had the practices of sharing and generosity imbued in them.

VIEW FROM ASSEMBLY HALL, CITY OF SCIENCE, XI'AN, CHINA

Given our commitment to the physical environment, we must evaluate the areas outlined here.

1. Decent, affordable housing for all citizens as a matter of right. Trump's presidency is, in some ways, an after-effect of the great recession brought on—in large part—by predatory financial practices. The mountain of mortgage debt and its "securitization" via high-risk financial junk collapsed, robbing millions of their homes and savings. We bailed out the banks but not the people. We now need robust means—including dramatic subsidy—to create genuine residential security for all Americans.

2. We face an emergency and we need radical steps to move us towards a post-carbon economy, to conserve energy, to use our precious planetary resources with the great care and most considered stewardship they demand.

3. Of course, we strongly support investment in our national physical infrastructure. This means jobs, an economic shot in the arm, increased competitiveness, and much else. But such an investment begs the question: "in what?"

AMSTERDAM AVENUE TRANSFORMED, NEW YORK CITY (STEADY) STATE

HOUGUAN LAKE ECOLOGICAL CITY, WUHAN, CHINA

5. Finally, can this tribune of wealth and disdain for "the other"—for people of color, the handicapped, Muslims, women, Hispanics—ever understand that many of us entered the design professions because we so clearly saw the capacity of our practices to influence and structure the way in which the world's resources are distributed and deployed?
—Michael Sorkin

MS: Infrastructure is generally considered to be a thing that is underneath and invisible and purely an artifact. **We must consider not simply physical infrastructure, but social and intellectual infrastructures, those "things" which contribute to the definition of what it means to build as a society.** During the great moment when America created more infrastructure than any other nation, the New Deal, it wasn't called infrastructure—it was called Public Work. Its urgent decree was that we return to the idea that we are a constituency of Publics who control this country.

MG: Quoting Risë Wilson from the Robert Rauschenberg Foundation's The Laundromat Project: "What's interesting to me in the wake of all this, what Equity means, is what are people willing to give up to stand up for their beliefs?"

We're so concerned about the identity of the architect—what he/she actually looks like, is, does. We want to say: This is what an architect is. This is what an architect always has been. And this is what an architect will always be.

BOSTANS AND NEW CONSTRUCTION, MAHALLE REGENERATION PROJECT, ISTANBUL

MM: A good way to describe much of what we have seen over the last couple of years.

Giancarlo De Carlo, from *Spazio e Società 1*, 1978: "Contemporary architecture tends to produce objects while its real role should be that of generating processes. This distortion has very serious consequences, for it confines architecture to a very narrow strip of the whole Spectrum, segregating it, leaving it open to the risks of dependency and megalomania, and leading it to social and political indifference."

AGRO-FORESTRY ON STATEN ISLAND, NEW YORK CITY (STEADY) STATE

MICHAEL **SORKIN**

GOWNTOWN STUDY AREA AND TRANSFORMATIONS, MANHATTAN, NY

MG: That's changing, whether we want it to or not, by outside forces that take over services and things that we do, that we're well qualified and should be doing. We sit and we wait and we don't do anything. We think change is outside of us.

BP: Architects have to work. They have to produce. They have to understand. They have to be accountable. They have to take responsibility. And they have to be able to deliver.

What must we do about the Trump regime? How do we reject authoritarianism, bigotry, and division?

Audience: We are in a profession where authoritarianism and a singular vision is usually lifted up above all else. We praise it within the firms that are successful. The multiplicity of aspects of design and the involvement of society is often a conversation we have amongst ourselves, and not something that we take out into the world. We're still putting someone's name on each act of defiance. We need to be part of the activism within communities at a social level, and we need to raise this collective to the national level over the next few years.

PS: We choose not to broaden the definition of architecture. We have a definition of architecture, and if something fits into it, it is good enough. If not, we don't want to deal with it. So **I have to resist this idea that there are things we can't do, or cannot afford to do, because we want children and family. We can have alliances.** I think we have to step outside of our practices and we have to be citizens. We have to go beyond architecture because every solution is not going to be architecture.

MS: **We must stop looking for solutions that are hermetic to the profession.** There are 150,000 architects for 300 million people. That's it! Clearly, the task of raising consciousness about the environment and equity does not fall exclusively to architects. Satisfying ourselves with marginal forms of alternative practice, however important, is not going to solve the big problem.

Is there an "apolitical" architecture?

Audience: My education in architecture was such that what an architect is goes beyond the profession. This question presupposes that there is a definition of a political architecture. What is this sort of undefined political architecture and, more specifically, what is apolitical professional architecture? Should a profession be political, or is there a broader idea of architecture as a discipline that can operate in a political sense?

MICHAEL **MURPHY**

MATERNITY WAITING VILLAGE, MALAWI

BUTARO HOSPITAL, RWANDA

MM: The equivocating that we may have done as practitioners between choosing something of ethics and something that is just neutral is not really a choice at all. **Architecture is never neutral.** Our great challenge is to determine which decisions that we're making are helping people and which are hurting people. It's a very hard thing that we have to reckon with, and it is not easy to manage. It's something that forces many practitioners to leave the profession.

Architects are paralyzed by the requirements to address social and economic inequality. The election has done a lot to reproduce the argument that we have a choice. The reproduction of that debate is dangerous theoretical work, and we have to call it out for what it is and not allow it to fester. We reproduce the idea that we aren't responsible and aren't accountable to the community that we serve.

Che Guevara, 1963: "Whoever says that a technician of whatever sort, be he an architect, doctor, engineer, scientist, etc., needs solely to work with his instruments, in his chosen specialty, while his countrymen are starving or wearing themselves out in the struggle, has de facto gone over to the other side. He is not apolitical: He has taken a political decision, but one opposed to the movements for liberation."

MM: The notion of the effort to make an apolitical project is, itself, potentially an act of violence.

Audience: I didn't come here for cocktails and polite conversation. I came here for a Revolution. We feel like we have no power. A lot of young people are searching now; they are young and newly un-apathetic and eager get involved. We want a movement to get behind. What can we do?

GHESKIO CHOLERA TREATMENT CENTER, HAITI

GHESKIO TUBERCULOSIS HOSPITAL, HAITI

MM: The call-out that we heard this week from all over the country in the wake of the election is that—**we care about the communities we're serving.**

Belmont Freeman's tweet in response to Robert Ivy's AIA election letter: *"We applaud any talk about investment in infrastructure—self-serving to our profession (no, our 'industry'), but what about social justice, including unequal distribution of economic gain, respect for a diverse population, inequitable housing policy, healthcare, and…the list goes on."*

Some things bubble to the top—human rights, the business ethics of our practice, sustainability and climate change, community partnerships, inequality in gender, racism, and diversity. Architecture and politics were mentioned 75% of the time. **Every single statement mentioned our core values.**

How should we spend a trillion dollars?

QR: I love this question because it forces us to forge a vision, a vision that includes the people in Youngstown, Ohio, with their shrinking city, and the increasing segregation and gentrification here in Sunset Park, Jackson Heights, East New York. These places have more in common than not, and it is an architectural, infrastructural issue. Somehow, our political conversation divides those people and divides us.

What jobs should we do and not do?

Audience: I think we should choose all projects and operate with integrity and ensure that the design that we do, does not infringe upon the rights or access of those who are vulnerable and take a stand on that when we accept those projects.

NATIONAL MEMORIAL FOR PEACE AND JUSTICE, EQUAL JUSTICE INITIATIVE, MONTGOMERY, AL

How do we define our own community? And how can we stand with and design for vulnerable populations?

MM: We do have an enormous amount of power. We need to keep in mind that architects are always aligned with those who have power. To build buildings is expensive. It takes an amazing amount of capital. The question we must ask is: How do we act to fundamentally restructure the power relationships in our built environment? There isn't a clear answer, but there are answers in how we teach, in the kinds of business models that we seek to push and engage with, in the types of clients and partnerships that we make in our work, and in the choices that we make in our profession. There are clear actions. I'm very encouraged by the things that were said, to mobilize, put your name on a piece of paper, sign up, and pay your dues.

NATIONAL MEMORIAL FOR PEACE AND JUSTICE, EQUAL JUSTICE INITIATIVE, MONTGOMERY, AL

For whom should we do projects?

Audience: I think that we are not accepting responsibility for what happened. The people who voted for Trump did so because they've been ignored. I think those of us who are empowered and included have, over time, ignored those people—**this profession has absolutely ignored those people.**

MM: Defining the populations that we serve is fundamental to how we redefine what we do as practitioners. And the notion of serving those who hire us is going back to the very sentiment of the Ivy letter—that the work is coming and we should respond by taking the job. On the other hand, we serve the public first and need to take a critical look at what the scope of work is. We have a fiduciary responsibility to the public, even those who might have voted for Trump are in our purview. We have to be accountable to all.

ILIMA PRIMARY SCHOOL, DEMOCRATIC REPUBLIC OF CONGO

MUBUGA PRIMARY SCHOOL, RWANDA

I don't think there is apolitical architecture. There isn't an architecture without social and political dimensions. We cannot unshackle ourselves from the social and political implications of our decisions because we make choices about labor and materials and the environment that, inevitably, affects the world we live in.

Some questions to think about:

What core values do we share? What values do we share with the other professions?

How do we assure our community values govern our work places and practices?

STEVEN HOLL

Steven Holl is founder and principal of **Steven Holl Architects**, an innovative architecture and urban design office based in New York City and Beijing. He is recognized for his ability to blend space and light with great contextual sensitivity, and to utilize unique qualities of a project to create a concept-driven design.

BARRY BERGDOLL

Barry Bergdoll is the Meyer Schapiro Professor of Modern Architectural History at **Columbia University**, and a curator in the Department of Architecture & Design at the **Museum of Modern Art**. He has also served as president of the Society of Architectural Historians, and was the 2010-11 Slade Professor of Fine Art at Cambridge University.

NEW SOCIAL CONDENSERS

SH: Social condenser is an old term. But I use it for what I am trying to do in my work. 1. To provide public spaces open to all 100% (not the 1% vs. the 99%). 2. To give spatial energy to this openness via a sense of invitation and urban porosity. 3. To excite potential creativity and interaction via architecture. 4. To carry this interactive energy beyond the boundary of the site to the campus, to the public streets. 5. To apply the most advanced science and technology so architecture serves as an environmental example for the future.

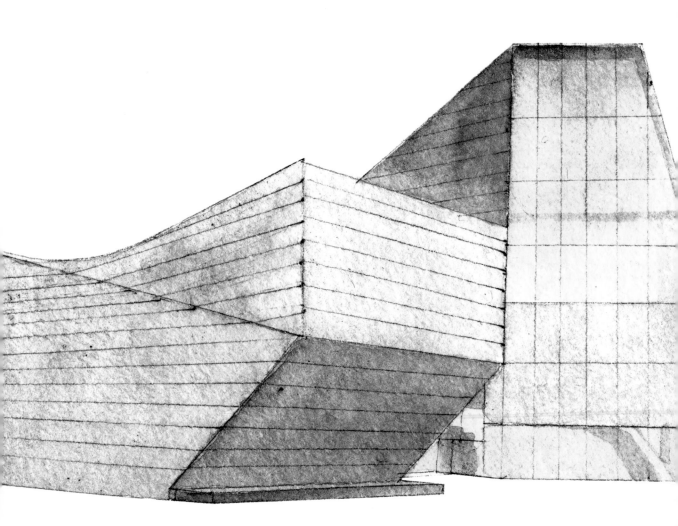

TWO NEGRONIS
By Eben Klemm

NEGRONI

1 oz. **Vodka**
1 oz. **Campari**
1 oz. **Punt E Mes**
Stir 20 times over ice in a mixing glass. Strain over large ice cube in rocks glass. Garnish with orange half-wheel.

CITRONI

1 1/2 oz. **Plymouth gin**
1/2 oz. **Cocchi Americano**
1/2 oz. **Contratto Bitter**
1/2 oz. **Giffard Pamplemousse**
Stir 20 times over ice in a mixing glass. Garnish with thin stick of grapefruit.

Steven Holl asked me to serve the Negroni his teacher made when he was studying in Rome in the '60s. I readily agreed, as the Negroni is more or less the gateway cocktail for most bartenders I know who love to invent new drinks. Its recent justly-deserved popularity is due to its perfect balance of bitter, sweet, and power. The recent appearance of heretofore unavailable Italian and French bittersweet liquors has allowed the advent of many variations on a theme, one of which I present here.

I was completely naïve. I mean really naïve! I was not a sensitive architect. I don't have any family with money. I'm not a Blue Blood. I', just a kid from Bremerton, Washington. By the way, there's not a single work of architecture in Bremerton. So luckily, I got to go to Rome as one of the first students in the University of Washington's Rome Architecture program.

Going to Rome absolutely changed my life. I learned how to cook and make a Negroni. That's why Rome and the Negroni are so important. I lived behind the Pantheon. I made a deal with the guard to let me in every day before he opened the doors, before the tourists could come in. Every day was different. I could see the change of the angle of the sun and, when it rained, the silver droplets would come down. The cuts in the marble where the drains go, and how the light would work. That was like a wordless education at the Pantheon, and that changed my life. It still took me 15 years to not have to sleep on a plywood shelf over my office, teaching for a living.

LEWIS ARTS COMPLEX, PRINCETON UNIVERSITY, PRINCETON, NJ

MAGGIE'S CENTER BARTS, LONDON, UK

I have our drawings organized. I can find every first drawing for every building we ever did in a catalog, like a second brain.

Conceptual density has to be there. I have projects that have 30 schemes before I get to the idea. We have pin-ups in our office, and everybody argues about what's on the wall. **The idea has to have a deep connection between the space, the life, the site, the program.** They all have to be lined up and have to connect. You can't get that every time. So there are many, many watercolors of really ugly buildings. You have to be able to say no. It's not a linear process.

What changed me was the Kiasma competition in Helsinki. One of the things about the program was that the lobby was very small, and when we entered the competition, we made the lobby 25 times larger than specified in the competition! We said, That's the social condenser. That's where everybody will come, and attendance is just as high as it was when it opened 20 years ago.

A concept drawing starts each project. An idea is something very powerful. To make it clear, you need as few lines as possible and maybe the smallest size. Something like 5x7 as a limitation is very good because you can't fit much on the page. I decided that a long time ago. It fits on an airplane tray. I can put it in my pocket. **It makes you reduce what you're doing to a statement, to a concept.**

INSTITUTE FOR CONTEMPORARY ART, VIRGINIA COMMONWEALTH UNIVERSITY, RICHMOND, VA

THE NELSON-ATKINS MUSEUM OF ART, KANSAS CITY, MO

Our first building in London, Maggie's Cancer Care Center, is a small building. The concept of a new social condenser doesn't have to be large. The public can come in. This becomes a meeting place for interaction, for social hope for terminal cancer victims. **I believe that architecture changes the way we live our lives.**

BB: I remember the story, which is a story that all architects must love, of the competition in Kansas City, at one of the great buildings on this continent, if not on this globe [Nelson-Atkins Museum of Art]. How you walked in and told them that you had ignored the program. Tell us about breaking the rules, about these risks you take in changing the program. What feels very in touch with that is the notion that there is some **agency of the architect.**

Every time we enter a competition we try to do what we think would be the ideal project. It may not be what they're asking for. In the case of Nelson-Atkins, it was a large 1933 neoclassical building. The rule was you could add to the north side of the building and nowhere else. Everybody did a box on the north side. Luckily, in that competition, we could present personally, which I think is very important. So I presented some sketches of different versions of things on the north side, and I said, "You shouldn't do this." Then I presented the scheme and said, "It should be something that lets all the elevations of the original 1933 building be free. You can go in on the side, underneath, you can connect perpendicularly, and you can merge with the landscape." I apologized, but I had the nerve to do it, because this was carved into the limestone façade of the building: **"The soul has greater need of the ideal than of the real"** [Victor Hugo]. I was just presenting the ideal solution.

HUNTERS POINT COMMUNITY LIBRARY, NEW YORK, NY

CAMPBELL SPORTS CENTER, COLUMBIA UNIVERSITY, NEW YORK, NY

My favorite material is light. In so many ways, it has the material of a spiritual presence. James Turrell is a good friend of mine. He came to the studio in 1990 and we built some of his models. He moved in the **deep spiritual dimension that light brings to architecture.** It's something that's also connected with the seasons and with a place. There's a different kind of light in every place you work. Texas is very different from Helsinki.

BB: I want to ask you if it's ever failed or flopped as a strategy.

One in 25 is what we went forward with—24 times you fail and just get up and do it again.

I think you go for the best, you go for the ideal, and just **hope that somebody on the other side of the table can see it, too**. So it wasn't me, it was the fact that somebody, who's on the client side saw the vision. **Every project that goes forward**, that has this kind of intensity and breaks the rules, **has someone besides the architect completely behind it.**

VISUAL ARTS BUILDING, UNIVERSITY OF IOWA, IOWA CITY, IA

VANKE CENTER HORIZONTAL SKYSCRAPER, SHENZHEN, CHINA

BB: What kinds of things carry over from one project to another?

The unique condition of a site, a circumstance, a client, a program—they should all add up to a unique work of architecture. My work is definitely about architecture looking towards the future. It's not about eclecticism, or saying that somehow what we did as modern architects needs to be completely trashed. In my work, I think you can see traces of the history of modern architecture, but somehow transformed. I believe Kenneth Frampton, who was my teacher, always said, "In any building, 25% of the cost is structure. If structure doesn't play a role in the concept, it's not great architecture."

126

JEANNE GANG

Founding principal of **Studio Gang**, an architecture and urban design practice with offices in Chicago, New York, and San Francisco. Known for an approach that foregrounds relationships between individuals, communities, and environments, Jeanne Gang is currently designing major projects throughout the Americas and Europe.

MICHAEL KIMMELMAN

As architecture critic at *The New York Times*, Michael Kimmelman's work often focuses on urban affairs, infrastructure, and social equity, as well as on new projects. He was awarded the Brendan Gill Prize for his "insightful candor and continuous scrutiny of New York's architectural environment" that is "journalism at its finest."

TRUTH IN ARCHITECTURE

JG: *The New York Times* is currently running a campaign: "Truth, it's more important now than ever." Today, in what some are calling our "post-truth" world, the question of truth is something we confront in many different parts of architectural practice. In addition to materials, we also engage it in terms of information, criticism, and representation—whether it's renderings that are so realistic they fool us, or the diversity (or lack thereof) of the people who are represented in our images. Finally, there is also the question of truth in architectural history, which has traditionally been so narrow. There are many more architectures than those we learned in school.

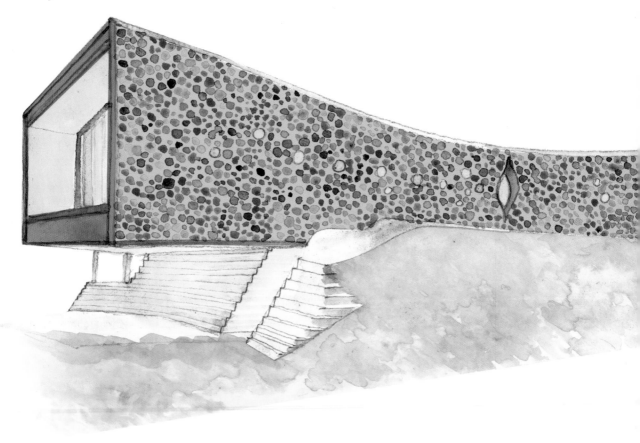

GIN AND PHONIC
By Eben Klemm

Build in Collins glass:
3/4 oz. **Greenhook Gin**
3/4 oz. **Beach Plum Gin**
1/2 oz. **Dry vermouth**
1/4 oz. **Rhubarb syrup**
Dash **celery bitters**
Dash **Absinthe**
Top with **Ginger ale**
Garnish with **Rhubarb ribbons**

Rhubarb syrup:
Simmer 2 cups chopped rhubarb in 2 cups water for 10 minutes. Dissolve in 2 cups white sugar. Remove from heat. When cool, purée in blender and strain.

There are never any shortages of ways to vary gin and tonics, especially when the mind starts thinking of them in the late winter, when spring just can't come soon enough. As you can see, local ingredients are a concept continually requested by the architects, and the request seemed especially germane taking into account Ms. Gang's work.

At Studio Gang we have a large model shop, and the work we do there is central to our design process. A key part of this work is experimenting with materials and exploring their properties. Whether it's in our shop or when I'm teaching a studio, often the first thing we do with a material is destroy it. This is because **looking at the way that things break teaches you a great deal about them.**

Material, with its multivalent qualities—which include the physical and the cultural—always plays a major role in my projects. With the Arcus Center for Social Justice Leadership in Kalamazoo, Michigan, for example, we tried to find a material consistent with the mission of the building: to create and sustain leaders in the fields of human rights and social justice. We stumbled upon a vernacular technique called cordwood masonry, in which logs are laid in a wall using a mortar matrix—they are load bearing, in the same way that brick or stone masonry is.

ARCUS CENTER FOR SOCIAL JUSTICE LEADERSHIP, KALAMAZOO, MI

CITY HYDE PARK, CHICAGO, IL

Today we have enough knowledge that we can reintroduce wood as a primary building material, which is especially important because it's a renewable material. For the Writers Theatre canopy walk, we worked with our fabricators to build a rig and test this structural system until failure. It turned out to be incredibly strong—the steel rig started to buckle before the wood did!

The canopy walk clearly expresses the way it's held up; I think architects and laypeople can read this. To me, this is an important achievement, because I've always felt that **making the structure of a building understandable makes it more approachable to people**—we intrinsically understand gravity.

This building method is highly sustainable. It uses all parts of the tree and, because the trees absorb and then sequester carbon within the wall, it reduces the carbon footprint. It also has incredible aesthetic qualities. As the wood ages, each log weathers in its own unique way, reflecting the diversity of human experiences that is central to the center's mission.

As the Arcus Center is a contemporary institutional building, to make the load-bearing walls high-performing, we added an air space and more insulation. For the wood, we chose white cedar that was grown locally in Michigan and sustainably harvested. Cordwood logs need to dry out for one year before they can be used in wood masonry construction, so we had to convince our client that this was the right material an entire year ahead of using it. They strongly connected with it particularly because wood masonry has a strong community-building aspect—historically, neighbors came together to help each other build this way, much like a barn raising.

We are always trying to **think about how a space will be built at the same time we're thinking about its materiality.** For our Writers Theatre project, which is a professional theater for a company located north of Chicago, the lobby space is formed by great timber trusses. From these trusses we literally hung the second-floor "canopy walk" using wood in tension. The custom detail at the bottom of each batten—which we named the "cat's paw"—expresses how the wood is hung. This is an unusual use for wood; for so long, building codes have prevented it from being used this thinly or this creatively because of fire concerns.

AQUA TOWER, CHICAGO, IL

MK: What does Truth mean when it comes to practice and the role of the architect?

My team and I try to use our skills to engage the city and the people in it; we try to use the tools and methods of design to make a positive impact. One of the projects in New York that we are currently working on is the Rescue Company 2 facility in Brownsville, Brooklyn, the home of FDNY's elite force of specialized rescue workers. This building is all about practice—it's designed as a tool for the rescue workers to use to practice their skills. Designing the project also led us to start thinking about the role of these public buildings within their neighborhoods and how they interact with residents. We noticed that the fire rescue workers are connected with their neighborhood; people like them and trust them. That same kind of trusting relationship, however, is not seen between residents and police.

UNIVERSITY OF CHICAGO CAMPUS, NORTH RESIDENTIAL COMMONS, CHICAGO, IL

WRITERS THEATRE, GLENCOE, IL

The Polis Station project is a great example of why it's important that we, as architects, start to learn how to engage people more directly. There's so much to learn from people's experiences. We need to be more responsive to the communities that we are working in. There is a continuum of ways to engage—the goal for us with these public projects is to get to the level where **we are empowering the people to shape the future of their neighborhood**, to realize their aspirations for themselves and their community. I do not think it cramps creativity at all to have these conversations and closely involve stakeholders. In the process of listening there's going to be good and bad ideas that surface. It's the role of the architect to sort through these ideas and bring them together with all of the other factors that influence a project, from program to infrastructure to climate to engineering. To weave them together into a future that people can imagine—to see the possibilities and communicate them in a compelling way—that's a skill that architects can bring to the table.

MK: Could architecture start to rebuild trust between the police and the community around them?

We initiated a project in Chicago called Polis Station to study this issue—to see how examining police stations could offer new insight into improving police-community relationships. We studied President Obama's Task Force on 21st-Century Policing report, which was a response to the events in Ferguson, Missouri, and then tried to apply the report's recommendations to North Lawndale, a real-life Chicago neighborhood. As part of the design process, we interviewed many people and held workshops with community members and police. We struck on the idea that **a police station could function more like a community center**, where officers and residents have more opportunities to interact in non-confrontational situations. A key part of our proposal was changing the "fortress" quality of many modern stations, which are surrounded by oceans of parking lots that separate the police from the community they serve. In addition, we started to think about how to bring new programs into the station's space, looking for activities and amenities that both the community and the police would enjoy. At North Lawndale, we came up with the idea of reusing a portion of the parking lot as a basketball court. We then worked with the local alderman, police officers, and residents to build the court. Since it opened in 2015 it's been quite successful—it's an important safe space for neighborhood youth to play, and sometimes the officers join in. We're now working with this same coalition to design an expansion that would bring more amenities and green space to the site.

WRITERS THEATRE, GLENCOE, IL

BARTHOLOMEW VOORSANGER

Bartholomew Voorsanger graduated from Princeton and Harvard Universities. He received an honorary Ph.D. in Architecture and Urbanism from Ion Mincu University of Architecture and Urbanism, Bucharest, Romania. He worked with Vincent Ponte and I.M. Pei & Partners before establishing Voorsanger & Mills, which was reorganized as **Voorsanger Architects.**

ALASTAIR GORDON

An award-winning critic and author, Alastair Gordon has written regularly about the built environment for *The New York Times* and the **Wall Street Journal**. His critically acclaimed books include *Naked Airport*, *Weekend Utopia*, and *Spaced Out*. He teaches critical writing at Harvard University Graduate School of Design.

HOW ARCHITECTURE SAVED MY LIFE

BV: When I was about 12 or 13, my mother would take us to see buildings, important buildings around the Bay Area in San Francisco. She took us to see the Maybeck's First Church of Christ, Scientist. I remember walking in—it had this celestial quality, and I remember saying, "I want to do something like this. I want to make this." It took me a while to figure out that I wanted to be an architect, but that was the commitment.

THE LAGUARDIA CONTROL TOWER SWIZZLE
By Toby Cecchini and David Moo

2 oz. **La Favorite Ambré Rhum Agricole**
3/4 oz. **Lime juice**
1/4 oz. **Quinine syrup**
5 dashes **Peychaud's bitters**

Build in a tall highball glass filled with pebble or crushed ice, adding first three ingredients, then swizzle with a bois lélé or a bar spoon. Dash the bitters atop and garnish with a cucumber and a wedge of lime.

Bart's body of work is immensely impressive, so I felt a little devious basing a drink on a single magnificent design he did for a helix-shaped control tower for LaGuardia Airport that, following 9/11, never got built. But he was magnanimous about it, laughing along. This called for a tall drink, not a far cry from the classic old Queen's Park Swizzle.

I started life as an abandoned child with an identical twin brother. The very first place that had a spatial impact on me was an amazing orphanage in the Bronx, which I think, at one point, was the largest building in North America. You go back and forth to homes and come back to a huge building that went on for blocks and blocks. My adoptive grandparents were first cousins of Herbert Lehman, the governor of New York, and Arthur Altschul, a famous art collector. Edith Lehman, who was chairwoman of the board of the orphanage, called my parents and asked, "Do you want these twins?" And my parents foolishly said yes. They came to New York, took us to San Francisco, and introduced us, the two twins, to my older brother Eric, and we were supposed to be a happy family thereafter.

ASIA SOCIETY & MUSEUM, NEW YORK, NY

NAPA VALLEY RESIDENCE, CA

I worked at I.M. Pei's office for 10 years. I was moonlighting on a house. It was actually a good experience with clients who berated each other. I was like the mediator between the husband and wife—you knew they were going to break up; it was just a matter of weeks or months. We photographed the house, and someone said, "Why don't you submit it to an award program?" I thought, "Oh, why not." So I submitted it to the AIA. It won a national award, which was given at the annual meeting in Atlanta.

My cousin was president of the Sierra Club for many years. When I was 15, he said, "You have to go to the mountains," and so we went to the mountains. Ansel Adams was a friend of the family and he asked me to carry his cameras. We would hike off to some place and Ansel would set up at what seemed to me just neutral locations. He was very precise and very careful—I didn't drop his cameras, of course. I never saw the final product, so I never quite understood the strategy or why he was doing what he was doing. He would come to our cocktail parties and he always wore a red flannel shirt and drank vodka, straight vodka.

WILDCAT RIDGE RESIDENCE, CO

BLUE RIDGE RESIDENCE, VA

When I got to LaGuardia, there was I.M. waiting to board the airplane. I said, "I.M." He turned to me and said, "Why are you here?" I said, "Well, I.M., why are you here?" And he said, "Well, I'm going to pick up an award for the Mile High Center in Denver." And I said, "I'm also picking up an award." I thought he was going to fire me right on the spot, but he didn't. He was very gracious, incredibly gracious. Wonderful guy.

AG: On September 21, 2001, only 10 days after the catastrophic terrorist attacks of 9/11, Voorsanger was asked by Robert Davidson, chief architect of the Port Authority, to visit Ground Zero in Lower Manhattan and organize a preservation process at the ruined site. There was concern that important pieces of wreckage were being trucked away to New Jersey and cut up for scrap metal.

No one trains you to do this kind of thing. There were moments when it was almost too emotional to go on. We were traumatized. What do we select? How do we choose what to keep? **We needed to find things that would resonate for generations.** I thought I was looking for the iconic piece, but I wasn't sure what that meant. It was just too complex. We needed to get other people involved. Eventually, **everyone at the site became a curator**.

ELIE TAHARI OFFICES, MILLBURN, NJ

When you're 21, 22, you're derivative. It's not wrong to be derivative. Emotionally, you will be derivative until your ego takes over, which is thought to be in your early 30s. When your ego takes over is when individuality is formed. And then the question is, do you end up supporting that, in terms of your work and your career, or do you suppress it? There are lots of complicated reasons for doing either, but I think what's incredibly important is to absolutely not suppress it.

The worst moments in my career have come when I abandoned the capacity for individualization.

NATIONAL WWII MUSEUM, NEW ORLEANS, LA,
VOORSANGER MATHES LLC.

We had what's called the **Last Column**. When it was brought to Hangar 17, the workers became very emotional—they started leaving notes on it, and adding notes to people who had died. We finally had to build an enclosure within the enclosure to protect the Last Column, basically freeze it in time and preserve it. The whole preservation thing became a large team of people, in terms of preserving a rusting I-beam weighing 40 tons, and all these handwritten notes and photographs glued to it, things like that.

LAGUARDIA AIRPORT CONTROL TOWER, QUEENS, NY

NATIONAL WWII MUSEUM, NEW ORLEANS, LA,
VOORSANGER MATHES LLC.

The moment you stop pleasing people is when you, in fact, do please people. The moment you stop, you don't even know when it happens—it's something that's transparent, it's invisible. But I think **the moment your ego finally does become free, at that point, emotion takes over.**

I take a look at architects I admire—I'm thinking of I.M., for example. The thing that's marvelous about I.M. is that when you visit his projects, his persona is there. You feel him there. I felt the same way about Louis Kahn when I went to the Salk Institute. Architecture is the cycle of life. At Salk, the pages of the book remain open and you can keep reading more and more into it. That's the essence of great art, and exactly what I've tried to find in my own work. **An open book.** Something that renews the human spirit and reveals the entire cycle of life and death.

PETER L. GLUCK

Peter Gluck is founder and principal of **GLUCK+** in New York. Most work is constructed by the firm through its unique approach to Architect-Led Design-Build. In 2014, *Fast Company*'s "World's Top 10 Most Innovative Companies in Architecture" list included GLUCK+ "for taking control of the entire building process."

INGA SAFFRON

As architecture critic for *The Philadelphia Inquirer* since 1999, Inga Saffron has written a weekly column called "*Changing Skyline*," which offers an insightful look at the urban design issues facing Philadelphia. She is the winner of the 2014 Pulitzer Prize in Criticism, and has been a finalist three times since 2004.

IN THE FRAY

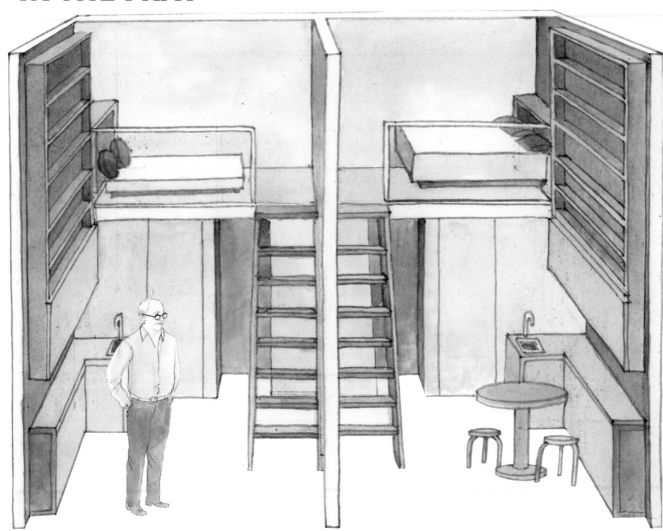

PLG: The architectural world tends to focus on the really high cost of buildings, the zip-a-dee-doo-dah buildings—music halls, museums, luxury condos, corporate centers. No one talks about how much these buildings cost while, simultaneously, the whole city is being silently rebuilt under our noses with a different set of criteria, different budgets. As part of our practice, although we do those zip-a-dee buildings, we seek projects that are not high-profile buildings with generous budgets, but more ordinary projects with ordinary budgets. One of the problems that developers and the real world face is a kind of fear of ambitious architects. When we're trying to do these kinds of projects, we're faced with the assumption that architects cause problems rather than adding value to their tightly budgeted project. The rap on architects in the real world is really not so great.

Architecture, in this context, is seen as an unaffordable kind of a luxury or worse. A path for many architects is to make problematic, costly buildings. I think, as architects, we really need to turn that vision around. The question for our profession is simply how do we, how can we add value in this context, and what is the framework within which we must operate.

WEST HARLEM
By Eben Klemm

2 oz. **Bourbon** or **rye**
1 oz. **West Harlem vermouth**
Stir ingredients over ice 20 times. Strain and serve, garnish with **dandelion leaf**.

West Harlem vermouth:
Combine one bottle Uncouth Vermouth Butternut Squash Vermouth, 1 bottle Malbec, 1 cup honey, 1 cup chopped dandelion leaf, 1 cup chopped arugula, 2 sprigs fresh basil, and macerate for 3 days. Strain out solids.

Peter Gluck wanted me to think about his work and studio in terms of its association with West Harlem. So I imagined the possibilities of making a vermouth with weeds found in the city streets and parks (I did not actually forage weeds in West Harlem for this drink).

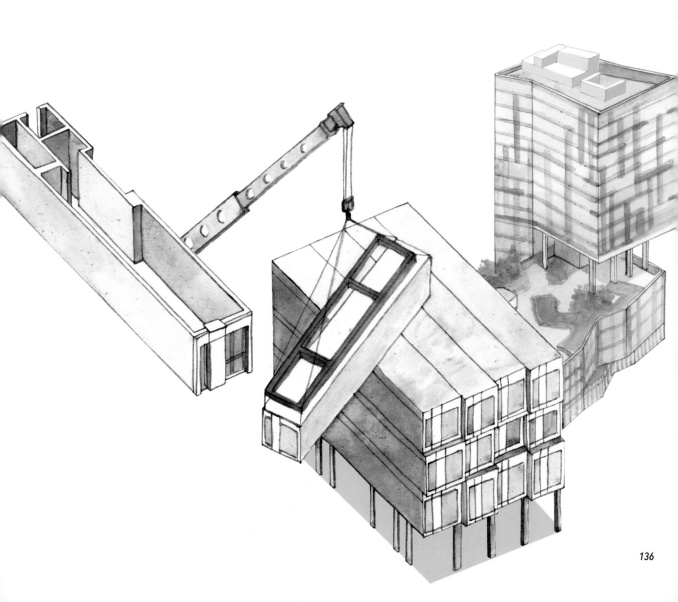

BRIDGE, PHILADELPHIA, PA

We are a design-build firm, but I don't like talking about it so much because everybody wants to just talk about it.

The way the construction process is organized is that the general contractor takes the architect's drawings, which are fixed and cannot be changed, to subcontractors. He's hamstrung. He can't really get any feedback from the construction world. **The whole secret is feedback from the construction world**. Similarly, it's feedback from the town, like the way we got a zoning change was by understanding what they were interested in. It's a dialogue.

Buzzwords such as "partnering" and "advocating for a client" mean developing a project framework and interpreting codes, rules, and best practices to maximize the allowable scope of a project. It requires knowledge of construction. It means understanding real estate values, doing test fits for alternate sites. It means taking responsibility for success rather than avoiding risk and remaining above the fray.

As architects, our role has always been to enhance the public realm, to create beautiful spaces, elegant forms that reflect their use. As modernists, our office is interested in housing within easy walking distance to public transportation, in space for community needs, schools, shopping—all the real stuff of life in the city.

BRIDGE, PHILADELPHIA, PA

TOWER HOUSE, CATSKILL, NY

Architects have given up their responsibility to deal with the construction process. They've been told that that's where all the liability is, so they don't do it. After years of not walking on a construction site, they have very little understanding of process; they've lost touch with these kinds of issues.

IS: How did you make the transition from doing architecture exclusively to being part of the building team, as in the case of the Bridge apartment tower in Philadelphia?

What's more fun and more exciting than construction? Buildings look great when they're under construction, and then they look terrible once they pull their pants up. The reality is that on a project like the Bridge, there's only one person who's personally liable if anything goes wrong, and that's me, the architect. I put that stamp on the drawings, so I'm liable.

HOUSE IN THE MOUNTAINS, ROCKY MOUNTAINS, CO

We understand the value of mixed-use buildings that express the inherent differentiation of use. We try to make more muscular buildings with appropriate materials that reflect the sky and create patterns of shade and light.

When it was finished, the NYC Department of Parks and Recreation had not yet started the adjacent exhibition courts, so they asked us to build the courts, which we did as a separate project.

The project is a series of platforms for watching tennis. The spaces for all the ancillary activities that occur around a tennis tournament—the award ceremonies, the people-watching—become a special precinct for the world of tennis in the center of the South Bronx.

CARY LEEDS CENTER FOR TENNIS & LEARNING, BRONX, NY

Why would I give that responsibility to some other person I don't know anything about, who might be a nefarious individual over whom I have no control. Why would I let him control my liability? **It always seemed to me that if I'm going to build a building, I'm going to make sure it's built right.** And if I have to build little buildings that way, then that's what I'll do. But it turns out you can build big buildings that way, too.

We recently finished the Cary Leeds Center for Tennis and Learning in the Bronx for Arthur Ashe's tennis program. Its mission is to get inner city kids into tennis and, through tennis, into doing their homework and ultimately into building their lives—as well as, of course, building their own strategies for tennis.

THE EAST HARLEM SCHOOL, NEW YORK, NY

LITTLE AJAX AFFORDABLE HOUSING, ASPEN, CO

*IS: In addition to all the construction challenges that you describe, finance really drives how buildings are built, and investors expect a certain return. Developers value-engineer a building. They cheapen the materials. There's a whole financial model built on how long the developer will actually hold a building if it's rental apartments, which impacts the quality of the architecture. I see a lot of buildings that look to me like they're built to last 30 years. It's kind of scary. **Are we building the slums of tomorrow?***

That's a good question. I have this theory that, in the early 1900s, buildings were designed to last for about 110 years. In the 1950s, buildings were designed to last about 60 years. In the 1980s, they were designed to last about 25 years, so next Tuesday the whole world is going to fall down. We don't really know what's going to happen. It's really interesting.

"How do you get this job?" is always a question architects ask when we show this kind of project. **We do not sit by the phone waiting for it to ring. We go into the community to understand what the needs are.** We worked on this project for 12 years.

We did test fits for six or seven sites while working for the non-profit organization. We did not work for free, but certainly not for profit. We built the Billie Jean King Clubhouse. We are a design-build office. We design and build most of our buildings.

DUKE UNIVERSITY MARINE LABORATORY, BEAUFORT, NC

DAVID PISCUSKAS

David Piscuskas is a founding principal of **1100 Architect**, a New York- and Frankfurt-based architecture firm. He served as the 2017 President of AIANY. David has completed many award-winning projects, including Perry World House, along with work for several universities, the City of New York, NY Public Library and a long roster of private clients.

DAVID HOLLENBERG

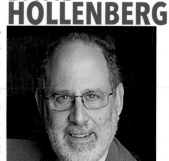

David Hollenberg is the University Architect, Special Projects at the **University of Pennsylvania**. In this role, he oversees the design of the physical development and preservation of the campus, and has managed several notable projects, including the Penn Connects Plan, Perry World House, the Music Building, Penn Park, the ARCH, and Golkin Hall.

COLLABORATION IN PLACE

DH: If you think of the life and death of a project as being from birth to ribbon cutting, a lot of decisions are made before the architect is hired, in some cases, 50% or 60% of the way into the life of a project. We have a phrase that I invented when we put in our request for proposals: "Come to the interview with your"—here's the phrase—"inclinations of design"—as opposed to bringing models and renderings. Because when you do that, it suggests, "We don't really need a client. We already have it figured out. We don't need you, and here it is." We've had people come to interviews with walkthroughs that they thought were going to blow us away. But it's really offensive when you get renderings and animations of a completed building, and all that's left for the client to do is pick a carpet. It just doesn't work. If you're good, you give an indication of the likely direction without pinning it down. And that helps.

BANANA TICKLER
By Toby Cecchini and David Moo

2 oz. **Anchor Old Tom gin** or
    Siete Leguas Reposado tequila
1/2 oz. **Giffard Banane du Brésil liqueur**
1/2 oz. **Cynar**
1 barspoon (7 ml.) **cinnamon tincture**
Combine all ingredients in a mixing glass over ice and stir until well chilled, up to 45 seconds. Strain into a double rocks glass with one large cube. Twist a peel of orange, skin side down, over it, and discard the peel.

Cinnamon tincture:
In a Mason jar or other sealable container, combine roughly 500 grams of cinnamon stick with one liter of a very strong neutral spirit, such as Everclear or 100-proof vodka. Leave for at least a week, shaking jar once a day or so. You can extract small amounts of the tincture, which will get stronger the longer you leave it on the cinnamon, and replace what you take with fresh spirit. Keeps indefinitely.

The two Davids' combined work was impossible to sum up in a single cocktail, so they asked that we conjure one cocktail that could function equally well with two different base spirits, Old Tom gin for David Hollenberg and tequila for David Piscuskas. Both were gratified with their respective cups.

When my partner Juergen Riehm and I started 1100 Architect, we would do any project as long as it was for an artist, where we worked directly with an artist who didn't answer to anyone else. We were incredibly lucky to get houses for Jasper Johns, Roy Lichtenstein, and Eric Fischl among others. The reason that it worked is that we've really been talking about the same things all the time in all of our work. **The work that we do is of material—the same as an artist.** And there's meaning in that material. There are details that bring materials together or separate them one from another. There's warmth, there's tactility, there's chilliness, there's brightness.

KOENIGSBLICK KINDERGARTEN, FRANKFURT AM MAIN, GERMANY

MAIN: EAST SIDE LOFTS, FRANKFURT AM MAIN, GERMANY

I'm fascinated when I look at our clients' work and the work of other artists—how they live with every mark they make. It's no different for an architect. The marks we make are made through others; we need to learn how to communicate that and to accept whatever outcome we get. In that respect, **we're always borrowing from others and learning from others**. I would say that our early work with artist-clients ensured that we would always accept that, and never worry that it was an indictment of purity or ideal or of our ability to deliver.

In every single case, we had several problems to solve, but it was never about the problems we were solving—**it was about the craft** that we were bringing to bear in doing that.

It's about **making our clients our collaborators**, merging their voices with ours, their concerns with ours. What I love about it is that within all of these different methodologies of communication and attitude and practice, there's a deep sense of commitment, history, integrity, and when you immerse yourself in it, you can't help but respect it.

We go on a journey with our clients, exploring our perspectives, our influences, and our values. We encourage them to communicate and we listen with great attentiveness. That's how we put the stuff together. With whomever we're working, we want to **communicate to them in the language that they understand.**

QUEENS CENTRAL LIBRARY, CHILDREN'S LIBRARY DISCOVERY CENTER, QUEENS, NY

RESIDENCE, IKEMA ISLAND, OKINAWA PREFECTURE, JAPAN

DH: As University Architect, my job is to look out for Penn as a place. I'm responsible for defining the place as it exists, for looking for the right architects for the right projects, for overseeing preservation, for dealing with the open space. Generally, anything that's physical on the campus is going to be my job. A wonderful part of that job is meeting lots of architects, figuring out what they can do, and if they would be right for us.

We're not a campus with a style. I like to say, "We don't have a style, we have an attitude." We tell the architects we hire that what we have is a tradition of architectural excellence that they're now a part of, and we want them to do the best contemporary buildings of our time.

DH: Maintaining the existing cottage porch [for Perry World House] triggered an interesting conversation about the nature of preservation and modern architecture and how they converge. We're keeping a fragment of the building, but that fragment is inevitably going to be misread, which is why, over time, I came to be more comfortable calling this project a collage rather than an addition.

I want to give a lot of credit to David because it took a lot of guts to say that this cottage prominently placed in the middle of the campus, but neglected for decades, could be realized again as a catalyst for good place-making.

PERRY WORLD HOUSE, UNIVERSITY OF PENNSYLVANIA,
PHILADELPHIA, PA

By watching how students moved around this site, we recognized what an opportunity it would be if we could: graft on a new building; turn the corner; face 38th Street (which is now a four-lane highway); gesture to a bridge; respect the fact that the President's house is right here and she comes and goes every day; face the dining commons; and anchor the west side of the campus. We think, based upon feedback we've gotten, that that's what this building does.

It also **speaks to the requirement that we have as architects to recognize our constituents**, the diversity within their community, and to be able to connect with each on their own terms.

PERRY WORLD HOUSE, UNIVERSITY OF PENNSYLVANIA,
PHILADELPHIA, PA

Programmatically, Perry World House is a venue for global engagement. People come from all over the world to participate in forums. It's electrifying to be at an event in this space, and be just an arm's length away from Vice President Biden, all part of the same community.

There were enormous political pressures on this project, and we were able to respectfully talk through them—that contributed greatly to the success of the building.

PERRY WORLD HOUSE, UNIVERSITY OF PENNSYLVANIA,
PHILADELPHIA, PA

PERRY WORLD HOUSE, UNIVERSITY OF PENNSYLVANIA,
PHILADELPHIA, PA

We make a book every month about our design progress, and we show A, B, or C. It's taken on the trips. It gets packed in the bag. It gets tucked under the pillow wherever it goes. It gets scribbled in. It gets marked on. I have a record. The team has embraced it as part of our process. I'm excited about it because it's **a process that works**. It's not unlike Jasper Johns making encaustic paintings, then suddenly painting with ink, then doing a print, then doing a drawing, and then sculpting it. This is one of the things we learned from our artist-clients—you do whatever the job requires, whatever you find yourself doing on the journey toward that thing that you chose.

TOM KUNDIG

Principal of **Olson Kundig** over the past three decades, Tom Kundig has received some of the world's highest design honors, from a National Design Award for Architecture from the Cooper Hewitt, Smithsonian Design Museum, to an Academy Award in Architecture from the American Academy of Arts & Letters.

CATHLEEN MCGUIGAN

Cathleen McGuigan is the editor-in-chief of **Architectural Record**, and former architecture critic and arts editor at *Newsweek*. She has taught at Columbia's Graduate School of Journalism and has been a Poynter Fellow at Yale and Loeb Fellow at Harvard. Under her leadership, *Record* won the Grand Neal award in 2012.

CONTEMPORARY CRAFT IN DESIGN

TK: Architecture is that wonderful intersection between the rational and the poetic. Working with different clients, working with different climates, working with different craftspeople, local craft, that's what gets me going.

THE TECHTONIC SHIFT
By Toby Cecchini

1 1/2 oz. **Blanche Armagnac Pellehaut**
1 1/2 oz. **Lustau Vermut Blanco**
Spritz of **Del Maguey Vida mezcal**
Twist of **pomelo**
In a mixing glass over ice, combine all ingredients and stir until well chilled. Strain into a double rocks glass with one large ice cube. Garnish with a twist of pomelo or grapefruit.

Tom's immense planes and Western scope demanded equally large and decisive flavors in a simple, forthright drink with varying thrusts. Marrying a white Armagnac to a Spanish vermouth, with an overlay of mezcal and citrus, brought the kind of surprising beauty Tom's magnificent structures conjure.

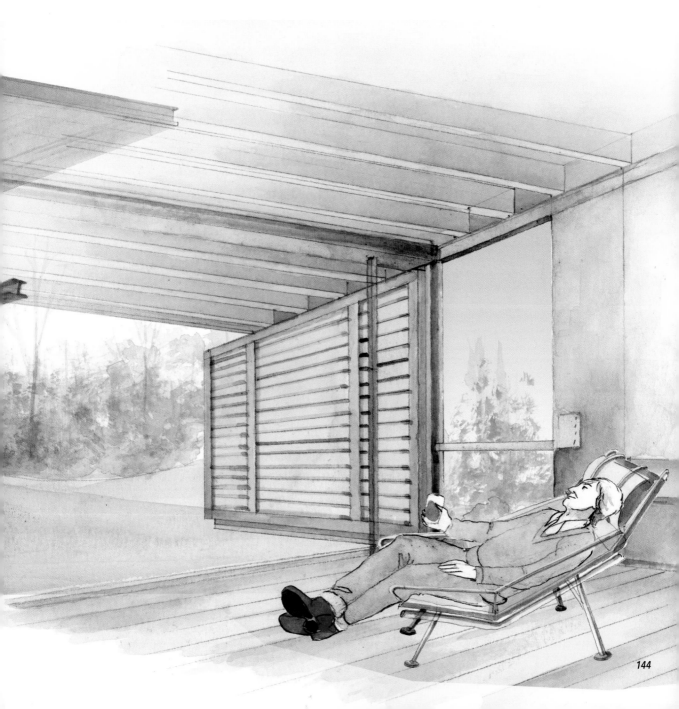

144

As I get older, I realize that the formative years are sometimes the most informative years for a lot of the work. They become your library to borrow from and be inspired by. I was lucky in many regards. I grew up around a lot of architects in an architectural community in a small town in Eastern Washington, and, frankly, I left that experience not wanting to be an architect. In fact, it was the last thing in the world I wanted to be. I found the architects to be rather entitled and arrogant, and not particularly interesting people to be around. But I was also around a lot of artists. Harold Balazs was a sculptor; I was able to work on his sculptures. I learned a lot about materials. I learned a lot about working hard. I learned a lot about doing the things that you're actually thinking about. In other words, as architects, we draw things but somebody else actually builds them. If you're an artist and you're actually making your work, you're actually making the work as you're thinking about it, and that was hugely important to me.

BERKSHIRE RESIDENCE, BERKSHIRES, MA

The biggest mistake large firms make is turning their back on small projects, because **small projects are where you can experiment**. You can also take kids who come out of school and don't know anything about what we do as practitioners, and put them on a team with a principal. With all the wisdom the principal brings and with all of the energy the kids bring, you can begin to help them understand the cycle of what design means, all the way through to the technical parts of a project. We're old school. We do not have a design department. We do not have a specification department. We do not have a construction administration department. Everybody in the office is expected to follow their projects all the way, from soup to nuts, and we expect people to draw, obviously, by hand. Unbelievably beautiful drawings come out of these kids, who are also super skilled at digital work. We insist that they follow the projects from beginning to end. You can do that with small projects.

MARTIN'S LANE WINERY, KELOWNA, BC, CANADA

Architecture is an unbelievable universe of possibilities because you can get training in architecture and take that training virtually anywhere you want to. Nicholas Negroponte, who started MIT Media Lab, got an undergraduate and a graduate degree in architecture. He said to me, "At MIT, there's a discussion about **architecture being possibly the most important, grounding education for kids in the future**," because of that rational and poetic overlay. Being on the West Coast, of course, we're hugely affected by Steve Job's legacy and his technology legacy. Steve was really the guy who came into the whole technology-engineering arena, and very clearly stated he didn't want to work with engineers, he wanted to work with architects. People would ask, "What do you mean?" And he would say, "I want to work with people who can think both as engineers and as artists."

SAWMILL, TEHACHAPI, CA

THE PIERRE, SAN JUAN ISLANDS, WA

The architect's first rule is that we are professional voyeurs. We look at things and try to understand them. That's why we have a research and development process for all our projects. What's the cultural research, what's the geographic research, what's the climatic research—what is happening there. Sometimes you can come in as an outsider and, if you have an interest and a discipline to understand a place, you may actually understand that place a little bit better than the people who have lived there for 10-20 years.

When we worked in Switzerland, in the mountains, the Swiss architects said that the farmers had it figured out. A farmer had to get a building up. They were there to farm, not to do architecture. But their buildings are really beautiful buildings, conceptually designed with super sustainable ideas about using material efficiently, engaging the climate efficiently, to lower maintenance.

We try to make architecture out of everything we work on, regardless of whether it's a super fancy house or really tough places that have all the cultural meaning in the world. Social meaning. Super important stuff.

Probably one of my biggest influences is working with craftspeople. I learn more from those people, or at least as much, as from my academic years at the University of Washington.

Harold Balazs, the artist I grew up with—he did it in his 50s and 60s. He did it with paper, graph paper, folding, shaping metal, just like a hot-rodder, basically, and he made these unbelievably complex shapes.

DELTA SHELTER, MAZAMA, WA

STUDHORSE, WINTHROP, WA

The big thing about rural sites is that they can be fragile. High deserts are fragile, mountainscapes are fragile, so you have to figure out **ways to assemble a building that are relatively light on the land**, and relatively small. That's another reason I like small buildings. I don't like doing big buildings in natural landscapes. I always try to convince clients who might think they want something large by saying, "No, you bought this place because of the landscape; you didn't buy it because of the architecture." So, how do you do an architecture that unfolds in that landscape and is light on that land?

The idea that everything has to be computer-generated is really not true. There are people who have been making complex shapes for a long time. We've seen it. Noguchi's work is like that. Sometimes the fascination with the computer as a tool is, to me, uninteresting.

I've gone to places where people have said to me, "No, we don't have any craftspeople here. We don't have any steel workers here." I would ask, "What do you mean? I've heard that in Austin, Texas, you have a hot rod culture, a culture where people take cars and completely personalize them in very bizarre, strange ways, very personal ways. That's an unbelievable skill right there." And they would say, "Well, I guess that's true ..." It was in their own backyard. We've actually hired some of those hot rod builders.

SHINSEGAE INTERNATIONAL, SEOUL, SOUTH KOREA

CHICKEN POINT CABIN, HAYDEN LAKE, ID

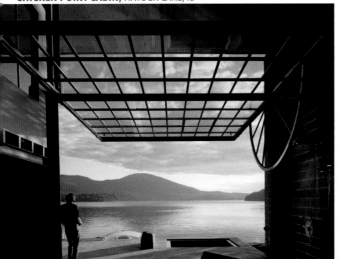

One of our favorite friends, Paul Schneider, interviewed me about a house for two days. And at the end of two days he said, "I actually don't like anything you've done. But I want to hire the brain that came up with that..." I knew immediately that he was going to be a great client, because that's exactly the kind of client I want. I want a client to push back and say, "OK, that's great. Now let's go on our own journey."

Those are the best clients.

TOD WILLIAMS

BILLIE TSIEN

Tod Williams and Billie Tsien founded **Tod Williams Billie Tsien Architects | Partners** in 1986. Their studio focuses on work for institutions such as schools, museums, and not-for-profits. A sense of rootedness, light, texture, detail, and most of all, experience are at the heart of what they design. Notable projects include the Barnes Foundation in Philadelphia, Asia Society Hong Kong Center, LeFrak Center in Prospect Park, Brooklyn, and the upcoming Obama Presidential Center in Chicago. Their practice has been recognized by numerous citations, including the National Medal of the Arts from President Obama, and the Firm of the Year Award from the American Institute of Architects.

THE SPACE BETWEEN

BT: We, as architects, are often so invested in what we're making, our designs, that we actually think that people who aren't architects really understand what we're showing them. I think that's a mistake. Most of what we show to other people is somewhat lost on them, but what they feel or do not feel is a connection with how you're presenting it and who you are.

KAREN STEIN

Karen Stein is an architectural advisor and executive director of the **George Nelson Foundation**. She serves on the board of The Architectural League of New York and the Chinati Foundation in Marfa, TX.

THE MID-CENTURY OLD FASHIONED
By Toby Cecchini and David Moo

2 oz. **Evan William's Single Barrel Bourbon**
1/2 oz. **Sour cherry spirit**
3 dashes **Angostura bitters**
1 Barspoon (7 ml.) **Maple syrup**
Wedge of **orange**
Twist of **lemon**

Muddle all ingredients together in a mixing glass. Add ice and stir to chill and dilute. Strain into a double rocks glass with a large ice cube and garnish with a fresh wedge of orange with a cherry picked to it, and a twist of lemon.

Toby Cecchini: David and I based Tod's drink on one single room that inspires us both: the entry hall of the Barnes Foundation in Philadelphia, a perfectly conjured midcentury modern hall that was built only recently. To suit, we wanted to update a midcentury cocktail, the latter version of the Old Fashioned, and bring it into the modern era using roughly the same ingredients.

THE KOMBUCHA QUAFFER
By Eben Klemm

3 oz. **Ginger Lemon Kombucha**
1 oz. **Lemon juice**
1/2 oz. **Cayenne agave syrup**

Peel a lemon completely, cut into a cube shape, and slice into thin cross sections. Squeeze a lemon peel into a Collins glass and fill with ice. Add all ingredients. Stir and garnish liberally with square lemon slices.

Cayenne agave syrup:
Add 2 tablespoons cayenne pepper to 1 cup agave nectar. Add 1 cup water and simmer 5 minutes. Strain through coffee filter.

Eben Klemm: Billie Tsien's low-alcohol cocktail is intended to be a light and zesty counter-balance to the weighty strength of Toby and David's mid-century Old Fashioned.

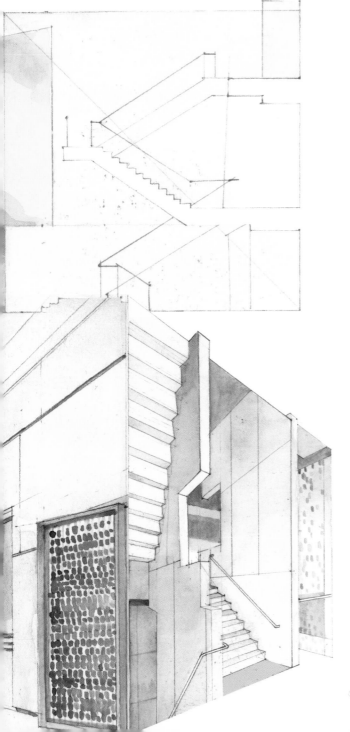

TW: I trained under Richard Meier, who so defined design as being the object that we architects thought of design as being pure and not relating to the landscape. So landscape architects have taken over the territory of infrastructure. It's a contested territory, and **I'm extremely interested in the infrastructural space.** I think most architects are not, while landscape architects, today, are. And because they are, they have every right to step into the world of the architect.

We're working on a Center for Theater and Dance at Exeter. You cannot work at Exeter without being humbled by Louis Kahn's presence. I thought this would be an interesting challenge because I believe he was interested in the space in between. That's why the final scheme is essentially as mute as it can be—we certainly knew that we couldn't exist in the heat of Kahn's work, but we needed to be in relation to it.

THE BARNES FOUNDATION, PHILADELPHIA, PA

TW: I've come humbly to this place that Billie so deeply believes in, and I absolutely believe in now, which is that it is truly about the process. That's actually what I, at least at my age and position in the world, feel is really exciting: continuously opening a world where I don't have to be a cartoon of myself, but where we can constantly see a new project together. This is thrilling.

THE CENTER FOR THE ADVANCEMENT OF PUBLIC ACTION,
BENNINGTON, VT

KS: For the Barnes, you were legally required to replicate the original galleries. You were given the sequence of rooms and their exact size, the exact position of each painting, and the exact materials to use. However, in some of the upper galleries, you found something you could do differently–the ceiling. So, in some cases, you raised it and added skylights. This relatively small change transformed the experience of the paintings. Many who knew the paintings from the original building thought they had been cleaned–and they hadn't.

LEFRAK CENTER AT LAKESIDE, PROSPECT PARK, BROOKLYN, NY

THE NEUROSCIENCES INSTITUTE, LA JOLLA, CA

BT: It's not as if we're sitting there sketching out buildings. I think where the hand now comes in is that drawings are printed out. Then Tod is always saying, "Where's my scale? Where's the scale, and where's the magic markers, and where's the white-out?" So we're drawing and using our hands on top of drawings that have been printed out. **Understanding space is still, for us, through small perspective drawings**, and Tod is usually scribbling around the edges.

TW: I think that drawings are not about beauty, they're about trying to find the answer. That's all there is to it. I do think that every person who has the capacity to draw on the computer and work with Revit has a more powerful muscle than we have. It's a muscle that doesn't exist in my body. At the same time, they all actually have the ability to draw. I only urge them all to continue to use their hand.

TW: I would say that's correct. I also think that they appreciated our general analysis, our openness to the campus idea, and our values. Billie has pushed the idea that words are important. It's very, very important for us to have simple, clear ideas that we can work with. I really subscribe to that.

BT: When we made our presentation to the President and Mrs. Obama, we first talked about values before we thought about design. He's very focused on the fact that this is not a monument to him. Of course it is, but it is really, for him, both his story and many people's stories. He's very clear that they don't want to be presented as finished, perfect people, but people who have found their way, and the idea of an of aspiration to rise. **It's about storytelling and storymaking.**

TW: When we first talked to them, we also said, "There are two things we want you to know about what we think of this Presidential Center. First, that, as a young organizer in Chicago, you enabled people, and we know that you want to continue to do that—to strengthen and give opportunities to young people, and to empower them as citizens. At the same time, you've ennobled the presidency like no other person by being the first Black president." We felt that this place needed to be both ennobling and enabling, and we put those two things together.

BT: In the past, all presidential libraries were archives, and held the papers of the presidency. In this particular case, it's a presidential center, and the archives will not be on site, they'll be digitized. So the idea of what happens there is much more about education and bringing in people, locally, nationally, and globally, to teach them about things like community organizing. What you can do to change the world. How do you pull people together? The Obamas have already started to do this with a series of summits.

THE ASIA SOCIETY HONG KONG CENTER, ADMIRALTY, HONG KONG

KS: *The Obama Presidential Center has been a project both followed and envied by many. One of the things that we all heard a lot about is how you were chosen out of a field of 140 architects. Why do you think they selected you?*

BT: There were other architects, partners and couples. I don't think it had so much to do with the design. We thought our design was really great until we saw the other models, and then we realized ours was probably the more quiet, less developed. I think it was about chemistry.

CRANBROOK NATATORIUM, BLOOMFIELD HILLS, MI

ANDLINGER CENTER FOR ENERGY & THE ENVIRONMENT, PRINCETON, NJ

TW: **The unexplored plane is always the space between two people.** I do think it is the space between two people, the dialogue that is so important. It's the space between the President and Michelle Obama. It's so terribly important to him and to them. I truly, deeply, believe that this is much more important than the object.

I believe it's a both/and situation. As an architect, you think: What is the territory I can inhabit? That's what we're constantly trying to do. What do we have to say that's of any value? **You need to find a place for your voice.** I do think it can be the space between. It's a rather simple idea.

MARK SIMON

Mark Simon was born into the world of the arts. After graduating from the Yale School of Architecture, he was hired by Charles Moore, his former teacher and dean. They collaborated on a number of projects, and Simon was named a principal at Moore Grover Harper, which became **Centerbrook Architects and Planners** in 1982.

JOHN RUBLE

John Ruble began his career as an architect and planner in the Peace Corps in Tunisia, where profound experiences with the culture, climate, and place became lasting influences on his work. At the University of California, LA, he studied and associated with Charles Moore. In 1977, John, Charles, and Buzz Yudell formed **Moore Ruble Yudell.**

REDISCOVERING CHARLES MOORE

JR: Charles Moore was born in Michigan. He went to Princeton University, then spent a year working for Louis Kahn before heading to UC Berkeley, where he chaired the architecture department, and co-founded Moore Lyndon Turnbull Whitaker. Everybody who worked with him in the San Francisco Bay Area era referred to Charles as Chuck. Years later, he moved east to head the Yale School of Architecture. There, everybody called him Charlie. His next move was west again, this time to UCLA, where I met him. Everybody in Los Angeles called him Charles. He moved to Texas in 1986—this was the last phase of his career—where he was known as Doctor Moore. He would answer the phone: "Hello, my name is Moore, Charles W."

151

PAUL MAKOVSKY

Paul Makovsky is the editorial director of award-winning *Metropolis magazine*. He was formerly managing editor of *2wice* magazine, and a Smithsonian Fellow at the Cooper Hewitt, Smithsonian Design Museum, where he worked on the exhibition and catalogue "Mixing Messages: Graphic Design in Contemporary Culture."

THE MOORETINI
By Toby Cecchini

2 oz. **Plymouth gin**
1 oz. **Dassai 50 Junmai Daiginjo Sake**
1/2 oz. **Lustau Vermut Blanco**
1 barspoon (7 ml.) **Tincture of bergamot and pomelo**

Combine all ingredients in a mixing glass over ice and stir well to chill, up to one minute. Strain into a chilled cocktail coupe. No garnish.

Mark and John having been students of Charles Moore, and Charles, having been not just a martini-only fellow, but also best friends with Hugh Hardy, I had to accede, again, to the martini. As Charles was an iconoclast who borrowed liberally from other cultures, and threw styles together in sometimes shocking fashion, his martini clearly needed some apostate influences that would come together to create a surprising cohesion. A rich junmai daiginjo sake and a vermouth made from a base of Moscatel and fino sherries, paired with a fresh tincture of bergamot and pomelo served perfectly, while never veering from being a real martini.

Immature poets imitate; mature poets steal; bad poets deface what they take, and good poets make it into something better, or at least something different. —T.S. Eliot, *The Sacred Wood*

MS: This is a wonderful opportunity to talk about our old teacher and mentor and partner, Charles Moore, a marvelous human being who died much too young, and who was, I think, the brightest man I ever met. I don't think I could ever match Charles's genius; it's difficult to follow in the footsteps of someone who was really quite extraordinary.

LANCASTER CAMPUS OF HISTORY, LANCASTER, PA

MARK **SIMON**

PARK SYNAGOGUE EAST, PEPPER PIKE, OH

Charles used walls a lot, which is something he got from his mentor, Louis Kahn. He created porches and overhangs to provide a sense of protection. He used gables for that, too. I completed a synagogue in Ohio about six years ago. I was very interested in making it feel like an Eastern European synagogue in a *shtetl*. When I first went to a service there, the rabbi blessed the congregation by creating an upside down heart with his hands. That stuck with me—and it became two sheltering canopies that both welcome and bless you as you come and go.

His own house in Orinda, California, was noted for structures within the larger house. He called these ***aediculae***. This, too, has stuck with me. In a traditional synagogue, there is a cabinet, the ark to hold the Torah, and a *bema*, a platform covered like a tent from which to read it; here, I combined them. I used the idea of a building within a building to create a structure that is both the ark and the *bema*.

Charles was a rebel, and he was rebelling against classic modernism in many ways. When *House Beautiful* asked him what style his work was, he told them that it was **Radical Eclectic Postmodern**. He looked to create a more humanist architecture, something that was based on the human body and the human experience rather than on a theory. I think he was concerned about the experience that people have individually and individual places. He was concerned about where a building was physically built—what its climate was like and what its culture was like.

Whereas the modernists may have been pleased with themselves for keeping out the wind and the rain and protecting you from the elements, Charles was very concerned about your emotional state as well—protecting you in an emotional way as well as a physical way.

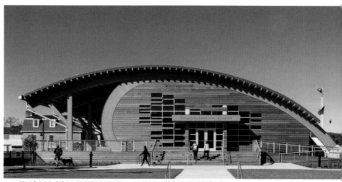

THOMPSON EXHIBITION BUILDING, MYSTIC, CT

THE TEMPLE-TIFERETH ISRAEL, BEACHWOOD, OHIO

Charles didn't mind building things that were ephemeral or temporary. He was concerned about human experience. **Just as humans change, so the setting for human experience can change.**

The buildings didn't always last as long as they could or should have, but they were markers of a time.

One very important thing Charles Moore said was that his ego was so big, **he could design anything that his client wanted and still make it beautiful.**

We were desperate for work in 1976. We were invited to apply for a job in Dayton, Ohio, to design the waterfront. The landscape architect Dan Kiley had been through—and the neighborhoods were furious with what he had done. Even though it was really beautiful, it didn't pay attention to them.

So we came up with the notion that we would open a downtown office and people could come in to tell us what they wanted and didn't want.

My partners Chad Floyd and Bill Grover came up with the idea that we would translate this to live television. We produced six shows and, out of that, we got approval for the redesign.

UNIVERSITY OF MICHIGAN SCHOOL OF PUBLIC HEALTH, ANN ARBOR, MI

LAKEWOOD HOUSE, NEW ENGLAND

But what you wouldn't see is how it was originally meant to represent the Italian business community of New Orleans. Here was someone who took an obscure organization that probably no one would be the least bit interested in except those who were part of it, and **he turned it into an icon.**

Charles was born in Michigan, but he grew up, in lots of ways, in California. His dedication to natural materials followed through in the work I did with him and in my own work. When I was at Yale, we were in the middle of the counterculture revolution. We wanted to go back to the Earth. Everything must be natural.

Perhaps the most famous of his early California projects was Sea Ranch. It has a form that fits the natural landscape. He imbued this with vernacular elements: barn siding and shed roofs.

Since then, it has slowly evolved from a series of cities and TV programs to get people involved in their own planning, to doing it at practically every campus we work on. I think it makes better buildings—it makes buildings and places that are localized and responsive.

Charles himself would make a distinction between what he thought of as his principles and his enthusiasms. Specific projects like Piazza d'Italia in New Orleans had to do with both. But I think a lot of people looking at the work saw only the enthusiasms and missed the deeper underlying principles. Look at Piazza d'Italia and you could see a lot of shiny metal interpretations of the orders of classical architecture, or the colors, or you could see the fact that it needs to be rebuilt every four years.

THE HOTCHKISS SCHOOL BIOMASS HEATING FACILITY, LAKEVILLE, CT

THE JACKSON LABORATORY FOR GENOMIC MEDICINE, FARMINGTON, CT

I did a house with Charles in a style we playfully called Japanese Gothic. It had the beginnings of an Irimoya roof with some Gothic touches. There was a two-story screened back porch which has stuck with me ever since. And here I am, 30 years later, doing a house with a three-story screened porch that's covered with logs.

Charles was always looking at creating layers of meaning. He was the only person I've ever known who could create a triple entendre off the top of his head. Not a double entendre, a triple entendre. He did this visually time and time again.

SUMMIT HOUSE, BERKELEY, CA

What we learned by working with Charles was the whole approach to thinking of **architecture as placemaking.**

I was thinking of some of the dimensions of placemaking, and the things that came to mind were:

Duality, Congeniality, and Improbability

Duality, in the sense of opposites that are brought together in different ways. That happens through all our work: inside/outside, old/new, order and accident, a rich interplay of things that are opposite to each other. **Congeniality**, in the old sense of the word: having kinship or maybe a common origin, which is the way we try to look at how our work fits in with the settings and different locales and environments that we work in. And finally, **improbability**, which Charles would call the fairy-tale dimension—the dimension of **wonder**.

JOHN **RUBLE**

JR: The first project that Charles and I worked on was St. Matthew's Church in Pacific Palisades, California, which was designed in close collaboration with the congregation. I think it was the investment of lots of people involved that created a kind of unexpected "life of its own quality" to the space. The rector loved to refer to it as the "wee kirche of the woods." Regarding the fairy-tale aspect, one of the dimensions Charles talked about was insides that are bigger than outsides, unexpected interiors that you would never imagine from what you see outside. And that's what happened at St. Matthew's. The interior has an amazing richness that comes from many different ideas being overlaid. There is an element of wonder and an element of unexplained quality in the way the work emerged.

SHANGHAI TECH LIBRARY, SHANGHAI, CHINA

It's very important to understand that Charles's view of architecture was really his view of the world. He had a way of looking at the world that, I think, influenced the way he thought about architecture. But the way he thought about architecture was by no means the only aspect of what he had to offer as a mentor and a teacher.

ENGINEERING 6, UNIVERSITY OF CALIFORNIA, LOS ANGELES, CA

BIOENGINEERING BUILDING, UCSB, SANTA BARBARA, CA

I was thinking back to Charles's ideas about the fairy-tale dimension in the architecture. He thought about the **spaces on to which openings open**, or the idea that you would **enter a vast domain through a tiny doorway**, like the cabinet in *The Lion, the Witch and the Wardrobe*.

We were doing a lot of houses in Los Angeles with very cheap materials, very common ordinary construction: drywall, wood. It was never about the primacy of materials. It wasn't about materials at all, except how they served to create a setting, to create something that was part of a deeper pursuit.

SHANGHAI TECH UNIVERSITY, SHANGHAI, CHINA

I think the idea of architecture is to make a place and to weave together elements of that place. It doesn't actually matter whether it's modernist or has other, more vernacular qualities. Whether it's made of wood or steel. The important thing is to link places in a multidimensional way.

The focus on how people experience places was always the inspiration. That's something that is fundamentally different from what you see today, where it's all about the means of production. Charles was all about: How do people experience a place? How do they form a connection? How do they behave in a space?

We see every project as a setting for people. Why are they there? What are they doing there? What does it mean to them? You could call it theatricality, but it's far more fundamental to address the way every person interacts with their world.

Once you get the concept, then all that matters is: How does it work? The concept is gone after—a day? Two or three days? A week? And what is there after that, after you've had that experience? You've seen the space, you've been dazzled by the light, you've been amazed at the construction. What is left after that? Where do you go from there?

Charles saw architecture as a medium for people to realize their values and their desires.

GEORGINA AVENUE HOUSE, SANTA MONICA, CA

FACULTY CLUB RENOVATION & GUEST HOUSE ADDITION, UNIVERSITY OF CALIFORNIA, SANTA BARBARA, CA

Mark wrote about the spirit of working with Charles, which always started out in Willy Wonka mode: "Want to change the world? There's nothin to it." And then four months later, you're in some kind of *Fitzcarraldo* situation.

Last year we finished restoring/remodeling Charles's famous Faculty Club at UC Santa Barbara. It was experimental at the time, especially in its use of color and neon. It's a beautiful, beautiful building with amazing things going on, and may be the best building on the campus. It probably should have been a temporary building that was going to be torn down. Rather than completely restoring it exactly the way it was, we transformed it into a more permanent building. We did it so that 20 years from now the university wouldn't find themselves back with the same problem and just say, "Okay, the hell with it. Let's get rid of this thing." I have mixed feelings; we gained some things in making a more permanent structure, and we lost some things.

ST. MATTHEW'S EPISCOPAL CHURCH, PACIFIC PALISADES, CA

LEE F. MINDEL

Lee F. Mindel and the late Peter Shelton founded **SheltonMindel** in 1978. The firm designs opulent settings, aiming to create minimal, streamlined spaces that are sophisticated and beautiful. The firm won the Cooper Hewitt, Smithsonian Design Museum's 2011 National Design Award, presented by Michelle Obama at the White House.

JOSEPH GIOVANNINI

A Pulitzer Prize nominee in criticism who trained in architecture at Harvard, Joseph Giovannini has led a career that spans three decades and two coasts. He served as the architecture critic for **New York magazine** and the *Los Angeles Herald Examiner*, and was long a design and architecture staff writer for *The New York Times*.

EQUAL TIME | INSIDE AND OUT

"Always design a thing by considering it in its next larger context—a chair in a room, a room in a house, a house in an environment, an environment in a city plan." -- Eliel Saarinen

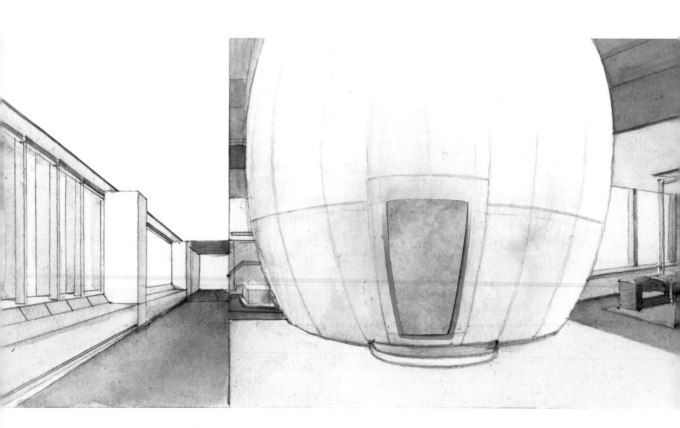

THE TURRELL TONIC
By Eben Klemm & Toby Cecchini

Build in an ice-filled Collins glass.
1 1/2 oz. Citadelle Gin
Fill with good bottled **tonic water** like **Q**
Top with **Aperol Slush** and garnish with **lime zest.**

Aperol Slush:
Add 1 cup Aperol to blender and add liquid nitrogen (or ice cubes) and flash blend, until blender drink consistency is reached.

Lee Mindel requested that I put together a cocktail that is evocative of James Turrell's projects with light. What I came up with required the use of liquid nitrogen, but duplicating the drink at home without it won't affect the flavor at all.

NEW YORK FAMILY OFFICE, NEW YORK, NY

JG: It seems like a perfectly obvious thing to do, but is, in fact, somewhat rare. When I was in architecture school, we didn't really discuss the decorative arts. Interior design was considered a no-no.

I didn't study interior design in school. Starting in a small practice, when you have small projects, you want to control everything out of necessity. There weren't many people doing that. If you look at the greats, they controlled their spaces. Alvar Aalto did it. Le Corbusier did it. Josef Hoffmann did it. How do you control your space to complete the message you're trying to convey? We're self-taught in trying to understand—with objects, furniture, lighting, materials—how that architectural idea could be completely realized and seamlessly integrated into the whole project.

JG: In your case, you studied design history and the decorative arts in a very broad way—it wasn't only French or Scandinavian furniture.

It was everything—art history and architectural history. I remember early in my career, a client would say, "Let's furnish this place." I couldn't go to the D & D Building. I couldn't get on the elevator. It was too random an experience. I didn't have enough "swatchismo" to enter.

JG: Is it because it was too commercial?

It seemed arbitrary. I thought that we could find works by masters that meant something, that resonated with our design philosophy. I started to explore Le Corbusier, Giacometti, and Alvar Aalto. I sought them all out. I went to their countries to explore their work and look at their buildings. We began to populate all our projects with works by Oscar Niemayer, Marcel Breuer, Mies van der Rohe, because those were the people we studied. **We were able to take our own education as a DNA and express it through objects that we would custom design and works by the masters that resonated with a similar point of view, instead of decorative objects that just filled space.** And that's how it started. It seemed to fill a niche in New York that was missing, because an architect and a decorator working together was not always a happy collaboration.

When we started our practice, we weren't getting big projects. We were getting kitchens and bathrooms. So we focused our macro-educations on a micro world, and didn't lose opportunities from the beginning.

Often, when the architect thinks the job at hand is complete, it is reassigned to a design or decoration consultant if the intended space does not deliver both programmatic and function and feel like a home. We try to avoid that conflict between the two by seamlessly integrating architecture and the interior.

NEW YORK FAMILY OFFICE, NEW YORK, NY

EUROPEAN HOME

I got to know Poul Kjærholm's family very well. I went to Denmark to see where he lived, which was a $10,000 house on the water. I went up to the window and pressed my nose against the glass. They weren't there. I was a stranger in a place I really admired. About eight months later, I got a call from them because MoMA was showing his furniture, and they knew that we were using it. They wanted to visit me when they came to see the MoMA show. Mrs. Kjærholm came to my loft where I had a lot of Poul's designs. She started to cry. She said she'd never seen anything like this.

And I realized that we are both an American political democracy and a design democracy. In Denmark, it's very homogeneous. But we're free to mix all cultures—politically, culturally, and design-wise. So it was my duty to introduce her husband's work to Le Corbusier's, Gio Ponti's, to have a conversation together. I realized that, as Americans, we are freer to do that than most people in other places. The next year, they invited me, as their guest, to the opening dinner for the Kjærholm retrospective at the Louisiana Museum of Modern Art [north of Copenhagen]. I couldn't believe that a year earlier, I was an outsider looking into a window of a place I couldn't get into, and a year later, I was an insider looking out, with the Kjærholms,. and couldn't believe how fortunate I was.

NEW ENGLAND ISLAND RETREAT, MARTHA'S VINEYARD, MA

OCEAN POND RESIDENCE, LONG ISLAND, NY

I went to the de Young Museum in San Francisco to photograph the underground Turrell, which had the same kind of entry—like an igloo leading into a chamber. Then I went to the Los Angeles County Museum of Art, and the Nasher Sculpture Center in Dallas to see the Turrells there. I sent my photographs to Turrell and his agent, and said that the de Young is beautiful. LACMA is beautiful. This might make sense underground. But we're in the air. On the 28th floor in New York, it seemed inappropriate. The client is a man who escaped the tyranny of the Holocaust, and we should rethink what this form should be. It should be lighter and more universal, and shouldn't be representational of something that might trigger the wrong emotion in the client. Turrell changed the form. I was very pleased by that.

SOHO PENTHOUSE DUPLEX, NEW YORK, NY

In 1991, we won a competition over Skidmore, Owings & Merrill and Kohn Pedersen Fox for Ralph Lauren's headquarters. They all showed up at the interviews wearing Ralph Lauren. I went wearing something the clients couldn't identify. They stopped me during the presentation and asked, "Whose suit are you wearing?" I knew exactly what they meant, and said I was wearing my own clothes. I got through two more slides. "Whose shoes are you wearing?" they asked. "They are my dad's shoes, actually." And it went on and on. The Skidmore people had Polo bowties and Samsonite luggage. I had a knapsack they couldn't identify. Somehow we made it through. The irony here is that Ralph wanted the interiors to cover all eras a and all decades. We were, perhaps, the only firm that could traverse traditionalism and modernism to create a campus for him. The center of the campus is finished in a chocolate palette and, like "ringstrasses," the spaces get lighter and whiter and more modern towards the perimeter. He was able to embrace both modernism and his men's club traditionalism.

The first New York installation of a James Turrell was commissioned for a philanthropic organization's family office. The entire space is designed around the egg-shaped sculpture, which occupies several floors. Most Turrell works are worlds unto themselves. Very rarely do you get a chance to interact with them.

There's a very interesting story about the form of Turrell's "egg." It was first presented to us on the 70th anniversary of Auschwitz, and our client had escaped the Holocaust. The form looked a lot like a gas chamber. I was very upset about it. I thought that to subject him to something that could be construed to be of the Holocaust could make him feel vulnerable. I thought I would try to change that section. I was a little nervous about interacting with the artist.

ERIC
OWEN MOSS

As principal of **Eric Owen Moss Architects**, Moss is an unrelenting voice in the search for new form and content in architecture. Building, writing, lecturing, and teaching around the world, he continues as a salient advocate of non-allegiance to those who forever attempt to standardize the definition of architecture.

TOM
KUNDIG

Over the past three decades, Tom Kundig, principal and owner of **Olson Kundig**, has received some of the world's highest design honors, from a National Design Award for Architecture from the Cooper Hewitt, Smithsonian Design Museum, to an Academy Award in Architecture from the American Academy of Arts and Letters.

THAT'S SO 20 MINUTES AGO...

EOM: The conceptual discourse ought to be premised on an enduring dissatisfaction with the world as we find it. How culture moves. How architecture moves. Not in a Darwinian sense, increment by increment—but cataclysmically, as an attack by one culture or one architect on another.

JAMES S. RUSSELL

James S. Russell is the director of Design Strategic Initiatives at the **NYC Department of Design & Construction**, where he produced Guiding Principles on Equity, Sustainability, Resiliency, and Healthy Living. He is an architectureal journalist, author, and consultant, and for nine years, was the architecture critic for *Bloomberg News*.

THE CULVER
By Eben Klemm & Toby Cecchini

2 oz. **London dry gin**
1/2 oz. **Kummel liqueur**
Stir ingredients over ice 20 times. Pour over large 1 1/2 ice cube into a rocks glass. Garnish with large **grapefruit** peel cut into a triangle, **orange peel** cut into a rectangle, **lime peel** twisted into a curl.

1 1/2 Ice cube:
Cut large ice cube in half with ice pick. Place pinch of salt on corner of another cube and press half cube together with second cube.

Eric Owen Moss is famously known for the challenging and angular constructions he's built in Culver City, an LA neighborhood that's practically inseparable from his work. He mentioned to me that he really only does his drinking in Berlin at 3am, and this gave me a good opportunity to annoy Toby by asking him for some Kummel.

I was just ruminating a little bit about the ubiquitous Friedrich Nietzsche, which is not to dump a lot of esoterica on anybody. But sometimes, notwithstanding reputations, people like that are of some use to people like us. And there was a line from *Thus Spoke Zarathustra* that went something like this: "Nobody tells me anything new." So I tell myself my own story. All of these discussions about art, and architecture, and what it means—there are many more discussions than there are progenitors. And the question is: If we try to talk to each other—because this is an exchange—is life private and personal and introverted, or is it exchangeable, transferable? Can we talk to each other? Can we hear a story? **I think we can hear a story.**

VESPERTINE, CULVER CITY, CA

UMBRELLA, CULVER CITY, CA

The Pterodactyl, an office building for an advertising agency in Culver City, California, raises a very interesting question about form and shape and space and utility. Because if you actually go into this damn thing, whatever your sense of it is, when you look at the building, and the meaning of the form, and the shape, it's incredibly efficient and operationally super-intelligible.

It works.

For a multi-city master plan located outside of Nanjing, China, there were topological issues, organizational issues that, in a sense, were a *priori*. That means they exist without form. They become topologies that have a form, but haven't yet landed at the site. Then they add the typography. So somewhere between the topology and the typography and the topography of the site, we integrated those pieces and began to develop four very different areas.

PTERODACTYL, CULVER CITY, CA

(W)RAPPER, CULVER CITY, CA

This is New Workplace stuff, where people who are engaged in that field welcome this kind of venue.

When we bent the glass panels for the canopy of the Umbrella, a performance and recording venue also in Culver City, everybody said, "You can't bend the glass. You can't draw it. You can't fabricate it. You can't install it. It will break. It will leak." That's what they said.

Every one of those things happened.

But the lawyers are gone. The owner is smiling.

And guess what?

It's up.

The (W)rapper office tower in Los Angeles is a difficult project because there's no building code that can account for it. It has no columns. It has no beams, in a conventional sense. So we have to write the program. We have to walk into a room with people from Arup and the City of Los Angeles Building Department. There are 21 people in the room and 22 points of view. And to make a case that this is intelligible in a constructional way and a structural way—we've now done that.

SAMITAUR TOWER , CULVER CITY, CA

I should say that Los Angeles probably has its own area for discourse in terms of what it is and how it's made.

One of the issues is that there is Hollywood, West Hollywood, Santa Monica, Beverly Hills, Burbank, Culver City, etc. So it's not a homogeneous jurisdiction. It's multiple jurisdictions.

The often used, not to say abused, term "fragmentation" probably applies to any attempt to plan what the city might be in a consistent way over long distances.

STEALTH, CULVER CITY, CA

CACTUS TOWER, CULVER CITY, CA

The way it works is that the curvilinear pieces on the exterior, which we call the "ribbons," are connected with elements we call "cords". The cords run from ribbon to ribbon. Sometimes they run into the core. An open plan, no internal structure. The girders are supported by the cords. The ribbons curve not only in one plane, but in two planes. There are very substantial questions about how to build this, how to put it up.

I have to acknowledge a very particular fascination with glass, and with the biblical admonition—I think it's an admonition—that life is understood not so clearly, but as if through a glass darkly.

The idea of glass, which is there and not there and can play both roles, and the tension between the possibilities is of great interest to me.

The hypothesis is to have planning obligate architecture. And reciprocally, have architecture do the same with planning.

There are other questions here. Los Angeles is zoned. But it's zoned with river beds, concrete river beds, freeways, and railway and power line rights-ofway. The premise here is that there is no single infrastructure.

The infrastructure belongs to the architecture.

And the architecture belongs to the infrastructure.

In a Hippodamus of Miletus sense of what the grid might be, the one thing that it doesn't seem to indicate is, in Yeats' old phrase, "The center cannot hold."

The grid has no center, although it might imply one with absence.

ABOUT THE BARTENDERS

TOBY CECCHINI, *Bartender & Author*
Toby Cecchini is a writer and bartender based in New York City. He has written about food, wine, and spirits for *GQ, Saveur, Food and Wine,* and, for over 10 years for *The New York Times* with his column "Case Study." His first book, *Cosmopolitan: A Bartender's Life,* was published in 2003. He began bartending at the Odeon in 1987, where he created the internationally-recognized version of the Cosmopolitan cocktail. He followed with stints in several bars including Passerby, which he owned until 2008. In 2013, he reopened the shuttered Long Island Bar in Cobble Hill, Brooklyn, and is currently at work on his second bar in downtown Brooklyn.

EBEN KLEMM, *Mixologist & Author*
Eben Klemm, a former research biologist, writes cocktail and wine lists for restaurant and hotel openings around the world. He began bartending in the last century in Upstate New York, and has trained thousands of servers and bartenders in beginning and advanced beverage service. His cocktail book for beginners, *The Cocktail Primer*, was published in 2009. He is cocktail editor for *World Policy Journal*, and his work has been featured in numerous publications. Eben currently divides his time between New York, Los Angeles, and Portland, OR.

DAVID MOO, *Bartender & Voice Actor*
David Moo is a 20-year veteran bartender whose cocktails and bar commentary have been widely published in books, magazines, and newspapers. In addition to his work consulting on bar design, bar operation, and menu design, he creates and prepares cocktails for a wide range of events like those detailed in this book. In his spare time, he is the owner and manager of The Quarter Brooklyn, the oldest post-revival cocktail bar in Brooklyn.

ABOUT THE CURATORS

ABBY SUCKLE, *Architect*

Abby Suckle, *FAIA,* is a practicing architect with a wide range of projects. She is president of cultureNOW, a nonprofit devoted to arts education and cultural tourism. She leads the Museum Without Walls project, an initiative to expand beyond gallery walls to understand place by creating an acoustic guide to the environment, blending art, architecture, and history. The iPhone app, developed as part of this effort, won a prize at the NYC Big Apps 2.0 in 2011, and the organization won the 2012 National AIA Collaborative Achievement Award. Her first book, *By Their Own Design*, was published by the Whitney Library of Design. She received her Masters in Architecture from Harvard University Graduate School of Design, and her undergraduate degree from the University of Pennsylvania.

WILLIAM SINGER, *Architect*

Since 2015, William M. Singer, *AIA*, a former partner at Gruzen Samton Architects, has supervised the NYC Deptartment of Buildings Brooklyn Plan Examination Unit as chief plan examiner. His 27 years of private sector work focused on civic architecture. His B.A. in Modern History and in English and French Literature from Duke University led to an M.A. in English Literature from UNC-Chapel Hill. He earned a Master of Architecture from the College of Design at NC State University. In 1993-94 he was a Senior Fulbright Scholar in Slovenia. Singer taught at NYU's Graduate Real Estate Program for 13 years, and currently serves on the board of trustees of the Penland School of Craft.

ANNE LEWISON, *Architect*

Anne Lewison, *AIA, MRAIC,* is a practicing architect with a focus on public buildings, primarily museums, and is currently architect advocate for the Museum of Contemporary Art, Toronto. She has been actively involved with cultureNOW since 2004. Her connection with Bing Thom and the David Geffen Hall - Lincoln Center competition brought his work to our attention.

KRITIKA DHANDA, *Architect & Experience Designer*

Kritika Dhanda, *Assoc. AIA,* is a recent graduate with a Master in Design Studies from Harvard University Graduate School of Design. She is interested in interactive and immersive design for public spaces, and has been working with cultureNOW as a project designer and manager since graduating in 2016. She has a bachelor's degree in architecture from the School of Planning and Architecture, New Delhi, India, where she worked as an architect and exhibition designer for five years.

BISHAKH SOM, *Architect & Artist*

Bishakh Som received her Masters in Architecture from Harvard University Graduate School of Design. Som's artwork has appeared in *The New Yorker, The Boston Review, VICE, The Brooklyn Rail, Buzzfeed, The Huffington Post,* and *The Graphic Canon, vol. 3.* Her comics will appear in *We're Still Here*, the first all-transgender comics anthology. Som's artwork has been exhibited at ArtLexis Gallery, the Bannister Gallery at Rhode Island College, the Grady Alexis Gallery, and the Society of Illustrators. Her paintings were featured in *A New York State of Mind: Stories from the Unusual Suspects*, a group show at the De Cacaofabriek in the Netherlands in 2018.

KRISTEN RICHARDS, *Consulting Editor*

Kristen Richards, *Hon. AIA, Hon. ASLA*, has written about the architecture and design industry, the firms, and the personalities for more than 25 years. She is co-founder and editor-in-chief of ArchNewsNow.com, launched in 2002, and from 2003 to 20016, served as editor-in-chief of *Oculus* magazine, the quarterly journal of the American Institute of Architects New York Chapter. These followed a 10-year tenure as news editor/feature writer for *Interiors* magazine, and as a freelance journalist and photographer for national and international design and business publications.

PHOTO CREDITS AND NAPKIN SKETCHES

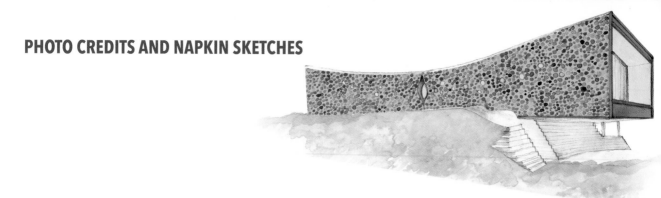

Charles Renfro - *Page 1-4*
Charles Renfro portrait - *©Geordie Wood*
Justin Davidson portrait - *©Ariella Budick*
The High Line; Institute of Contemporary Art; The Broad; Roy & Diana Vagelos Education Center; Zaryadye Park - *©Iwan Baan*
Lincoln Center for the Performing Arts - *©Nanette Melville*
Blur Building - *©Beat Widmer*

Claire Weisz - *Page 5-8*
Claire Weisz portrait - *©Sioux Nesi*
James S. Russell portrait - *Courtesy James S. Russell*
Bronx Charter School for the Arts; SeaGlass Carousel; Far Rockaway Park - *©Albert Vecerka/Esto*
Spring Street Manhattan Districts 1/2/5 Garage & Salt Shed - *with Dattner Architects, ©Albert Vecerka/Esto*
WXY Urban Furniture Systems in New York - *©Wade Zimmerman*
Times Square Visitors Center; Bronx EMS Ambulance Station - *©Paul Warchol*
Xinjin Bridge - *Courtesy WXY*

Audrey Matlock - *Page 9-12*
Audrey Matlock portrait; Medeu Sports Center; Armstrong Visitor Center; 57 Irving Place - *Courtesy Audrey Matlock Architect*
Jason Sheftell portrait - *Courtesy New York Daily News*
Bar House; Catskill Mountain House - *©Peter Aaron/OTTO*
Chelsea Modern - *©Bruce Damonte*

Brad Cloepfil - *Page 13-16*
Brad Cloepfil portrait - *©Grace Rivera*
David van der Leer portrait - *Courtesy Van Alen Institute*
National Veterans Memorial and Museum; U.S. Embassy Mozambique - *Image by MIR, courtesy Allied Works Architecture*
Dutchess County Residence Guest House; Clyfford Still Museum (all images); Sokol Blosser Winery Tasting Room; National Music Centre of Canada
- *©Jeremy Bittermann*

Richard Weller - *Page 17-20*
Richard Weller portrait - *Courtesy Richard Weller*
William Menking portrait - *Courtesy William Menking*
The Garden of Australian Dreams (all images) - *Courtesy National Museum of Australia*
Tsunami Memorial Competition (all images) - *Courtesy Richard Weller / University of Pennsylvania*

Rob Rogers - *Page 21-24*
Rob Rogers portrait; Atlanta's Park Over GA400; Constitution Garden - *Courtesy ROGERS PARTNERS Architects+Urban Designers*
Susan S. Szenasy portrait - *Courtesy Susan S. Szenasy*
SandRidge Commons (landscape and building) - *©Scott Shigley Photography*
The Elevated Acre at 55 Water Street - *©Nathan Sayers*
Henderson-Hopkins High School - *©Albert Vecerka/Esto*

Todd Schliemann - *Page 25-28*
Todd Schliemann portrait; Marina Bay Integrated Resort Competition - *Courtesy Ennead Architects*
Clifford Pearson portrait - *Courtesy Clifford Pearson*
The Standard; National History Museum (all images); American Museum of Natural History; University of Texas at Austin Cockrell School of
Engineering Education and Research Center - *Jeff Goldberg/Esto*
University of Michigan, Biological Science Building - *Courtesy Aislinn Weidele/Ennead Architects*

Calvin Tsao - *Page 29-32*
Calvin Tsao portrait - *Courtesy Tsao + McKown*
Karen Stein portrait - *Courtesy Karen Stein*
Bhutan Elder Sangha Sanctuary - *Courtesy Tsao + McKown*
Berkshire Mountain House - *©Eric Laignel*
Sagaponac House - *©Michael Moran*
Astrid Hill House; William Beaver House - *©Richard Bryant*
Jianfu Palace Museum Exterior View - *©China Heritage Fund*
Jianfu Palace Museum Interior View - *©Cheng Shouqi*

William Pedersen - *Page 33-36*
William Pedersen portrait; 10 & 30 Hudson Yards; One Jackson Square; Gannett USA Today Headquarters; 333 Wacker Drive; Shanghai World
Financial Center; Loop de Loop - *Courtesy Kohn Pedersen Fox Associates*
Carol Willis portrait - *Courtesy The Skyscraper Museum*

Hugh Hardy - *Page 37-40*
Hugh Hardy portrait - *Courtesy H3*
James Sanders portrait - *©Natalie Holt, Courtesy James Sanders + Associates*
Maritime and Seafood Industry Museum; Claire Tow Theater - *©Francis Dzikowski/OTTO*
Langworthy House - 18 W 11th st - *©Eduard Hueber/archphoto*
Bridgemarket - *©Peter Aaron/OTTO*
Central Synagogue Renovation - *©Peter Aaron/OTTO*
Wright State University, Schuster Hall renovation - *©Brad Feinknopf/OTTO*
Two River Theater - *©Robert Polidori*

Belmont Freeman - *Page 41-44*
Belmont Freeman portrait - *Courtesy Belmont Freeman Architects*
Cathleen McGuigan portrait - *©Jenna-Beth Lyde Parish Photography*
Kowalewski Residence; Riverside Drive Penthouse; Uris Hall, Columbia Business School; The Carriage House; Ezra and Cecile Zilkha Gallery
Renovation - *©Christopher Wesnofske*
Sushi Yasuda - *©Alexander Gryger*
The Four Seasons Restoration - *©Jennifer Calais Smith*
Gertrude Ederle Recreation Center - *©Jody Kivort*

Enrique Norten - *Page 45-48*
Enrique Norten portrait - *©Sarah Silver*
Pedro Gadanho portrait - *©Pedro Guimarães photographer*
Chopo Museum; Musevi - *©Luis Gordoa*
Mercedes House - *©Evan Joseph*
New York Public Library 53rd Street - *©TEN Arquitectos*
Casita - *©Hannah Cooper*
Museo Amparo - *©Agustin Garza*
Rutgers Business School - *©Peter Aaron/OTTO*
Centro - *©Jaime Navarro*

Joel Sanders - *Page 49-52*
Joel Sanders portrait; University of Pennsylvania, Institute of Contemporary Art Concept Study; Woodstock Library Annex - *Courtesy JSA (Joel
Sanders Architect)*
Barry Bergdoll portrait - *©Robin Holland/Museum of Modern Art*
New Canaan Residence; Capsule Loft; Broadway Penthouse; 25 Columbus Circle; House on Mt. Merino; Princeton Julian Street Library; NYU Bobst
Library Pixel Veil - *©Peter Aaron/OTTO*
Seongbukdong Residences - *©ChaiSoo Ok*

Massimiliano Fuksas & Gregg Pasquarelli - *Page 53-58*
Massimiliano Fuksas portrait - *©Gianmarco Chieregato*
Gregg Pasquarelli portrait; Midtown Center; Uber Headquarters; Pier 17; American Copper Buildings - *Courtesy SHoP Architects*
Paul Goldberger portrait - *Courtesy Paul Goldberger*
111 West 57th Street (street view) - *©Hayes Davidson*
111 West 57th Street (aerial view) - *©JDS Development Group*
Barclays Center - *©Bruce Damonte*
The Porter House - *©Seong Kwon*
Shenzhen Bao'an International Airport–Terminal 3 (interior view) - *©Archivio Fuksas*
Shenzhen Bao'an International Airport–Terminal 3 (exterior view); New Rome-Eur Convention Centre "The Cloud" (exterior day view) - *©Leonardo
Finotti*
Tbilisi Public Service Hall; New Rome-Eur Convention Centre "The Cloud" (interior night view) - *©Moreno Maggi*
Rhike Park, Music Theatre and Exhibition Hall - *©Joel Rookwood*
New National Archives of France - *©Kamal Khalfi_Archiv. Nationales*

Morris Adjmi - *Page 59-62*
Morris Adjmi portrait - *©Lisa Mahar*
William Higgins portrait - *Courtesy William Higgins*
520 West 20th Street (all images) - *Courtesy Morris Adjmi Architects*
Wythe Hotel (all images) - *©Jimi Billingsley*
837 Washington Street (exterior) - *©Matthew Williams*
837 Washington Street (detail) - *©Timothy Schenck*

Ken Smith - *Page 63-66*
Ken Smith portrait; Cowles Commons - *©Tobias Klotke, courtesy Ken Smith Workshop*
Alan G. Brake portrait - *©Catherine Gavin*
BAM Arts District TFANA Arts Plaza - *©David Sundberg/Esto*
WallFlowers; Silverstein Family Park; East River Waterfront Esplanade and Piers - *©Peter Mauss/Esto*
Croton Water Filtration Plant - *©Alex MacLean*
Pacific Coast Residence hand rail - *©Trevor Tondro*

Frances Halsband - *Page 67-70*
Frances Halsband portrait; Ambulatory Surgical Facility - *Courtesy Kliment Halsband Architects*
Michael J. Crosbie portrait - *Courtesy Michael J. Crosbie*
FDR Presidential Visitor & Education Center (all images) - *©Cervin Robinson*
University of Chicago, Neubauer Collegium for Culture & Society - *©Tom Rossiter*
Rockefeller University Welch Hall Library; Johns Hopkins University, Gilman Hall (all images) - *©Peter Mauss/Esto*

Daniel Libeskind - *Page 71-74*
Daniel Libeskind portrait - *©Stefan Ruiz*
Brett Littman portrait - *©Mari Juliano*
World Trade Center Master Plan Site - *Courtesy Studio Libeskind*
Denver Art Museum Extension - *©BitterBredt*
Jewish Museum Berlin - *©www.guenterschneider.de*
All hand-drawn sketches - *©Daniel Libeskind*

Deborah Berke - *Page 75-78*
Deborah Berke portrait - ©*Winnie Au*
Cathleen McGuigan portrait - ©*Jenna-Beth Lyde Parish Photography*
21c Museum Hotel, Bentonville (all images) - ©*Timothy Hursley*
Rockefeller Arts Center (all images); Cummins Indy Distribution Headquarters - ©*Chris Cooper*
21c Museum Hotel, Nashville - ©*Mike Schwartz*
Marianne Boesky Gallery - ©*Eduard Hueber*

Scott Marble & David Benjamin - *Page 79-84*
Scott Marble portrait - ©*Spencer Starnes*
David Benjamin portrait - *Courtesy David Benjamin*
Kenneth Frampton - *Courtesy Kenneth Frampton*
Glen Oaks Branch Library (all images) - ©*Eduard Hueber, ArchPhoto, Inc.*
Greenpoint Library and Environmental Education Center; The Schomburg Center for Research in Black Culture - *Courtesy Marble Fairbanks Architects*
Hy-Fi at MoMA PS1 (exterior view) - ©*Amy Barkow*
Hy-Fi at MoMA PS1 (interior view) - ©*Kris Graves*
Hy-Fi at MoMA PS1 (detail); Embodied Computation Lab (side wall elevation); Pier 35 EcoPark; Bionic Partition - ©*The Living*
Embodied Computation Lab (exterior view) - ©*Michael Moran*
Embodied Computation Lab (interior view) - ©*Pablo Marvel*

David Adjaye - *Page 85-88*
David Adjaye portrait; Dirty House; Moscow School of Management; Idea Store Whitechapel - ©*Ed Reeve*
Thomas Campbell portrait - *Courtesy The Metropolitan Museum of Art*
Gwangju Pavilion - ©*Kyungsub Shin*
Sugar Hill - ©*Wade Zimmerman*
Smithsonian NMAAHC - ©*Darren Bradley*
Smithsonian NMAAHC (detail) - ©*Steve Hall/Hedrich Blessing*

Louisa Hutton - *Page 89-92*
Louisa Hutton portrait - ©*Valerie Bennett*
Barry Bergdoll portrait - ©*Robin Holland/Museum of Modern Art*
Jessop West Building; Federal Environment Agency (exterior view) - ©*Jan Bitter*
Immanuel Church and Parish Center - ©*Margot Gottschling*
GSW Headquarters; Federal Environment Agency (interior view) - ©*Annette Kisling*
Brandhorst Museum - ©*Andreas Lechtape*

Andrea Leers & Jane Weinzapfel - *Page 93-96*
Andrea Leers and Jane Weinzapfel portraits - *Courtesy Leers Weinzapfel Associates*
Susan S. Szenasy portrait - *Courtesy Susan S. Szenasy*
Paul S. Russell, MD Museum of Medical History and Innovation; Dudley Square Neighborhood Police Station; University of Connecticut Social Science and Classroom Building - ©*Anton Grassl/Esto*
Franklin County Courthouse - ©*Brad Feinknopf/OTTO*
Harvard Science Center Expansion - ©*Alan Karchmer/OTTO*
University of Pennsylvania Gateway Complex - ©*Peter Aaron/OTTO*
Ohio State University East Regional Chilled Water Plant - ©*Brad Feinknopf/OTTO*
University of Massachusetts, John W. Oliver Design Building - ©*Albert Vecerka/Esto*

Marion Weiss & Michael Manfredi - *Page 97-100*
Marion Weiss and Michael Manfredi portraits - ©*Shuli Sade / Sade Studio, courtesy Weiss/Manfredi*
Julian Zugazagoitia portrait - *Courtesy Bob Greenspan*
Nelson-Atkins Cultural Arts District - *Courtesy Weiss/Manfredi*
Seattle Art Museum: Olympic Sculpture Park - ©*Benjamin Benschneider, courtesy Weiss/Manfredi*
Hunter's Point South Waterfront Park; Kent State Center for Architecture & Environmental Design; Barnard College Diana Center; Brooklyn Botanic Garden Visitor Center; Krishna P. Singh Center for Nanotechnology; Novartis Visitor Reception Pavilion - ©*Albert Vecerka/Esto, courtesy Weiss/Manfredi*
Women's Memorial and Education Center - ©*Jeff Goldberg/Esto, courtesy Weiss/Manfredi*
The Tata Innovation Center - ©*Iwan Baan, courtesy Weiss/Manfredi*

Tom Balsley - *Page 101-104*
Tom Balsley portrait; Balsley Park; Capitol Plaza; Gantry Plaza State Park; Curtis Hixon Waterfront Park; Main Street Garden Park; Macombs Dam Park at Yankee Stadium; Intercontinental Hotel Courtyard - *Courtesy SWA/Balsley*
Matt Shaw portrait - *Courtesy Matt Shaw*
Hunter's Point South Waterfront Park - ©*Albert Vecerka/Esto*; Park Designers - *SWA/Balsey & Weiss/Manfredi*; Prime Consultant & Infrastructure Designer – *ARUP*; Architect - *Weiss/Manfredi*

Bing Thom & Michael Heeney - *Page 105-108*
Bing Thom portrait; The Butterfly; Xiqu Centre (all images) - *Courtesy Revery Architecture*
Michael Heeny portrait - *Courtesy Surrey City Development Corporation*
Gina Pollara portrait - *Courtesy Gina Pollara*
Surrey City Centre Library (all images); Guildford Aquatic Centre (all images) - ©*Ema Peter*
Arena Stage (all images) - ©*Nic Lehoux*

Frank Harmon - *Page 109-112*
Frank Harmon portrait; all project images - *Courtesy Frank Harmon Architect*
Frank Harmon Watercolor - *Courtesy Frank Harmon*
Suzanne Stephens portrait - ©*Jenna-Beth Lye Parish Photography 2016*

Shohei Shigematsu - *Page 113-116*
Shohei Shigematsu portrait - *Courtesy OMA*
Amanda Dameron portrait - *©Amy Elisabeth Spasoff*
Milstein Hall; Faena Forum - *©Iwan Baan*
Audrey Irmas Pavilion - *Courtesy OMA/Luxigon*
Pierre Lassonde Pavilion - *©Bruce Damonte*
121 East 22nd Street - *Courtesy OMA/ENCORE*
Manus x Machina - *©Albert Vecerka/Esto*
7 Screen Pavilion - *©Philippe Ruault*
"An Occupation of Loss" with Taryn Simon - *©Naho Kubota*

Michael Murphy & Michael Sorkin - *Page 117-122*
Michael Murphy portrait; Equal Justice Initiative, Memorial to Peace and Justice (all images); Ilima Primary School - *Courtesy MASS Design Group*
Michael Sorkin portrait - *Courtesy Michael Sorkin Studio/Terreform*
Amsterdam Avenue Transformed - *©Terreform 2010*
Hotel Jellyfish; Honguan Lake Ecological City - *©Michael Sorkin Studio, 2010*
Bostans and New Construction, Mahalle Regeneration Project - *©Michael Sorkin Studio, 2012*
City of Science - *©Michael Sorkin Studio, 2015*
Agro-Forestry on Staten Island; Gowntown: A 197-X Plan for Upper Manhattan - *©Terreform 2015*
Maternity Waiting Village; Butaro Hospital; Gheskio Cholera Treatment Center; Gheskio Tuberculosis Hospital; Mubuga Primary School - *©Iwan Baan*

Steven Holl - *Page 123-126*
Steven Holl portrait; Hunters Point Community Library - *Courtesy Steven Holl Architects*
Barry Bergdoll portrait - *©Robin Holland/Museum of Modern Art*
Lewis Arts Complex, Princeton University - *©Paul Warchol*
Maggie's Centre Barts; The Nelson-Atkins Museum of Art; Institute for Contemporary Art, Virginia Commonwealth University; Campbell Sports Center, Columbia University; Visual Arts Building, University of Iowa; Vanke Center Horizontal Skyscraper - *©Iwan Baan*

Jeanne Gang - *Page 127-130*
Jeanne Gang portrait - *©Sally Ryan*
Michael Kimmelman portrait - *Courtesy Michael Kimmelman*
Arcus Center for Social Justice Leadership; City Hyde Park; Aqua Tower; Writers Theatre (all images) - *©Steve Hall/Hedrich Blessing*
University of Chicago Campus North Residential Commons - *©Tom Harris Photography*

Bartholomew Voorsanger - *Page 131-134*
Bartholomew Voorsanger portrait - *©Patrik Andersson*
Alastair Gordon portrait - *Courtesy Alastair Gordon*
Asia Society and Museum - *©Thomas Loof*
Napa Valley Residence; Wildcat Ridge Residence; National WWII Museum, New Orleans (exterior view) - *©Thomas Damgaard*
Blue Ridge Residence; Elie Tahari Offices - *©Elizabeth Felicella*
National WWII Museum, New Orleans (3D) - *Courtesy National World War II Museum*
LaGuardia Airport Control Tower - *Courtesy Voorsanger Architects/University of St. Thomas Department of Art History*

Peter L. Gluck - *Page 135-138*
Peter L. Gluck portrait - *©Theo Morrison*
Inga Saffron portrait - *©Gene Smirov*
Bridge (aerial view) - *Philly By Drone, courtesy GLUCK+*
Bridge (street view) - *©Timothy Hursley*
Tower House; Cary Leeds Center for Tennis & Learning; Duke University Marine Laboratory - *©Paul Warchol*
House in the Mountains; Little Ajax Affordable Housing - *©Steve Mundinger*
The East Harlem School - *©Erik Freeland*

David Piscuskas - *Page 139-142*
David Piscuskas and David Hollenberg portraits - *Courtesy 1100 Architect*
Koenigsblick Kindergarten - *©Jean-Luc Valentin*
Main: East Side Lofts - *©Nikolas Koenig*
Queens Central Library - *©Michael Moran*
Residence, Ikema Island- *©Shinichi Sato*
University of Pennsylvania, Perry World House (all images) - *©Peter Aaron/OTTO*

Tom Kundig - *Page 143-146*
Tom Kundig portrait - *Courtesy Rafael Soldi*
Cathleen McGuigan portrait - *©Jenna-Beth Lyde Parish Photography*
Berkshire Residence; Studhorse; Chicken Point Cabin - *©Benjamin Benschneider*
Martin's Lane Winery - *©Nic Lehoux*
Sawmill; Shinsegae International - *©Olson Kundig/Kevin Scott*
The Pierre - *©Dwight Eschliman*
Delta Shelter - *©Olson Kundig/Tim Bies*

Tod Williams & Billie Tsien - *Page 147-150*
Tod Williams and Billie Tsien portraits - *©TaylorJewell*
Karen Stein portrait - *Courtesy Karen Stein*
The Barnes Foundation; The Center for the Advancement of Public Action; Lefrak Center at Lakeside; The Neurosciences Institute; The Asia Society Hong Kong Center; Andlinger Center for Energy & the Environment; Cranbrook Natatorium - *©Michael Moran/OTTO*

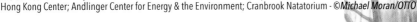

Mark Simon & John Ruble - *Page 151-156*
Mark Simon portrait - *©Derek Hayn*
John Ruble portrait - *Courtesy Moore Ruble Yudell*
Paul Makovsky portrait - *©Sheila Kim*
Lancaster Campus of History; The Temple-Tifereth Israel; Lakewood House - *©Peter Aaron/OTTO*

Park Synagogue East - *©Scott Frances*
Thompson Exhibition Building - *©Jeff Goldberg/Esto*
School of Public Health; Biomass Heating Facility - *©David Sundberg/Esto*
The Jackson Laboratory for Genomic Medicine - *©Robert Benson*
Summit House; Georgina Avenue House; Engineering 6, University of California; BioEngineering Building, UCSB; Shanghai Tech University; Shanghai Tech Library; Faculty Club Renovation & Guest House Addition - *©Colins Lozada*
St. Matthew's Episcopal Church - *©Tim Hursley*

Lee F. Mindel - *Page 157-160*
Lee Mindel portrait - *Courtesy Shelton Mindel*
Joseph Giovannini portrait - *©Tom Bonner Photography*
New York Family Office (all images); European Home; New England Island Retreat; Ocean Pond Residence; SOHO Penthouse Duplex - *©Michael Moran*

Eric Owen Moss & Tom Kundig - *Page 161-164*
Eric Owen Moss portrait - *Courtesy Eric Owen Moss Architects*
Tom Kundig portrait - *©Rafael Soldi*
James S. Russell portrait - *Courtesy James S. Russell*
Vespertine; Umbrella; Pterodactyl; (W)rapper; Samitaur Tower; Stealth; Cactus Tower - *©Tom Bonner Photography*

Curators and Bartenders
Abby Suckle portrait - *Courtesy Abby Suckle*
William Singer portrait - *Courtesy William Singer*
Anne Lewison portrait - *Courtesy Anne Lewison*
Kritika Dhanda portrait - *Courtesy Kritika Dhanda*
Bishakh Som portrait - *Courtesy Bishakh Som*
Kristen Richards portrait - *©Emma Abbate*
Toby Cecchini portrait - *©Marc Falzon*
Eben Klemm portrait - *©Marc Falzon*
David Moo portrait - *Courtesy David Moo*
All Cocktail & Bar photographs - *©Marc Falzon*
All Cocktails and Conversation event photographs - *Courtesy AIANY*

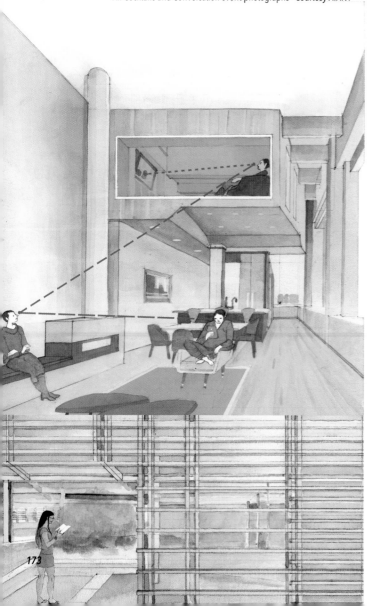

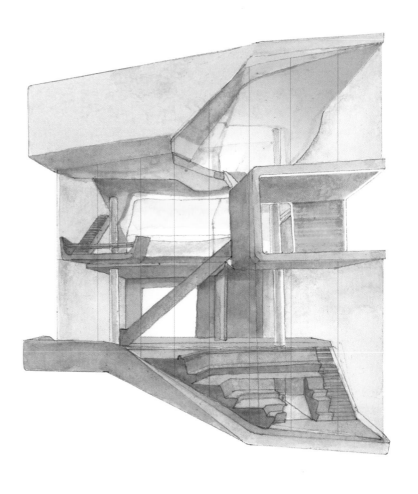

LEE MINDEL

LOUISA HUTTON

MARK SIMON

WHEW!

BARTHOLOMEW VOORSANGER

OPENING CANOPY u will hut.

DANIEL LIBESKIND

ROM TORONTO